MW00575018

CONTENTS

BREAKFAST & BRUNCH RECIPES

1. Spinach Frittata(2)

INGREDIENTS for Servings: 6

8 eggs	1 tbsp curry powder
1 1/4 cup mushrooms, sliced	1/4 cup onion, diced
	Pepper
1 tbsp olive oil	Salt
2 cups spinach	

DIRECTIONS and Cooking Time: 8 Minutes

Preheat the air fryer to 325 F.   Heat oil in a pan over medium-high heat.   Add onion and mushrooms to the pan and sauté for 5-8 minutes.   Add spinach and cook for 2 minutes.   In a large bowl, whisk eggs, curry powder, pepper, and salt.   Transfer pan mixture into the air fryer baking dish. Pour egg mixture over vegetables and stir well.   Place dish in the air fryer and cook for 8 minutes or until eggs are set   Serve and enjoy.

2. Air Fryer Bacon

INGREDIENTS for Servings: 6

½ tablespoon olive oil	6 bacon strips

DIRECTIONS and Cooking Time: 9 Minutes

Preheat the Air fryer to 350F and grease an Air fryer basket with olive oil.   Cook for about 9 minutes and flip the bacon.   Cook for 3 more minutes until crispy and serve warm.

3. Cherry And Almond Scones

INGREDIENTS for Servings: 4

⅓ cup sugar	¼ cup cold butter, cut into cubes
2 tsp baking powder	
½ cup sliced almonds	½ cup milk
¾ cup chopped cherries, dried	1 egg
	1 tsp vanilla extract

DIRECTIONS and Cooking Time: 30 Minutes

Line air fryer basket with baking paper. Mix together flour, sugar, baking powder, almonds, and dried cherries. Rub the butter into the dry ingredients with hands to form a sandy, crumbly texture. Whisk together egg, milk, and vanilla extract.   Pour into the dry ingredients and stir to combine. Sprinkle a working board with flour, lay the dough onto the board and give it a few kneads. Shape into a rectangle and cut into 9 squares. Arrange the squares in the air fryer's basket and cook for 14 minutes at 390 F. Serve immediately.

4. Eggless Spinach And Bacon Quiche

INGREDIENTS for Servings: 2

1 cup fresh spinach, chopped	1 cup Parmesan cheese, shredded
4 slices of bacon, cooked and chopped	4 dashes Tabasco sauce
½ cup mozzarella cheese, shredded	Salt and black pepper, to taste
4 tablespoons milk	

DIRECTIONS and Cooking Time: 10 Minutes

Preheat the Air fryer to 325F and grease a baking dish lightly.   Mix together all the ingredients in a bowl and transfer the mixture into prepared baking dish. Place in the Air fryer and cook for about 10 minutes. Dish out and serve warm.

5. Sausage Breakfast Casserole

INGREDIENTS for Servings: 4

1 pound hash browns	4 eggs
1 pound ground breakfast sausage	1 tablespoon olive oil
3 bell peppers, diced	Salt and black pepper, to taste
¼ cup sweet onion, diced	

DIRECTIONS and Cooking Time: 20 Minutes

Preheat the Air fryer to 355F and grease the casserole dish with olive oil.   Place the hash browns on the bottom of the casserole dish and top with sausages, bell peppers and onions.   Transfer into the Air fryer and cook for about 10 minutes.   Crack eggs into the casserole dish and cook for 10 more minutes. Season with salt and black pepper and serve warm.

6. Grilled Steak With Parsley Salad

INGREDIENTS for Servings: 4

1 ½ pounds flatiron steak	2 cups parsley leaves
	½ cup parmesan cheese, grated
3 tablespoons olive oil	
Salt and pepper to taste	1 tablespoon fresh lemon juice

DIRECTIONS and Cooking Time: 45 Minutes

Preheat the air fryer at 390F.   Place the grill pan accessory in the air fryer.   Mix together the steak, oil, salt and pepper.   Grill for 15 minutes per batch and make sure to flip the meat halfway through the cooking time.   Meanwhile, prepare the salad by combining in a bowl the parsley leaves, parmesan cheese and lemon juice. Season with salt and pepper.

7. Garlic Feta Asparagus

INGREDIENTS for Servings: 4

2 lbs asparagus, trimmed	½ tsp dried oregano
2 tbsp fresh parsley, chopped	3 garlic cloves, minced
	1 tsp lemon zest
4 oz feta cheese, crumbled	¼ cup olive oil
	1 lemon juice
½ tsp red pepper flakes	Pepper
	Salt

DIRECTIONS and Cooking Time: 15 Minutes
In a bowl, whisk together oil, oregano, red pepper flakes, garlic, and lemon zest.   Add asparagus, crumbled cheese, pepper, and salt and toss well. Transfer asparagus mixture into the air fryer basket and cook at 350 F for 8 minutes.   Drizzle asparagus with lemon juice and sprinkle with parsley.   Serve and enjoy.

8. Air Fried Calzone

INGREDIENTS for Servings: 4

4 oz cheddar cheese, grated	1 egg, beaten
1 oz mozzarella cheese	4 tbsp tomato paste
	1 tsp basil
1 oz bacon, diced	1 tsp oregano
2 cups cooked and shredded turkey	Salt and pepper, to taste

DIRECTIONS and Cooking Time: 20 Minutes
Preheat the air fryer to 350 F. Divide the pizza dough into 4 equal pieces so you have the dough for 4 small pizza crusts. Combine the tomato paste, basil, and oregano in a small bowl.   Brush the mixture onto the crusts, just make sure not to go all the way and avoid brushing near the edges on one half of each crust, place ½ turkey, and season the meat with some salt and pepper. Top the meat with bacon. Divide mozzarella and cheddar cheeses between pizzas. Brush the edges with beaten egg. Fold the crust and seal with a fork. Cook for 10 minutes.

9. Tofu And Mushroom Omelet

INGREDIENTS for Servings: 2

¼ of onion, chopped	2 teaspoons canola oil
8 ounces silken tofu, pressed and sliced	1 garlic clove, minced
3½ ounces fresh mushrooms, sliced	Salt and black pepper, to taste
3 eggs, beaten	
2 tablespoons milk	

DIRECTIONS and Cooking Time: 28 Minutes
Preheat the Air fryer to 360F and grease an Air Fryer pan.   Heat oil in the Air Fryer pan and add garlic and onion.   Cook for about 3 minutes and stir in the tofu and mushrooms.   Season with salt and black pepper and top with the beaten eggs.   Cook for about 25 minutes, poking the eggs twice in between.   Dish out and serve warm.

10. Bacon And Eggs Cup

INGREDIENTS for Servings: 2

1 bacon slice	2 tablespoons milk
2 eggs	½ teaspoon red pepper
1 tablespoon Parmesan cheese, grated	1 teaspoon marinara sauce
2 bread slices, toasted and buttered	Freshly ground black pepper, to taste

DIRECTIONS and Cooking Time: 26 Minutes
Preheat the Air fryer at 355F and place the bacon in it. Cook for about 18 minutes and remove from the Air fryer.   Cut the bacon into small pieces and divide into 2 ramekins.   Crack 1 egg over bacon in each ramekin and pour milk evenly over eggs.   Sprinkle with black pepper and top with marinara sauce.   Layer with the Parmesan cheese and transfer the ramekins in the Air fryer.   Cook for about 8 minutes and serve alongside the bread slices.

11. Balsamic Asparagus Salad

INGREDIENTS for Servings: 4

1 bunch asparagus, trimmed	1 tablespoon balsamic vinegar
1 cup baby arugula	A pinch of salt and black pepper
1 tablespoon cheddar cheese, grated	Cooking spray

DIRECTIONS and Cooking Time: 10 Minutes
Put the asparagus in your air fryer's basket, grease with cooking spray, season with salt and pepper and cook at 360 degrees F for 10 minutes. In a bowl, mix the asparagus with the arugula and the vinegar, toss, divide between plates and serve hot with cheese sprinkled on top

12. Caprese On Toast

INGREDIENTS for Servings: 1

4 tomato slices	1 tbsp chopped basil
4 mozzarella slices	Salt and pepper, to taste
1 tbsp olive oil	

DIRECTIONS and Cooking Time: 7 Minutes

Preheat air fryer to 370 F. Arrange two tomato slices on each bread slice. Season with salt and pepper. Top each slice with 2 mozzarella slices. Put in the air fryer and cook for 3 minutes. Drizzle the toasts with olive oil and top with chopped basil to serve.

13. Sausage Bacon Beans Cancan

INGREDIENTS for Servings: 6

6 medium sausages	4 eggs
6 bacon slices	1 can baked beans
6 bread slices, toasted	Salt and black pepper, to taste

DIRECTIONS and Cooking Time: 20 Minutes
Preheat the Air fryer at 320F and place the bacon and sausages in a fryer basket. Cook for about 10 minutes and dish out. Place the baked beans in first ramekin. Place the eggs whisked with salt and black pepper in another ramekin. Set the Air fryer to 390 degrees F and transfer the ramekins in it. Cook for about 10 more minutes and divide the bread slices, sausage mixture, beans and eggs in 6 serving plates to serve.

14. Asparagus Frittata

INGREDIENTS for Servings: 4

6 eggs	1 cup mozzarella cheese, shredded
3 mushrooms, sliced	
10 asparagus, chopped	1 tsp pepper
	1 tsp salt
1/4 cup half and half	
2 tsp butter, melted	

DIRECTIONS and Cooking Time: 10 Minutes
Toss mushrooms and asparagus with melted butter and add into the air fryer basket. Cook mushrooms and asparagus at 350 F for 5 minutes. Shake basket twice. Meanwhile, in a bowl, whisk together eggs, half and half, pepper, and salt. Transfer cook mushrooms and asparagus into the air fryer baking dish. Pour egg mixture over mushrooms and asparagus. Place dish in the air fryer and cook at 350 F for 5 minutes or until eggs are set. Slice and serve.

15. Spinach Spread

INGREDIENTS for Servings: 4

2 tablespoons coconut cream	2 tablespoons bacon, cooked and crumbled
3 cups spinach leaves	Salt and black pepper to the taste
2 tablespoons cilantro	

DIRECTIONS and Cooking Time: 10 Minutes
In a pan that fits the air fryer, combine all the ingredients except the bacon, put the pan in the machine and cook at 360 degrees F for 10 minutes.

Transfer to a blender, pulse well, divide into bowls and serve with bacon sprinkled on top.

16. Nutty Zucchini Bread

INGREDIENTS for Servings: 16

3 cups all-purpose flour	3 eggs
2 teaspoons baking powder	1 tablespoon ground cinnamon
	1 teaspoon salt
2 cups zucchini, grated	2¼ cups white sugar
	1 cup vegetable oil
1 cup walnuts, chopped	3 teaspoons vanilla extract

DIRECTIONS and Cooking Time: 20 Minutes
Preheat the Air fryer to 320F and grease two (8x4-inch) loaf pans. Mix together the flour, baking powder, cinnamon and salt in a bowl. Whisk together eggs with sugar, vanilla extract and vegetable oil in a bowl until combined. Stir in the flour mixture and fold in the zucchini and walnuts. Mix until combined and transfer the mixture into the prepared loaf pans. Arrange the loaf pans in an Air fryer basket and cook for about 20 minutes. Remove from the Air fryer and place onto a wire rack to cool. Cut the bread into desired size slices and serve.

17. Mozzarella Cups

INGREDIENTS for Servings: 2

2 eggs	1 teaspoon coconut oil, melted
2 oz Mozzarella, grated	
	¼ teaspoon chili powder
1 oz Parmesan, grated	

DIRECTIONS and Cooking Time: 6 Minutes
Crack the eggs and separate egg yolks and egg whites. Then whisk the egg whites till the soft peaks. Separately whisk the egg yolks until smooth and add chili powder. Then carefully add egg whites, Parmesan, and Mozzarella. Stir the ingredients. Brush the silicone egg molds with coconut oil. Then put the cheese-egg mixture in the molds with the help of the spoon. Transfer the molds in the air fryer and cook at 385F for 6 minutes.

18. Spiced Pumpkin Bread

INGREDIENTS for Servings: 4

¼ cup coconut flour	1/8 teaspoon salt
2 tablespoons stevia blend	¼ cup canned pumpkin
1 teaspoon baking powder	2 large eggs
	2 tablespoons unsweetened almond milk
¾ teaspoon pumpkin pie spice	

¼ teaspoon ground cinnamon	1 teaspoon vanilla extract

DIRECTIONS and Cooking Time: 25 Minutes
In a bowl, mix together the flour, stevia, baking powder, spices, and salt. In another large bowl, add the pumpkin, eggs, almond milk, and vanilla extract. Beat until well combined. Then, add in the flour mixture and mix until just combined Set the temperature of air fryer to 350 degrees F. Line a cake pan with a greased parchment paper. Place the mixture evenly into the prepared pan. Arrange the pan into an air fryer basket. Air fry for about 25 minutes or until a toothpick inserted in the center comes out clean. Remove the pans from air fryer and place onto a wire rack for about 5 minutes. Carefully, take out the bread from pan and put onto a wire rack to cool for about 5-10 minutes before slicing. Cut the bread into desired size slices and serve.

19. Breakfast Spinach Pie

INGREDIENTS for Servings: 4

7 ounces white flour	2 tablespoons milk
7 ounces spinach, torn	3 ounces mozzarella cheese, crumbled
2 tablespoons olive oil	
2 eggs, whisked	Salt and black pepper to taste
	1 red onion, chopped

DIRECTIONS and Cooking Time: 19 Minutes
In your food processor, mix the flour with 1 tablespoon of the oil, eggs, milk, salt, and pepper; pulse, then transfer to a bowl. Knead the mixture a bit, cover, and keep in the fridge for 10 minutes. Heat up a pan with the remaining 1 tablespoon of oil over medium heat, and then add all remaining ingredients. Stir, cook for 4 minutes, and remove from heat. Divide the dough into 4 pieces, roll each piece, and place in the bottom of a ramekin. Divide the spinach mixture between the ramekins, place them in your air fryer's basket, and cook at 360 degrees F for 15 minutes. Serve and enjoy!

20. Ham And Cheese Mini Quiche

INGREDIENTS for Servings: 8

3 oz chopped ham	¼ tsp garlic powder
½ cup grated cheese	¼ tsp salt
4 eggs, beaten	¼ tsp black pepper
3 tbsp Greek yogurt	

DIRECTIONS and Cooking Time: 30 Minutes
Preheat the air fryer to 330 F. Take 8 ramekins and sprinkle them with flour to avoid sticking. Cut the shortcrust pastry into 8 equal pieces to make 8 mini quiches. Line the ramekins with the pastry. Combine all of the other ingredients in a bowl. Divide the filling

between the ramekins and cook for 20 minutes in the air fryer.

21. Air Fryer Breakfast Casserole

INGREDIENTS for Servings: 2

3 red potatoes	¼ cup cheddar cheese
3 eggs	1 tablespoon milk
2 turkey sausage patties	Olive oil cooking spray

DIRECTIONS and Cooking Time: 25 Minutes
Preheat the Air fryer to 400 ° F and grease a baking dish with cooking spray. Place the potatoes in the Air fryer basket and cook for about 10 minutes. Whisk eggs with milk in a bowl. Put the potatoes and sausage in the baking dish and pour egg mixture on top. Sprinkle with cheddar cheese and arrange in the Air fryer. Cook for about 15 minutes at 350 ° F and dish out to serve warm.

22. Bacon Pockets

INGREDIENTS for Servings: 6

6 wontons wrap	1 egg yolk, whisked
2 oz bacon, chopped, cooked	1 teaspoon sesame oil
½ cup Edam cheese, shredded	½ teaspoon ground black pepper

DIRECTIONS and Cooking Time: 4 Minutes
Put the chopped bacon in the bowl. Add Edam cheese and ground black pepper. Stir the ingredients gently with the help of the fork. After this, put the mixture on the wonton wrap and fold it in the shape of the pocket. Repeat the steps with remaining filling and wonton wraps. Preheat the air fryer to 400F. Brush every wonton pocket with whisked egg yolk. Then brush the air fryer with sesame oil and arrange the pockets inside. Cook the meal for 2 minutes from each side.

23. Cheesy Mustard Toasts

INGREDIENTS for Servings: 4

2 tablespoons cheddar cheese, shredded	4 bread slices
	1 tablespoon mustard
2 eggs, whites and yolks, separated	1 tablespoon paprika

DIRECTIONS and Cooking Time: 15 Minutes
Set the temperature of Air Fryer to 355 degrees F. Place the bread slices in an Air fryer basket. Air Fry for about 5 minutes or until toasted. Add the egg whites in a clean glass bowl and beat until they form soft peaks. In another bowl, mix together the cheese, egg yolks, mustard, and paprika. Gently, fold in the egg whites. Spread the mustard mixture over the

toasted bread slices.   Air Fry for about 10 minutes. Serve warm!

24. Breakfast Creamy Donuts

INGREDIENTS for Servings: 8

4 tablespoons butter, softened and divided	1 pinch baking soda
2 large egg yolks	1/3 cup caster sugar
2¼ cups plain flour	1 teaspoon cinnamon
1½ teaspoons baking powder	½ cup sugar
	1 teaspoon salt
	½ cup sour cream

DIRECTIONS and Cooking Time: 18 Minutes
Preheat the Air fryer to 355F.   Mix together sugar and butter in a bowl and beat until crumbly mixture is formed.   Whisk in the egg yolks and beat until well combined.   Sift together flour, baking powder, baking soda and salt in another bowl.   Add the flour mixture and sour cream to the sugar mixture.   Mix well to form a dough and refrigerate it.   Roll the dough into 2-inch thickness and cut the dough in half. Coat both sides of the dough with the melted butter and transfer into the Air fryer.   Cook for about 8 minutes until golden brown and remove from the Air fryer.   Sprinkle the donuts with the cinnamon and caster sugar to serve.

25. Ground Pork Bake

INGREDIENTS for Servings: 2

1 tablespoon keto tomato sauce	8 oz ground pork
½ teaspoon dried basil	½ teaspoon butter, melted
1/3 cup Mozzarella, shredded	¼ teaspoon dried oregano
	Cooking spray

DIRECTIONS and Cooking Time: 12 Minutes
Preheat the air fryer to 365F. Then spray the air fryer basket with cooking spray. In the mixing bowl mix up ground pork, marinara sauce, dried basil, oregano, butter, and Mozzarella. Put the mixture in the air fryer basket and spread gently with the help of the spatula. Cook the morning pizza for 12 minutes.

26. Cinnamon Toasts

INGREDIENTS for Servings: 4

10 bread slices	4 tbsp. sugar
1 pack salted butter	½ tsp. vanilla extract
2 tsp. ground cinnamon	

DIRECTIONS and Cooking Time: 15 Minutes
In a bowl, combine the butter, cinnamon, sugar, and vanilla extract. Spread onto the slices of bread.   Set

your Air Fryer to 380°F. When warmed up, put the bread inside the fryer and cook for 4 – 5 minutes.

27. Tofu & Mushroom Omelet

INGREDIENTS for Servings: 2

2 teaspoons canola oil	3½ ounces fresh mushrooms, sliced
¼ of onion, chopped	Salt and freshly ground black pepper, as needed
1 garlic clove, minced	
8 ounces silken tofu, pressed and sliced	
	3 eggs, beaten

DIRECTIONS and Cooking Time: 29 Minutes
Set the temperature of Air Fryer to 355 degrees F.   In an Air Fryer pan, add the oil, onion, and garlic. Air Fry for about 4 minutes.   Add the tofu and mushrooms and sprinkle with salt and black pepper.   Place the beaten eggs evenly on top.   Air Fry for about 25 minutes, opening after every 8 minutes to poke the eggs.   Serve hot.

28. Scotch Eggs

INGREDIENTS for Servings: 4

4 large eggs	8 slices thick-cut bacon
1 package Jimmy Dean's Pork Sausage (12 oz)	4 toothpicks

DIRECTIONS and Cooking Time: 40 Minutes
Hard-boil the eggs, peel the shells and let them cool. Slice the sausage into four parts and place each part into a large circle.   Put an egg into each circle and wrap it in the sausage.   Place inside your refrigerator for 1 hour.   Make a cross with two pieces of thick-cut bacon.   Place a wrapped egg in the center, fold the bacon over top of the egg and secure with a toothpick. Cook inside your fryer at 450°F/230°C for 25 minutes. Enjoy!

29. Easy & Tasty Salsa Chicken

INGREDIENTS for Servings: 4

1 lb chicken thighs, boneless and skinless	Pepper
	Salt
1 cup salsa	

DIRECTIONS and Cooking Time: 30 Minutes
Preheat the air fryer to 350 F.   Place chicken thighs into the air fryer baking dish and season with pepper and salt. Top with salsa.   Place in the air fryer and cook for 30 minutes.   Serve and enjoy.

30. Espresso Oatmeal

INGREDIENTS for Servings: 4

1 cup steel cut oats	2 tsp. vanilla extract
1 cup milk	2 ½ cups water
1 tsp. espresso powder	2 tbsp. sugar

DIRECTIONS and Cooking Time: 27 Minutes
In a pan that fits your air fryer, mix oats with water, sugar, milk and espresso powder; stir, introduce in your air fryer and cook at 360 °F, for 17 minutes.   Add vanilla extract, stir; leave everything aside for 5 minutes; divide into bowls and serve for breakfast.

31. Sausage Quiche

INGREDIENTS for Servings: 4

12 large eggs	1 tsp black pepper
1 cup heavy cream	2 cups shredded cheddar cheese
12 oz sugar-free breakfast sausage	

DIRECTIONS and Cooking Time: 35 Minutes
Preheat your fryer to 375°F/190°C.   In a large bowl, whisk the eggs, heavy cream, salad and pepper together.   Add the breakfast sausage and cheddar cheese.   Pour the mixture into a greased casserole dish.   Bake for 25 minutes.   Cut into 12 squares and serve hot.

32. Banana Chia Seed Pudding

INGREDIENTS for Servings: 1

1 medium- or small-sized banana, ripe	1 can full-fat coconut milk
½ tsp cinnamon	1 tsp vanilla extract
	¼ cup chia seeds

DIRECTIONS and Cooking Time: 1-2 Days
In a bowl, mash the banana until soft.   Add the remaining ingredients and mix until incorporated. Cover and place in your refrigerator overnight. Serve!

33. Posh Soufflé

INGREDIENTS for Servings: 4

¼ cup flour	4 egg yolks
⅓ cup butter	6 egg whites
1 cup milk	1 oz. sugar
1 tsp. vanilla extract	1 tsp. cream of tartar

DIRECTIONS and Cooking Time: 25 Minutes
Set your Air Fryer at 320°F and allow to warm.   In a bowl, mix together the butter and flour until a smooth consistency is achieved.   Pour the milk into a saucepan over a low-to-medium heat. Add in the and allow to dissolve before raising the heat to boil the milk.   Pour in the flour and butter mixture and stir

rigorously for 7 minutes to eliminate any lumps. Make sure the mixture thickens. Take off the heat and allow to cool for 15 minutes.   Spritz 6 soufflé dishes with oil spray.   Place the egg yolks and vanilla extract in a separate bowl and beat them together with a fork. Pour in the milk and combine well to incorporate everything.   In a smaller bowl mix together the egg whites and cream of tartar with a fork. Fold into the egg yolks-milk mixture before adding in the flour mixture. Transfer equal amounts to the 6 soufflé dishes.   Put the dishes in the fryer and cook for 15 minutes.

34. Cherry Tomato Frittata

INGREDIENTS for Servings: 2

½ of Italian sausage	1 teaspoon fresh parsley, chopped
4 cherry tomatoes, halved	1 tablespoon olive oil
3 eggs	Salt and black pepper, to taste
1 tablespoon Parmesan cheese, shredded	

DIRECTIONS and Cooking Time: 10 Minutes
Preheat the Air fryer to 360F.   Place the sausage and tomatoes in a baking pan and transfer in the Air fryer. Cook for about 5 minutes until done and remove the baking dish from oven.   Whisk together eggs with Parmesan cheese, oil, parsley, salt and black pepper and beat until combined.   Drizzle this mixture over sausage and tomatoes and place in the Air fryer. Cook for about 5 minutes and serve warm.

35. Mushroom Frittata

INGREDIENTS for Servings: 1

1 cup egg whites	2 tbsp parmesan cheese, grated
1 cup spinach, chopped	Salt
2 mushrooms, sliced	

DIRECTIONS and Cooking Time: 13 Minutes
Spray pan with cooking spray and heat over medium heat.   Add mushrooms and sauté for 2-3 minutes. Add spinach and cook for 1-2 minutes or until wilted. Transfer mushroom spinach mixture into the air fryer pan.   Whisk egg whites in a mixing bowl until frothy. Season with a pinch of salt.   Pour egg white mixture into the spinach and mushroom mixture and sprinkle with parmesan cheese.   Place pan in air fryer basket and cook frittata at 350 F for 8 minutes.   Slice and serve.

36. Crispy Bread Rolls

INGREDIENTS for Servings: 4

5 large potatoes, boiled and mashed 2 small onions, chopped finely 2 green chilies, seeded and chopped finely 8 bread slices, trimmed 2 tablespoons olive oil, divided	2 tablespoons fresh cilantro, chopped finely ½ teaspoon ground turmeric ½ teaspoon mustard seeds 1 teaspoon curry powder Salt, to taste

DIRECTIONS and Cooking Time: 20 Minutes
Heat 1 tablespoon of olive oil on medium heat in a large skillet and add mustard seeds. Sauté for about 30 seconds and add onions. Sauté for about 5 minutes and add curry leaves and turmeric. Sauté for about 30 seconds and add the mashed potatoes and salt. Mix until well combined and remove from the heat. Transfer into a bowl and keep aside to cool. Stir in the chilies and cilantro and divide the mixture into 8 equal-sized portions Shape each portion into an oval patty. Wet the bread slices with water and squeeze the moisture with your palms. Place one patty in the center of each bread slice and roll the bread around the patty. Seal the edges to secure the filling and coat the rolls evenly with the remaining olive oil. Preheat the Air fryer at 390F and grease the Air fryer basket with some oil. Transfer the rolls into the prepared basket and cook for about 13 minutes until golden.

37. Pineapple Cornbread

INGREDIENTS for Servings: 5

1 (8½-ounces) package Jiffy corn muffin 7 ounces canned crushed pineapple	1/3 cup canned pineapple juice 1 egg

DIRECTIONS and Cooking Time: 15 Minutes
In a bowl, mix together all the ingredients. Set the temperature of Air Fryer to 330 degrees F. Grease a round cake pan. (6"x 3") Place the mixture evenly into the prepared pan. Arrange the cake pan into an Air Fryer basket. Air Fry for about 15 minutes or until a toothpick inserted in the center comes out clean. Remove from Air Fryer and place the pan onto a wire rack for about 10-15 minutes. Carefully, take out the bread from pan and put onto a wire rack until it is completely cool before slicing. Cut the bread into desired size slices and serve.

38. Avocado And Cabbage Salad

INGREDIENTS for Servings: 4

2 cups red cabbage, shredded A drizzle of olive oil	1 small avocado, peeled, pitted and sliced

1 red bell pepper, sliced	Salt and black pepper to the taste

DIRECTIONS and Cooking Time: 15 Minutes
Grease your air fryer with the oil, add all the ingredients, toss, cover and cook at 400 degrees F for 15 minutes. Divide into bowls and serve cold for breakfast.

39. Baked Eggs

INGREDIENTS for Servings: 3

3 eggs ½ teaspoon ground turmeric ¼ teaspoon salt	3 bacon slices 1 teaspoon butter, melted

DIRECTIONS and Cooking Time: 10 Minutes
Brush the muffin silicone molds with ½ teaspoon of melted butter. Then arrange the bacon in the silicone molds in the shape of circles. Preheat the air fryer to 400F. Cook the bacon for 7 minutes. After this, brush the center of every bacon circle with remaining butter. Then crack the eggs in every bacon circles, sprinkle with salt and ground turmeric. Cook the bacon cups for 3 minutes more.

40. Peppers And Cream Cheese Casserole

INGREDIENTS for Servings: 2

2 medium green peppers 1 chili pepper, chopped 4 oz chicken, shredded	1 tablespoon cream cheese ½ cup mozzarella, shredded ¼ teaspoon chili powder

DIRECTIONS and Cooking Time: 5 Minutes
Remove the seeds from the bell peppers. After this, preheat the air fryer to 375F. Meanwhile, in the bowl mix up chili pepper, shredded chicken, cream cheese, and shredded Mozzarella. Add chili powder and stir the mixture until homogenous. After this, fill the bell peppers with chicken mixture and wrap in the foil. Put the peppers in the preheated air fryer and cook for 5 minutes.

41. Cristy's Pancakes

INGREDIENTS for Servings: 1

1 scoop of genX Vanilla 2 tbsp water	1 tbsp or hazelnut meal 1 egg

DIRECTIONS and Cooking Time: 10 Minutes

Add the ingredients together in a bowl and mix together. Pour the mixture into a frying pan, cook on a medium heat for approximately 2 to 3 minutes on each side. (Watch carefully as it may burn quickly.) Serve buttered with a handful of mixed berries.

42. Chi Spacca's Bistecca

INGREDIENTS for Servings: 4

2 pounds bone-in rib eye steak	1 packet Italian herb mix
Salt and pepper to taste	1 tablespoon olive oil

DIRECTIONS and Cooking Time: 45 Minutes
Preheat the air fryer at 390F. Place the grill pan accessory in the air fryer. Season the steak with salt, pepper, Italian herb mix, and olive oil. Cover top with foil. Grill for 45 minutes and flip the steak halfway through the cooking time.

43. Green Beans And Eggs

INGREDIENTS for Servings: 4

1 pound green beans, roughly chopped	2 eggs, whisked
Cooking spray	1 tablespoon sweet paprika
Salt and black pepper to the taste	4 ounces sour cream

DIRECTIONS and Cooking Time: 20 Minutes
Grease a pan that fits your air fryer with the cooking spray and mix all the ingredients inside. Put the pan in the Air Fryer and cook at 360 degrees F for 20 minutes. Divide between plates and serve.

44. Bacon And Egg Bite Cups

INGREDIENTS for Servings: 4

6 large eggs	3 slices bacon, cooked and crumbled
½ cup red peppers, chopped	2 tablespoons heavy whipping cream
¼ cup fresh spinach, chopped	Salt and black pepper, to taste
¾ cup mozzarella cheese, shredded	

DIRECTIONS and Cooking Time: 15 Minutes
Preheat the Air fryer to 300F and grease 4 silicone molds. Whisk together eggs with cream, salt and black pepper in a large bowl until combined. Stir in rest of the ingredients and transfer the mixture into silicone molds. Place in the Air fryer and cook for about 15 minutes. Dish out and serve warm.

45. Yummy Ham Rolls

INGREDIENTS for Servings: 4

1 sheet puff pastry	8 ham slices; chopped
4 handful gruyere cheese; grated	4 tsp. mustard

DIRECTIONS and Cooking Time: 20 Minutes
Roll out puff pastry on a working surface, divide cheese, ham and mustard, roll tight and cut into medium rounds. Place all rolls in air fryer and cook for 10 minutes at 370 degrees F. Divide rolls on plates and serve for breakfast.

46. Egg Yolks With Squid

INGREDIENTS for Servings: 4

½ cup self-rising flour	2 green chilies, seeded and chopped
14 ounces squid flower, cleaned and pat dried	2 curry leaves stalks
	4 raw salted egg yolks
Salt and freshly ground black pepper	½ cup chicken broth
	2 tablespoons evaporated milk
1 tablespoon olive oil	
2 tablespoons butter	1 tablespoon sugar

DIRECTIONS and Cooking Time: 20 Minutes
Set the temperature of Air Fryer to 355 degrees F. Grease an Air Fryer pan. In a shallow dish, add the flour. Sprinkle the squid flower evenly with salt and black pepper. Coat the squid evenly with flour and then shake off any excess flour. Place the squid into the prepared pan in a single layer. Air Fry for about 9 minutes. Remove from the Air Fryer and set aside Now, heat the oil and butter in a skillet over medium heat and sauté the chilies and curry leaves for about 3 minutes. Add the egg yolks and cook for about 1 minute, stirring continuously. Gradually, add the chicken broth and cook for about 3-5 minutes, stirring continuously. Add in the milk and sugar and mix until well combined. Add the fried squid and toss to coat well. Serve hot.

47. Roasted Asparagus With Serrano & Parmesan

INGREDIENTS for Servings: 4

2 tbsp polive oil	12 slices Serrano ham
¼ cup Parmesan cheese, grated	Salt and black pepper to taste

DIRECTIONS and Cooking Time: 15 Minutes
Preheat your Air Fryer to 350 F. Spray the air fryer basket with cooking spray. Season asparagus with salt and black pepper. Wrap each ham slice around each asparagus spear one end to the other end. Drizzle with olive oil and arrange on the air fryer basket. Cook for 10 minutes, shaking once halfway

through. When ready, scatter with Parmesan cheese to serve.

48. Yummy Savory French Toasts

INGREDIENTS for Servings: 2

¼ cup chickpea flour	½ teaspoon red chili
3 tablespoons onion,	powder
chopped finely	¼ teaspoon ground
2 teaspoons green	turmeric
chili, seeded and	¼ teaspoon ground
chopped finely	cumin
Water, as required	Salt, to taste
4 bread slices	

DIRECTIONS and Cooking Time: 4 Minutes
Preheat the Air fryer to 375F and line an Air fryer pan with a foil paper. Mix together all the ingredients in a large bowl except the bread slices. Spread the mixture over both sides of the bread slices and transfer into the Air fryer pan. Cook for about 4 minutes and remove from the Air fryer to serve.

49. Blueberry Cream Cheese With French Toast

INGREDIENTS for Servings: 4

4 slices bread	¼ tsp nutmeg
3 tbsp sugar	4 tbsp berry-flavored
1½ cups corn flakes	cheese
⅓ cup milk	¼ tsp salt

DIRECTIONS and Cooking Time: 15 Minutes
Preheat your air fryer to 400 F. In a bowl, mix sugar, eggs, nutmeg, salt and milk. In a separate bowl, mix blueberries and cheese. Take 2 bread slices and pour the blueberry mixture over the slices. Top with the milk mixture. Cover with the remaining two slices to make sandwiches. Dredge the sandwiches over cornflakes to coat thoroughly. Lay the sandwiches in your air fryer's cooking basket and cook for 8 minutes. Serve with berries and syrup.

50. Scrambled Mug Eggs

INGREDIENTS for Servings: 1

1 mug	Shredded cheese
2 eggs	Your favorite buffalo
Salt and pepper	wing sauce

DIRECTIONS and Cooking Time: 5 Minutes
Crack the eggs into a mug and whisk until blended. Put the mug into your microwave and cook for 1.5 – 2 minutes, depending on the power of your microwave. Leave for a few minutes and remove from the microwave. Sprinkle with salt and pepper. Add your desired amount of cheese on top. Using a fork, mix everything together. Then add your favorite buffalo or hot sauce and mix again. Serve!

51. Broccoli Stuffed Peppers

INGREDIENTS for Servings: 2

4 eggs	1 tsp dried thyme
1/2 cup cheddar	1/4 cup feta cheese,
cheese, grated	crumbled
2 bell peppers, cut in	1/2 cup broccoli,
half and remove seeds	cooked
1/2 tsp garlic powder	1/4 tsp pepper
	1/2 tsp salt

DIRECTIONS and Cooking Time: 40 Minutes
Preheat the air fryer to 325 F. Stuff feta and broccoli into the bell peppers halved. Beat egg in a bowl with seasoning and pour egg mixture into the pepper halved over feta and broccoli. Place bell pepper halved into the air fryer basket and cook for 35-40 minutes. Top with grated cheddar cheese and cook until cheese melted. Serve and enjoy.

52. Mushroom Leek Frittata

INGREDIENTS for Servings: 4

6 eggs	1 cup leeks, sliced
6 oz mushrooms,	Salt
sliced	

DIRECTIONS and Cooking Time: 32 Minutes
Preheat the air fryer to 325 F. Spray air fryer baking dish with cooking spray and set aside. Heat another pan over medium heat. Spray pan with cooking spray. Add mushrooms, leeks, and salt in a pan sauté for 6 minutes. Break eggs in a bowl and whisk well. Transfer sautéed mushroom and leek mixture into the prepared baking dish. Pour egg over mushroom mixture. Place dish in the air fryer and cook for 32 minutes. Serve and enjoy.

53. Almond Crust Chicken

INGREDIENTS for Servings: 2

2 chicken breasts,	¼ cup almonds
skinless and boneless	Pepper
1 tbsp Dijon mustard	Salt
2 tbsp mayonnaise	

DIRECTIONS and Cooking Time: 25 Minutes
Add almond into the food processor and process until finely ground. Transfer almonds on a plate and set aside. Mix together mustard and mayonnaise and spread over chicken. Coat chicken with almond and place into the air fryer basket and cook at 350 F for 25 minutes. Serve and enjoy.

54. Avocado Salad

INGREDIENTS for Servings: 4

1 avocado, peeled, pitted and roughly sliced	½ teaspoon olive oil
½ teaspoon minced garlic	¼ teaspoon salt
¼ teaspoon chili flakes	1 teaspoon cilantro, chopped
1 tablespoon lime juice	1 cup baby spinach
	1 cup cherry tomatoes halved
	Cooking spray

DIRECTIONS and Cooking Time: 3 Minutes
Preheat the air fryer to 400F. Then spray the air fryer basket with cooking spray from inside. Combine all the ingredients inside, cook for 3 minutes, divide into bowls and serve.

55. Taco Wraps

INGREDIENTS for Servings: 4

1 tbsp. water	2 cobs grilled corn kernels
4 pc commercial vegan nuggets, chopped	4 large corn tortillas
1 small yellow onion, diced	Mixed greens for garnish
1 small red bell pepper, chopped	

DIRECTIONS and Cooking Time: 30 Minutes
Pre-heat your Air Fryer at 400°F. Over a medium heat, water-sauté the nuggets with the onions, corn kernels and bell peppers in a skillet, then remove from the heat. Fill the tortillas with the nuggets and vegetables and fold them up. Transfer to the inside of the fryer and cook for 15 minutes. Once crispy, serve immediately, garnished with the mixed greens.

56. Breakfast Tea

INGREDIENTS for Servings: 1

16 oz water	1 tbsp coconut oil
2 tea bags	½ tsp vanilla extract
1 tbsp ghee	

DIRECTIONS and Cooking Time: 5 Minutes
Make the tea and put it to one aside. In a bowl, melt the ghee. Add the coconut oil and vanilla to the melted ghee. Pour the tea from a cup into a Nutribullet cup. Screw on the lid and blend thoroughly.

57. Exquisite German Pancake

INGREDIENTS for Servings: 4

2 tbsp unsalted butter	½ cup flour
2 tbsp sugar, powdered	½ cup milk
	1½ cups fresh strawberries, sliced

DIRECTIONS and Cooking Time: 30 Minutes
Preheat your air fryer to 330 F. Add butter to a pan and melt over low heat. In a bowl, mix flour, milk, eggs and vanilla until fully incorporated. Add the mixture to the pan with melted butter. Place the pan in your air fryer's cooking basket and cook for 12-16 minutes until the pancake is fluffy and golden brown. Drizzle powdered sugar and toss sliced strawberries on top.

58. Oregano And Coconut Scramble

INGREDIENTS for Servings: 4

2 tablespoons oregano, chopped	8 eggs, whisked
Salt and black pepper to the taste	2 tablespoons parmesan, grated
	¼ cup coconut cream

DIRECTIONS and Cooking Time: 20 Minutes
In a bowl, mix the eggs with all the ingredients and whisk. Pour this into a pan that fits your air fryer, introduce it in the preheated fryer and cook at 350 degrees F for 20 minutes, stirring often. Divide the scramble between plates and serve for breakfast.

59. Herb Mushrooms

INGREDIENTS for Servings: 2

10 mushrooms, stems remove	1 tbsp olive oil
1 tbsp dill, chopped	½ tbsp oregano
1 tbsp parmesan cheese, grated	½ tsp dried basil
	Pepper
	Salt

DIRECTIONS and Cooking Time: 12 Minutes
Add mushrooms into the bowl and toss with oil, oregano, basil, pepper, and salt. Add mushrooms into the air fryer basket and cook at 360 F for 6 minutes. Add dill and cheese and toss well and cook for 6 minutes more. Serve and enjoy.

60. Cream Bread

INGREDIENTS for Servings: 12

1 cup milk	4½ cups bread flour
1 large egg	¾ cup whipping cream
½ cup all-purpose flour	1 teaspoon salt
2 tablespoons milk powder	¼ cup fine sugar
	3 teaspoons dry yeast

DIRECTIONS and Cooking Time: 55 Minutes

Preheat the Air fryer to 375F and grease 2 loaf pans. Mix together all the dry ingredients with the wet ingredients to form a dough. Divide the dough into 4 equal-sized balls and roll each ball into a rectangle. Roll each rectangle like a Swiss roll tightly and place 2 rolls into each prepared loaf pan. Keep aside for about 1 hour and place the loaf pans into an air fryer basket. Cook for about 55 minutes and remove the bread rolls from pans. Cut each roll into desired size slices and serve warm.

61. Bacon & Egg Cups

INGREDIENTS for Servings: 2

1 bacon slice	1 tablespoon
2 eggs	Parmesan cheese,
2 tablespoons milk	grated
Freshly ground black pepper, to taste	1 tablespoon fresh parsley, chopped
1 teaspoon marinara sauce	2 bread slices, toasted and buttered

DIRECTIONS and Cooking Time: 23 Minutes
Set the temperature of Air Fryer to 355 degrees F. Place the bacon in an Air Fryer basket and Air Fry for about 10-15 minutes or until tender. Remove from the Air Fryer and cut into small pieces. Divide the bacon into 2 ramekins. Crack 1 egg in each ramekin over the bacon. Pour the milk evenly over eggs and sprinkle with black pepper. Top with marinara sauce, followed by the Parmesan cheese. Place the ramekins in an Air Fryer basket and air fryer for 8 minutes or until desired doneness. Sprinkle with parsley and serve alongside the toasts.

LUNCH & DINNER RECIPES

62. Lamb Satay

INGREDIENTS for Servings: 2

¼ tsp. cumin	2 boneless lamb
1 tsp ginger	steaks
½ tsp. nutmeg	Olive oil cooking spray
Salt and pepper	

DIRECTIONS and Cooking Time: 25 Minutes
Combine the cumin, ginger, nutmeg, salt and pepper in a bowl.   Cube the lamb steaks and massage the spice mixture into each one.   Leave to marinate for ten minutes, then transfer onto metal skewers.   Pre-heat the fryer at 400°F.   Spritz the skewers with the olive oil cooking spray, then cook them in the fryer for eight minutes.   Take care when removing them from the fryer and serve with the low-carb sauce of your choice.

63. Cheeseburger Sliders

INGREDIENTS for Servings: 3

1 lb. ground beef	6 dinner rolls
6 slices cheddar	Salt and pepper
cheese	

DIRECTIONS and Cooking Time: 20 Minutes
Pre-heat the Air Fryer to 390°F.   With your hands, shape the ground beef into 6 x 5-oz. patties. Sprinkle on some salt and pepper to taste.   Place the burgers in the cooking basket and cook for 10 minutes. Take care when removing them from the Air Fryer.   Top the patties with the cheese. Put them back in the Air Fryer and allow to cook for another minute before serving.

64. 'i Love Bacon'

INGREDIENTS for Servings: 4

30 slices thick-cut	10 oz pork sausage
bacon	4 oz cheddar cheese,
12 oz steak	shredded

DIRECTIONS and Cooking Time: 90 Minutes
Lay out 5 x 6 slices of bacon in a woven pattern and bake at 400°F/200°C for 20 minutes until crisp. Combine the steak, bacon and sausage to form a meaty mixture.   Lay out the meat in a rectangle of similar size to the bacon strips. Season with salt/peppe.   Place the bacon weave on top of the meat mixture. Place the cheese in the center of the bacon.   Roll the meat into a tight roll and refrigerate.   Make a 7 x 7 bacon weave and roll the bacon weave over the meat, diagonally.   Bake at 400°F/200°C for 60 minutes or

165°F/75°C internally.   Let rest for 5 minutes before serving.

65. Pasta Salad

INGREDIENTS for Servings: 8

4 tomatoes, medium and cut in eighths	½ cup Italian dressing, fat-free
3 eggplants, small	8 tbsp. parmesan, grated
3 zucchinis, medium sized	2 tbsp. extra virgin olive oil
2 bell peppers, any color	2 tsp. pink Himalayan salt
4 cups large pasta, uncooked in any shape	1 tsp. basil, dried
1 cup cherry tomatoes, sliced	High quality cooking spray

DIRECTIONS and Cooking Time: 2 Hours 25 Minutes
Wash and dry the eggplant. Cut off the stem and throw it away. Do not peel the eggplant. Cut it into half-inch-thick round slices.   Coat the eggplant slices with 1 tbsp. of extra virgin olive oil, and transfer to the Air Fryer basket.   Cook the eggplant for 40 minutes at 350°F. Once it is tender and cooked through, remove from the fryer and set to one side.   Wash and dry the zucchini. Cut off the stem and throw it away. Do not peel the zucchini. Cut the zucchini into half-inch-thick round slices.   Combine with the olive oil to coat, and put it in the Air Fryer basket.   Cook the zucchini for about 25 minutes at 350°F. Once it is tender and cooked through, remove from the fryer and set to one side.   Wash the tomatoes and cut them into eight equal slices. Transfer them to the fryer basket and spritz lightly with high quality cooking spray. Cook the tomatoes for 30 minutes at 350°F. Once they have shrunk and are beginning to turn brown, set them to one side.   Cook the pasta and drain it. Rinse with cold water and set it aside to cool.   Wash, dry and halve the bell peppers. Remove the stems and seeds.   Wash and halve the cherry tomatoes.   In a large bowl, mix together the bell peppers and cherry tomatoes. Stir in the roasted vegetables, cooked pasta, pink Himalayan salt, dressing, chopped basil leaves, and grated parmesan, ensuring to incorporate everything well. Let the salad cool and marinate in the refrigerator. Serve the salad cold or at room temperature.

66. Chickpea & Avocado Mash

INGREDIENTS for Servings: 4

1 medium-sized head of cauliflower, cut into florets	2 tbsp. lemon juice
	Salt and pepper to taste
1 can chickpeas,	4 flatbreads, toasted

drained and rinsed 1 tbsp. extra-virgin olive oil	2 ripe avocados, mashed

DIRECTIONS and Cooking Time: 30 Minutes

Pre-heat the Air Fryer at 425°F. In a bowl, mix together the chickpeas, cauliflower, lemon juice and olive oil. Sprinkle salt and pepper as desired. Put inside the Air Fryer basket and cook for 25 minutes. Spread on top of the flatbread along with the mashed avocado. Sprinkle on more pepper and salt as desired and enjoy with hot sauce.

67. Chicken Fillets & Brie

INGREDIENTS for Servings: 4

4 slices turkey, cured 2 large chicken fillets 4 slices brie cheese	1 tbsp. chives, chopped Salt and pepper to taste

DIRECTIONS and Cooking Time: 40 Minutes

Pre-heat Air Fryer to 360°F. Slice each chicken fillet in half and sprinkle on salt and pepper. Coat with the brie and chives. Wrap the turkey around the chicken and secure with toothpick. Cook for 15 minutes until a brown color is achieved.

68. Corn Stew

INGREDIENTS for Servings: 4

2 leeks, chopped 2 tablespoons butter, melted 2 tomatoes, cubed 2 garlic cloves, minced 4 cups corn ¼ cup chicken stock	1 teaspoon olive oil 4 tarragon sprigs, chopped Salt and black pepper to taste 1 tablespoon chives, chopped

DIRECTIONS and Cooking Time: 15 Minutes

Grease a pan with the oil, and then add all the ingredients and toss. Place the pan in the fryer and cook at 370 degrees F for 15 minutes. Divide the stew between bowls and serve.

69. Pork And Eggs Bowls

INGREDIENTS for Servings: 4

2 eggs, whisked 1 and ½ pounds pork meat, ground 2 teaspoons olive oil	½ cup keto tomato sauce Salt and black pepper to the taste

DIRECTIONS and Cooking Time: 15 Minutes

Heat up a pan that fits the Air Fryer with the oil over medium-high heat, add the meat and brown for 3-4 minutes. Add the rest of the ingredients, toss, put the pan in the machine and cook at 370 degrees F for 12

minutes. Divide into bowls and serve for lunch with a side salad.

70. Lemon Cauliflower And Spinach

INGREDIENTS for Servings: 4

1-pound cauliflower head 1 tablespoon olive oil 1 teaspoon lemon juice 1 teaspoon salt 1 teaspoon chili flakes 2 cups of water	6 bacon slices ½ cup spinach, chopped ½ cup Cheddar cheese, shredded ½ teaspoon minced garlic 1 egg, beaten 1 tablespoon mascarpone

DIRECTIONS and Cooking Time: 20 Minutes

Pour water in the saucepan and bring it to boil. Then add olive oil, lemon juice, salt, and chili flakes. Put the cauliflower head in the boiling water and simmer it for 10 minutes with the closed lid. Meanwhile, mix up minced ginger, egg, mascarpone, Cheddar cheese, and spinach. You should get a smooth and homogenous mixture. After this, cool the cooked cauliflower head and fill it with the spinach mixture. After this, wrap the cauliflower head in the bacon. Preheat the air fryer to 400F. Place the wrapped cauliflower head in the air fryer basket and cook it for 10 minutes or until bacon is light brown. Cut the cooked cauliflower head on 4 servings.

71. Pork And Okra Stew

INGREDIENTS for Servings: 4

1 and ½ pounds pork stew meat, cubed and browned 2 teaspoons sweet paprika 1 cup okra	1 tablespoon olive oil Salt and black pepper to the taste 3 garlic cloves, minced

DIRECTIONS and Cooking Time: 20 Minutes

In your air fryer's pan, combine the meat with the remaining ingredients, toss, cover and cook at 370 degrees F for 20 minutes. Divide the stew into bowls and serve.

72. Air Fryer Bacon Pudding

INGREDIENTS for Servings: 6

4 bacon strips; cooked and chopped. 1 tbsp. butter; soft 2 cups corn 3 eggs; whisked	3 cups bread; cubed 1/2 cup red bell pepper; chopped. 1 tsp. thyme; chopped. 2 tsp. garlic; minced

4 tbsp. parmesan; grated 1 yellow onion; chopped. 1/4 cup celery; chopped.	1/2 cup heavy cream 1 ½ cups milk Cooking spray Salt and black pepper to the taste

DIRECTIONS and Cooking Time: 40 Minutes
Grease your air fryer's pan with cooking spray.   In a bowl; mix bacon with butter, corn, onion, bell pepper, celery, thyme, garlic, salt, pepper, milk, heavy cream, eggs and bread cubes; toss, pour into greased pan and sprinkle cheese all over   Add this to your preheated air fryer at 320 degrees and cook for 30 minutes. Divide among plates and serve warm for a quick lunch.

73. Eggplant Sandwich

INGREDIENTS for Servings: 2

1 large eggplant ½ cup mozzarella, shredded 1 tablespoon fresh basil, chopped	1 teaspoon minced garlic 1 teaspoon salt 1 tablespoon nut oil 1 tomato

DIRECTIONS and Cooking Time: 7 Minutes
Slice the tomato on 4 slices. Then slice along the eggplant on 4 slices. Then rub every eggplant slice with salt, minced garlic, and brush with nut oil. Preheat the air fryer to 400F. Put the eggplant slices in one layer and cook for 2 minutes at 400F. Then flip the vegetables on another side and cook for 2 minutes more. Transfer the cooked eggplant slices on the plate. Sprinkle 2 eggplant slices with basil and mozzarella. Then add 2 tomato slices on 2 eggplant slices. Cover the tomato slices with the remaining 2 eggplant slices and put in the air fryer basket. Cook the sandwich for 3 minutes at 400F.

74. Blue Cheese Chicken Wedges

INGREDIENTS for Servings: 4

Blue cheese dressing 2 tbsp crumbled blue cheese 2 chicken breasts (boneless)	4 strips of bacon 3/4 cup of your favorite buffalo sauce

DIRECTIONS and Cooking Time: 45 Minutes
Boil a large pot of salted water.   Add in two chicken breasts to pot and cook for 28 minutes.   Turn off the heat and let the chicken rest for 10 minutes. Using a fork, pull the chicken apart into strips.   Cook and cool the bacon strips and put to the side.   On a medium heat, combine the chicken and buffalo sauce. Stir until hot.   Add the blue cheese and buffalo pulled chicken. Top with the cooked bacon crumble.   Serve and enjoy.

75. Sausage Balls

INGREDIENTS for Servings: 6

12 oz Jimmy Dean's Sausage 6 oz. shredded cheddar cheese	10 cubes cheddar (optional)

DIRECTIONS and Cooking Time: 25 Minutes
Mix the shredded cheese and sausage.   Divide the mixture into 12 equal parts to be stuffed.   Add a cube of cheese to the center of the sausage and roll into balls.   Fry at 375°F/190°C for 15 minutes until crisp. Serve!

76. Italian Style Eggplant Sandwich

INGREDIENTS for Servings: 4

1 eggplant; sliced 2 tsp. parsley; dried 1/2 cup breadcrumbs 1/2 tsp. Italian seasoning 1/2 tsp. garlic powder 1/2 tsp. onion powder 2 tbsp. milk	4 bread slices Cooking spray 1/2 cup mayonnaise 3/4 cup tomato sauce 2 cups mozzarella cheese; grated Salt and black pepper to the taste

DIRECTIONS and Cooking Time: 26 Minutes
Season eggplant slices with salt and pepper, leave aside for 10 minutes and then pat dry them well.   In a bowl; mix parsley with breadcrumbs, Italian seasoning, onion and garlic powder, salt and black pepper and stir.   In another bowl; mix milk with mayo and whisk well.   Brush eggplant slices with mayo mix, dip them in breadcrumbs, place them in your air fryer's basket, spray with cooking oil and cook them at 400 °F, for 15 minutes; flipping them after 8 minutes.   Brush each bread slice with olive oil and arrange 2 on a working surface.   Add mozzarella and parmesan on each, add baked eggplant slices; spread tomato sauce and basil and top with the other bread slices, greased side down. Divide sandwiches on plates; cut them in halves and serve for lunch.

77. Fried Potatoes

INGREDIENTS for Servings: 1

1 medium russet potatoes, scrubbed and peeled 1 tsp. olive oil ¼ tsp. onion powder A dollop of vegan butter	1/8 tsp. salt A dollop of vegan cream cheese 1 tbsp. Kalamata olives 1 tbsp. chives, chopped

DIRECTIONS and Cooking Time: 55 Minutes

Pre-heat the Air Fryer at 400°F. In a bowl, coat the potatoes with the onion powder, salt, olive oil, and vegan butter. Transfer to the fryer and allow to cook for 40 minutes, turning the potatoes over at the halfway point. Take care when removing the potatoes from the fryer and enjoy with the vegan cream cheese, Kalamata olives and chives on top, plus any other vegan sides you desire.

78. Honey Chicken Thighs

INGREDIENTS for Servings: 4

1½ pounds chicken thighs, skinless and boneless Salt and black pepper to taste ¾ cup honey	½ cup chicken stock 2 teaspoons sweet paprika ½ teaspoon basil, dried

DIRECTIONS and Cooking Time: 25 Minutes
In a bowl, make a mixture with all the ingredients except the chicken thighs; whisk well. Add the chicken thighs to this mix and toss until the wings are coated. Put the chicken in your air fryer's basket and cook at 380 degrees F for 25 minutes. Divide between plates, serve, and enjoy.

79. Italian Lamb Chops

INGREDIENTS for Servings: 2

2 lamp chops 2 tsp. Italian herbs 2 avocados	½ cup mayonnaise 1 tbsp. lemon juice

DIRECTIONS and Cooking Time: 20 Minutes
Season the lamb chops with the Italian herbs, then set aside for five minutes. Pre-heat the fryer at 400°F and place the rack inside. Put the chops on the rack and allow to cook for twelve minutes. In the meantime, halve the avocados and open to remove the pits. Spoon the flesh into a blender. Add in the mayonnaise and lemon juice and pulse until a smooth consistency is achieved. Take care when removing the chops from the fryer, then plate up and serve with the avocado mayo.

80. Mac & Cheese

INGREDIENTS for Servings: 2

1 cup cooked macaroni ½ cup warm milk 1 tbsp. parmesan cheese	1 cup grated cheddar cheese Salt and pepper, to taste

DIRECTIONS and Cooking Time: 15 Minutes
Pre-heat the Air Fryer to 350°F. In a baking dish, mix together all of the ingredients, except for Parmesan.

Put the dish inside the Air Fryer and allow to cook for 10 minutes. Add the Parmesan cheese on top and serve.

81. Beef And Sauce

INGREDIENTS for Servings: 4

1 pound lean beef meat, cubed and browned 2 garlic cloves, minced	Salt and black pepper to the taste Cooking spray 16 ounces keto tomato sauce

DIRECTIONS and Cooking Time: 20 Minutes
Preheat the Air Fryer at 400 degrees F, add the pan inside, grease it with cooking spray, add the meat and all the other ingredients, toss and cook for 20 minutes. Divide into bowls and serve for lunch.

82. Almond Chicken Curry

INGREDIENTS for Servings: 2

10 oz chicken fillet, chopped 1 teaspoon ground turmeric ½ cup spring onions, diced 1 teaspoon salt ½ teaspoon curry powder	½ teaspoon garlic, diced ½ teaspoon ground coriander ½ cup of organic almond milk 1 teaspoon Truvia 1 teaspoon olive oil

DIRECTIONS and Cooking Time: 15 Minutes
Put the chicken in the bowl. Add the ground turmeric, salt, curry powder, diced garlic, ground coriander, and almond Truvia. Then add olive oil and mix up the chicken. After this, add almond milk and transfer the chicken in the air fryer pan. Then preheat the air fryer to 375F and place the pan with korma curry inside. Top the chicken with diced onion. Cook the meal for 10 minutes. Stir it after 5 minutes of cooking. If the chicken is not cooked after 10 minutes, cook it for an additional 5 minutes.

83. Salmon Salad

INGREDIENTS for Servings: 4

4 salmon fillets, boneless 2 tablespoons olive oil Salt and black pepper to the taste	3 cups kale leaves, shredded 2 teaspoons balsamic vinegar

DIRECTIONS and Cooking Time: 8 Minutes
Put the fish in your air fryer's basket, season with salt and pepper, drizzle half of the oil over them, cook at 400 degrees F for 4 minutes on each side, cool down and cut into medium cubes. In a bowl, mix the kale

with salt, pepper, vinegar, the rest of the oil and the salmon, toss gently and serve for lunch.

84. Tomato And Peppers Stew

INGREDIENTS for Servings: 4

4 spring onions, chopped	Salt and black pepper to the taste
2 pound tormatoes, cubed	2 red bell peppers, cubed
1 teaspoon sweet paprika	1 tablespoon cilantro, chopped

DIRECTIONS and Cooking Time: 15 Minutes
In a pan that fits your air fryer, mix all the ingredients, toss, introduce the pan in the fryer and cook at 360 degrees F for 15 minutes. Divide into bowls and serve for lunch.

85. Prosciutto & Potato Salad

INGREDIENTS for Servings: 8

4 lb. potatoes, boiled and cubed	15 oz. sour cream
15 slices prosciutto, diced	2 tbsp. mayonnaise
	1 tsp. salt
	1 tsp. black pepper
2 cups shredded cheddar cheese	1 tsp. dried basil

DIRECTIONS and Cooking Time: 15 Minutes
Pre-heat the Air Fryer to 350°F. Place the potatoes, prosciutto, and cheddar in a baking dish. Put it in the Air Fryer and allow to cook for 7 minutes. In a separate bowl, mix together the sour cream, mayonnaise, salt, pepper, and basil using a whisk. Coat the salad with the dressing and serve.

86. Italian Chicken Mix

INGREDIENTS for Servings: 4

Salt and black pepper to taste	1 cup chicken stock
8 chicken drumsticks, bone-in	28 ounces canned tomatoes, chopped
1 teaspoon garlic powder	1 teaspoon oregano, dried
1 yellow onion, chopped	½ cup black olives, pitted and sliced

DIRECTIONS and Cooking Time: 20 Minutes
Add all the ingredients to a baking dish that fits your air fryer and toss. Place the dish in your air fryer and cook at 380 degrees F for 20 minutes. Divide the mix into bowls and serve.

87. Rosemary Rib Eye Steaks

INGREDIENTS for Servings: 2

¼ cup butter	Salt and pepper
1 clove minced garlic	¼ cup rosemary, chopped
1 ½ tbsp. balsamic vinegar	2 ribeye steaks

DIRECTIONS and Cooking Time: 40 Minutes
Melt the butter in a skillet over medium heat. Add the garlic and fry until fragrant. Remove the skillet from the heat and add in the salt, pepper, and vinegar. Allow it to cool. Add the rosemary, then pour the whole mixture into a Ziploc bag. Put the ribeye steaks in the bag and shake well, making sure to coat the meat well. Refrigerate for an hour, then allow to sit for a further twenty minutes. Pre-heat the fryer at 400°F and set the rack inside. Cook the ribeyes for fifteen minutes. Take care when removing the steaks from the fryer and plate up. Enjoy!

88. Cheese & Macaroni Balls

INGREDIENTS for Servings: 2

2 cups leftover macaroni	1 cup milk
	½ cup flour
1 cup cheddar cheese, shredded	1 cup bread crumbs
	½ tsp. salt
3 large eggs	¼ tsp. black pepper

DIRECTIONS and Cooking Time: 25 Minutes
In a bowl, combine the leftover macaroni and shredded cheese. Pour the flour in a separate bowl. Put the bread crumbs in a third bowl. Finally, in a fourth bowl, mix together the eggs and milk with a whisk. With an ice-cream scoop, create balls from the macaroni mixture. Coat them the flour, then in the egg mixture, and lastly in the bread crumbs. Pre-heat the Air Fryer to 365°F and cook the balls for about 10 minutes, giving them an occasional stir. Ensure they crisp up nicely. Serve with the sauce of your choice.

89. Lamb Stew

INGREDIENTS for Servings: 4

1 cup eggplant, cubed	1 pound lamb stew meat, cubed
2 garlic cloves, minced	
3 celery ribs, chopped	1 tablespoon olive oil
½ cups keto tomato sauce	Salt and black pepper to the taste

DIRECTIONS and Cooking Time: 30 Minutes
Heat up a pan that fits the air fryer with the oil over medium-high heat, add the lamb, salt, pepper and the garlic and brown for 5 minutes. Add the rest of the ingredients, toss, introduce the pan in the machine and cook at 370 degrees F for 25 minutes. Divide into bowls and serve for lunch.

90. Bacon Pancetta Casserole

INGREDIENTS for Servings: 4

2 cups cauliflower, shredded	½ cup heavy cream
3 oz pancetta, chopped	1 teaspoon salt
2 oz bacon, chopped	1 teaspoon cayenne pepper
1 cup Cheddar cheese, shredded	1 teaspoon dried oregano

DIRECTIONS and Cooking Time: 20 Minutes
Put bacon and pancetta in the air fryer and cook it for 10 minutes at 400F. Stir the ingredients every 3 minutes to avoid burning. Then mix up shredded cauliflower and cooked pancetta and bacon. Add salt and cayenne pepper. Mix up the mixture. Add the dried oregano. Line the air fryer pan with baking paper and put the cauliflower mixture inside. Top it with Cheddar cheese and sprinkle with heavy cream. Cook the casserole for 10 minutes at 365F.

91. Pesto Gnocchi

INGREDIENTS for Servings: 4

1 package [16-oz.] shelf-stable gnocchi	⅓ cup parmesan cheese, grated
1 medium-sized onion, chopped	1 tbsp. extra virgin olive oil
3 cloves garlic, minced	Salt and black pepper to taste
1 jar [8 oz.] pesto	

DIRECTIONS and Cooking Time: 30 Minutes
Pre-heat the Air Fryer to 340°F. In a large bowl combine the onion, garlic, and gnocchi, and drizzle with the olive oil. Mix thoroughly. Transfer the mixture to the fryer and cook for 15 – 20 minutes, stirring occasionally, making sure the gnocchi become lightly brown and crispy. Add in the pesto and Parmesan cheese, and give everything a good stir before serving straightaway.

92. Herbed Butter Beef Loin

INGREDIENTS for Servings: 4

1 tbsp. butter, melted	1 tsp. garlic salt
¼ dried thyme	¼ tsp. dried parsley
	1 lb. beef loin

DIRECTIONS and Cooking Time: 25 Minutes
In a bowl, combine the melted butter, thyme, garlic salt, and parsley. Cut the beef loin into slices and generously apply the seasoned butter using a brush. Pre-heat your fryer at 400°F and place a rack inside. Cook the beef for fifteen minutes. Take care when removing it and serve hot.

93. Butternut Squash Stew

INGREDIENTS for Servings: 5

1½ pounds butternut squash, cubed	½ cup celery, chopped
½ cup green onions, chopped	15 ounces canned tomatoes, chopped
3 tablespoons butter, melted	Salt and black pepper to taste
½ cup carrots, chopped	⅛ teaspoon red pepper flakes, dried
1 garlic clove, minced	1 cup quinoa, cooked
½ teaspoon Italian seasoning	1½ cups heavy cream
	1 cup chicken meat, already cooked and shredded

DIRECTIONS and Cooking Time: 15 Minutes
Place all the ingredients in a pan that fits your air fryer and toss. Put the pan into the fryer and cook at 400 degrees F for 15 minutes. Divide the stew between bowls, serve, and enjoy.

94. Turmeric Chicken

INGREDIENTS for Servings: 2

2 chicken thighs, boneless, skinless	½ teaspoon ground turmeric
½ cup spring onions, chopped	¼ teaspoon garam masala
1 green bell pepper, chopped	1 tablespoon olive oil
½ teaspoon chili powder	1 teaspoon keto tomato sauce
¼ teaspoon salt	

DIRECTIONS and Cooking Time: 14 Minutes
Rub the chicken thighs with chili powder, ground turmeric, garam masala, salt, and tomato sauce. Then preheat the air fryer to 365F. Mix up spring onion and bell pepper and place the vegetables in the air fryer. Chop the chicken thighs roughly and put over the vegetables. Cook the meal for 7 minutes. Then shake the ingredients and cook the meal for 7 minutes more.

95. Black Bean Chili

INGREDIENTS for Servings: 6

1 tbsp. olive oil	2 cans diced tomatoes
1 medium onion, diced	2 chipotle peppers, chopped
3 cloves of garlic, minced	2 tsp. cumin
1 cup vegetable broth	2 tsp. chili powder
3 cans black beans, drained and rinsed	1 tsp. dried oregano
	½ tsp. salt

DIRECTIONS and Cooking Time: 25 Minutes
Over a medium heat, fry the garlic and onions in a little oil for 3 minutes. Add in the remaining ingredients,

stirring constantly and scraping the bottom to prevent sticking. Pre-heat your Air Fryer at 400°F. Take a heat-resistant dish small enough to fit inside the fryer and place the mixture inside. Put a sheet of aluminum foil on top. Transfer to the air fryer and cook for 20 minutes. When ready, plate up and serve with diced avocado, chopped cilantro, and chopped tomatoes.

96. Chili Potato Wedges

INGREDIENTS for Servings: 4

1 lb. fingerling potatoes, washed and cut into wedges	1 tsp. black pepper
	1 tsp. cayenne pepper
	1 tsp. nutritional yeast
1 tsp. olive oil	½ tsp. garlic powder
1 tsp. salt	

DIRECTIONS and Cooking Time: 50 Minutes
Pre-heat the Air Fryer at 400°F. Coat the potatoes with the rest of the ingredients. Transfer to the basket of your fryer and allow to cook for 16 minutes, shaking the basket at the halfway point.

97. Cast-iron Cheesy Chicken

INGREDIENTS for Servings: 4

4 chicken breasts	2 green onions
4 bacon strips	4 oz cheddar cheese
4 oz ranch dressing	

DIRECTIONS and Cooking Time: 10 Minutes
Pour the oil into a skillet and heat on high. Add the chicken breasts and fry both sides until piping hot. Fry the bacon and crumble it into bits. Dice the green onions. Put the chicken in a baking dish and top with soy sauce. Toss in the ranch, bacon, green onions and top with cheese. Cook until the cheese is browned, for around 4 minutes. Serve.

98. Oregano Cod And Arugula Mix

INGREDIENTS for Servings: 4

2 tablespoons fresh cilantro, minced	1 pound cod fillets, boneless, skinless and cubed
1 spring onion, chopped	½ teaspoon oregano, ground
Salt and black pepper to the taste	A drizzle of olive oil
½ teaspoon sweet paprika	2 cups baby arugula

DIRECTIONS and Cooking Time: 12 Minutes
In a bowl, mix the cod with salt, pepper, paprika, oregano and the oil, toss, transfer the cubes to your air fryer's basket and cook at 360 degrees F for 12 minutes. In a salad bowl, mix the cod with the remaining ingredients, toss, divide between plates and serve.

99. Pork And Potatoes Recipe

INGREDIENTS for Servings: 2

2 red potatoes; cut into medium wedges	2 lbs. pork loin
	1 tsp. parsley; dried
1/2 tsp. garlic powder	A drizzle of balsamic vinegar
1/2 tsp. red pepper flakes	Salt and black pepper to the taste

DIRECTIONS and Cooking Time: 35 Minutes
In your air fryer's pan; mix pork with potatoes, salt, pepper, garlic powder, pepper flakes, parsley and vinegar; toss and cook at 390 °F, for 25 minutes. Slice pork, divide it and potatoes on plates and serve for lunch.

100. Quinoa And Spinach Salad

INGREDIENTS for Servings: 4

1½ cups quinoa, cooked	2 tomatoes, chopped
	½ cup chicken stock
1 red bell pepper, chopped	½ cup black olives, pitted and chopped
3 celery stalks, chopped	½ cup feta cheese, crumbled
Salt and black pepper to taste	⅓ cup basil pesto
	¼ cup almonds, sliced
4 cups spinach, torn	

DIRECTIONS and Cooking Time: 15 Minutes
In a pan that fits your air fryer, combine the quinoa, bell peppers, celery, salt, pepper, spinach, tomatoes, chicken stock, olives, and basil pesto. Sprinkle the almonds and the cheese on top, and then place the pan in the air fryer and cook at 380 degrees F for 15 minutes. Divide between plates and serve.

101. Garlic Pork And Sprouts Stew

INGREDIENTS for Servings: 4

2 tablespoons olive oil	2 tomatoes, cubed
2 garlic cloves, minced	¼ cup veggie stock
½ pound Brussels sprouts, halved	¼ cup keto tomato sauce
1 pound pork stew meat, cubed	Salt and black pepper to the taste
	1 tablespoon chives, chopped

DIRECTIONS and Cooking Time: 25 Minutes
Heat up a pan that fits the air fryer with the oil over medium-high heat, add the meat, garlic, salt and pepper, stir and brown for 5 minutes. Add all the other ingredients except the chives, toss, introduce in the

fryer and cook at 380 degrees F for 20 minutes. Divide the stew into bowls and serve with chives sprinkled on top.

102.   Chicken Rolls

INGREDIENTS for Servings: 4

2 large zucchini	1 teaspoon salt
½ cup Cheddar cheese, shredded	2 spring onions, chopped
1-pound chicken breast, skinless, boneless	1 teaspoon ground paprika
1 teaspoon dried oregano	½ teaspoon ground turmeric
½ teaspoon olive oil	½ cup keto tomato sauce

DIRECTIONS and Cooking Time: 18 Minutes
Preheat the skillet well and pour the olive oil inside. Put the onions in it and sprinkle with salt, ground paprika, and ground turmeric. Cook the onion for 5 minutes over the medium-high heat. Stir it from time to time. Meanwhile, shred the chicken. Add it in the skillet. Then add oregano. Stir well and cook the mixture for 2 minutes. After this, remove the skillet from the heat. Cut the zucchini into halves (lengthwise). Then make the zucchini slices with the help of the vegetable peeler. Put 3 zucchini slices on the chopping board overlapping each of them. Then spread the surface of them with the shredded chicken mixture. Roll the zucchini carefully in the shape of the roll. Repeat the same steps with remaining zucchini and shredded chicken mixture. Line the air fryer pan with parchment and put the enchilada rolls inside. Sprinkle them with tomato sauce Preheat the air fryer to 350F. Top the zucchini rolls (enchiladas) with Cheddar cheese and put in the air fryer basket. Cook the meal for 10 minutes.

103.   Nearly Pizza

INGREDIENTS for Servings: 4

4 large portobello mushrooms	1 cup shredded mozzarella cheese
4 tsp olive oil	10 slices sugar-free pepperoni
1 cup marinara sauce	

DIRECTIONS and Cooking Time: 30 Minutes
Preheat your fryer to 375°F/190°C.   De-steam the 4 mushrooms and brush each cap with the olive oil, one spoon for each cap.   Place on a baking sheet and bake stem side down for 8 minutes.   Take out of the fryer and fill each cap with 1 cup marinara sauce, 1 cup mozzarella cheese and 3 slices of pepperoni.   Cook for another 10 minutes until browned.   Serve hot.

104.   Mushroom Pizza Squares

INGREDIENTS for Servings: 10

1 vegan pizza dough	¼ red bell pepper, chopped
1 cup oyster mushrooms, chopped	2 tbsp. parsley
1 shallot, chopped	Salt and pepper

DIRECTIONS and Cooking Time: 20 Minutes
Pre-heat the Air Fryer at 400°F.   Cut the vegan pizza dough into squares.   In a bowl, combine the oyster mushrooms, shallot, bell pepper and parsley. Sprinkle some salt and pepper as desired.   Spread this mixture on top of the pizza squares.   Cook in the Air Fryer for 10 minutes.

105.   Salsa Chicken Mix

INGREDIENTS for Servings: 4

4 chicken breasts, skinless, boneless and cubed	1 onion, chopped
	Salt and black pepper to taste
2 tablespoons olive oil	2 tablespoons parsley, dried
3 garlic cloves, minced	
16 ounces jarred chunky salsa	1 teaspoon garlic powder
20 ounces canned tomatoes, peeled and chopped	1 tablespoon chili powder
	12 ounces canned black beans, drained

DIRECTIONS and Cooking Time: 17 Minutes
Place all ingredients into a pan that fits your air fryer and toss.   Put the pan in the fryer and cook at 380 degrees F for 17 minutes.   Divide into bowls, serve, and enjoy.

106.   Bacon Scallops

INGREDIENTS for Servings: 6

12 scallops	Salt and pepper to taste
12 thin bacon slices	
12 toothpicks	½ tbsp oil

DIRECTIONS and Cooking Time: 10 Minutes
Heat a skillet on a high heat while drizzling in the oil. Wrap each scallop with a piece of thinly cut bacon— secure with a toothpick.   Season to taste.   Cook for 3 minutes per side.   Serve!

107.   Rocket Salad

INGREDIENTS for Servings: 4

8 fresh figs, halved	2 tbsp. extra-virgin olive oil
1 ½ cups chickpeas, cooked	Salt and pepper to taste
1 tsp. cumin seeds, roasted then crushed	

4 tbsp. balsamic vinegar	3 cups arugula rocket, washed and dried

DIRECTIONS and Cooking Time: 35 Minutes
Pre-heat the Air Fryer to 375°F. Cover the Air Fryer basket with aluminum foil and grease lightly with oil. Put the figs in the fryer and allow to cook for 10 minutes. In a bowl, combine the chickpeas and cumin seeds. Remove the cooked figs from the fryer and replace with chickpeas. Cook for 10 minutes. Leave to cool. In the meantime, prepare the dressing. Mix together the balsamic vinegar, olive oil, salt and pepper. In a salad bowl combine the arugula rocket with the cooled figs and chickpeas. Toss with the sauce and serve right away.

108. Chicken And Coconut Casserole

INGREDIENTS for Servings: 4

1 lb. chicken breast; skinless, boneless and cut into thin strips	1-inch piece; grated
	4 Thai chilies; chopped.
4 lime leaves; torn	4 tbsp. fish sauce
1 cup veggie stock	6 oz. coconut milk
1 lemongrass stalk; chopped	1/4 cup lime juice
	1/4 cup cilantro; chopped
8 oz. mushrooms; chopped.	Salt and black pepper to the taste

DIRECTIONS and Cooking Time: 35 Minutes
Put stock into a pan that fits your air fryer; bring to a simmer over medium heat, add lemongrass, ginger and lime leaves; stir and cook for 10 minutes. Strain soup, return to pan, add chicken, mushrooms, milk, chilies, fish sauce, lime juice, cilantro, salt and pepper; stir, introduce in your air fryer and cook at 360 °F, for 15 minutes. Divide into bowls and serve.

109. Zucchini Pasta

INGREDIENTS for Servings: 4

½ cup ground beef	2 tablespoons mascarpone
¼ teaspoon salt	
½ teaspoon chili flakes	1 teaspoon olive oil
	½ teaspoon ground black pepper
¼ teaspoon dried dill	
2 zucchinis, trimmed	Cooking spray

DIRECTIONS and Cooking Time: 14 Minutes
In the mixing bowl mix up ground beef, salt, chili flakes, and dill. Then make the small meatballs. Preheat the air fryer to 365F. Spray the air fryer basket with cooking spray and place the meatballs inside in one layer. Cook the meatballs for 12 minutes. Shake them after 6 minutes of cooking to avoid burning. Then remove the meatballs from the air fryer.

With the help of the spiralizer make the zucchini noodles and sprinkle them with olive oil and ground black pepper. Place the zucchini noodles in the air fryer and cook them for 2 minutes at 400F. Then mix up zucchini noodles and mascarpone and transfer them in the serving plates. Top the noodles with cooked meatballs.

110. Tomato And Eggplant Casserole

INGREDIENTS for Servings: 4

2 eggplants, cubed	Salt and black pepper to the taste
1 hot chili pepper, chopped	2 teaspoons olive oil
4 spring onions, chopped	½ cup cilantro, chopped
½ pound cherry tomatoes, cubed	4 garlic cloves, minced

DIRECTIONS and Cooking Time: 20 Minutes
Grease a baking pan that fits the air fryer with the oil, and mix all the ingredients in the pan. Put the pan in the preheated air fryer and cook at 380 degrees F for 20 minutes, divide into bowls and serve for lunch.

111. Ribs

INGREDIENTS for Servings: 4

1 lb. pork ribs	1 tbsp. apple cider vinegar
1 tbsp. barbecue dry rub	
	1 tsp. sesame oil
1 tsp. mustard	

DIRECTIONS and Cooking Time: 60 Minutes
Chop up the pork ribs. Combine the dry rub, mustard, apple cider vinegar, and sesame oil, then coat the ribs with this mixture. Refrigerate the ribs for twenty minutes. Preheat the fryer at 360°F. When the ribs are ready, place them in the fryer and cook for 15 minutes. Flip them and cook on the other side for a further fifteen minutes. Then serve and enjoy!

112. Mustard Chicken

INGREDIENTS for Servings: 4

2 tablespoons Dijon mustard	1 and ½ pounds chicken thighs, bone-in
A pinch of salt and black pepper	
	Cooking spray

DIRECTIONS and Cooking Time: 30 Minutes
In a bowl, mix the chicken thighs with all the other ingredients and toss. Put the chicken in your Air Fryer's basket and cook at 370 degrees F for 30 minutes shaking halfway. Serve these chicken thighs for lunch.

113.   Rosemary Lamb

INGREDIENTS for Servings: 4

1 tablespoon olive oil	¼ cup keto tomato
2 garlic clove, minced	sauce
1 tablespoon	1 and ½ pounds lamb,
rosemary, chopped	cubed
1 cup baby spinach	Salt and black pepper
	to the taste

DIRECTIONS and Cooking Time: 30 Minutes
Heat up a pan that fits the air fryer with the oil over medium heat, add the lamb and garlic and brown for 5 minutes. Add the rest of the ingredients except the spinach, introduce the pan in the fryer and cook at 390 degrees F for 15 minutes, shaking the machine halfway. Add the spinach, cook for 10 minutes more, divide between plates and serve for lunch.

114.   Falafel

INGREDIENTS for Servings: 8

1 tsp. cumin seeds	3 cloves garlic
½ tsp. coriander seeds	¼ cup coriander,
2 cups chickpeas from	chopped
can, drained and	½ onion, diced
rinsed	1 tbsp. juice from
½ tsp. red pepper	freshly squeezed
flakes	lemon
¼ cup parsley,	3 tbsp. flour
chopped	½ tsp. salt cooking
	spray

DIRECTIONS and Cooking Time: 30 Minutes
Fry the cumin and coriander seeds over medium heat until fragrant.   Grind using a mortar and pestle.   Put all of ingredients, except for the cooking spray, in a food processor and blend until a fine consistency is achieved.   Use your hands to mold the mixture into falafels and spritz with the cooking spray.   Preheat your Air Fryer at 400°F.   Transfer the falafels to the fryer in one single layer.   Cook for 15 minutes, serving when they turn golden brown.

115.   Sausage-chicken Casserole

INGREDIENTS for Servings: 8

2 cloves minced garlic	½ tbsp. salt
10 eggs	¼ tbsp. pepper
1 cup broccoli,	¾ cup whipping
chopped	cream
1 cup cheddar,	1 x 12-oz. package
shredded and divided	cooked chicken
	sausage

DIRECTIONS and Cooking Time: 30 Minutes

Pre-heat the Air Fryer to 400°F.   In a large bowl, beat the eggs with a whisk. Pour in the whipping cream and cheese. Combine well.   In a separate bowl, mix together the garlic, broccoli, salt, pepper and cooked sausage.   Place the chicken sausage mix in a casserole dish. Top with the cheese mixture. Transfer to the Air Fryer and cook for about 20 minutes.

116.   Pork And Mushrooms Mix

INGREDIENTS for Servings: 4

1 pound pork stew	1 teaspoon Italian
meat, ground	seasoning
1 cup mushrooms,	½ teaspoon garlic
sliced	powder
2 spring onions,	1 tablespoon olive oil
chopped	
Salt and black pepper	
to the taste	

DIRECTIONS and Cooking Time: 20 Minutes
Heat up a pan that fits the air fryer with the oil over medium high heat, add the meat and brown for 3-4 minutes. Add the rest of the ingredients, stir, put the pan in the Air Fryer, cover and cook at 360 degrees F for 15 minutes. Divide between plates and serve for lunch.

117.   Cauliflower Rice Chicken Curry

INGREDIENTS for Servings: 4

2 lb chicken (4	1 packet curry paste
breasts)	½ cup heavy cream
3 tbsp ghee (can	1 head cauliflower
substitute with	(around 1 kg/2.2 lb)
butter)	

DIRECTIONS and Cooking Time: 40 Minutes
Melt the ghee in a pot. Mix in the curry paste.   Add the water and simmer for 5 minutes.   Add the chicken, cover, and simmer on a medium heat for 20 minutes or until the chicken is cooked.   Shred the cauliflower florets in a food processor to resemble rice.   Once the chicken is cooked, uncover, and incorporate the cream.   Cook for 7 minutes and serve over the cauliflower.

118.   Amazing Beef Stew

INGREDIENTS for Servings: 4

2 lbs. beef meat; cut	1-quart veggie stock
into medium chunks	A handful thyme;
2 carrots; chopped	chopped
4 potatoes; chopped	Salt and black pepper
	to the taste

1/2 tsp. smoked paprika	

DIRECTIONS and Cooking Time: 30 Minutes
In a dish that fits your air fryer; mix beef with carrots, potatoes, stock, salt, pepper, paprika and thyme; stir, place in air fryer's basket and cook at 375 °F, for 20 minutes. Divide into bowls and serve right away for lunch.

119.   Dill Egg Salad

INGREDIENTS for Servings: 3

1 avocado, peeled, pitted 5 eggs 1 tablespoon ricotta cheese 1 tablespoon heavy cream	1 teaspoon mascarpone cheese ½ teaspoon minced garlic 1 pickled cucumber 1 tablespoon fresh dill, chopped

DIRECTIONS and Cooking Time: 17 Minutes
Put the eggs in the air fryer basket and cook them for 17 minutes at 250F. Meanwhile, cut the avocado into cubes and put them in the salad bowl. In the shallow bowl whisk together ricotta cheese, mascarpone, and minced garlic. Grate the pickled cucumber and add it in the cheese mixture. Add dill and stir the mixture well. When the eggs are cooked, cool them in the ice water and peel. Cut the eggs into the cubes and add in the avocado. Add cheese mixture and stir the salad well.

120.   Thanksgiving Sprouts

INGREDIENTS for Servings: 6

1 ½ lb. Brussels sprouts, cleaned and trimmed	3 tbsp. olive oil 1 tsp. salt 1 tsp. black pepper

DIRECTIONS and Cooking Time: 20 Minutes

Pre-heat the Air Fryer to 375°F. Cover the basket with aluminum foil and coat with a light brushing of oil. In a mixing bowl, combine all ingredients, coating the sprouts well.   Put in the fryer basket and cook for 10 minutes. Shake the Air Fryer basket throughout the duration to ensure even cooking.

121.   Roasted Garlic, Broccoli & Lemon

INGREDIENTS for Servings: 6

2 heads broccoli, cut into florets 2 tsp. extra virgin olive oil 1 tsp. salt	½ tsp. black pepper 1 clove garlic, minced ½ tsp. lemon juice

DIRECTIONS and Cooking Time: 25 Minutes
Cover the Air Fryer basket with aluminum foil and coat with a light brushing of oil.   Pre-heat the fryer to 375°F.   In a bowl, combine all ingredients save for the lemon juice and transfer to the fryer basket. Allow to cook for 15 minutes.   Serve with the lemon juice.

122.   'oh So Good' Salad

INGREDIENTS for Servings: 2

½ tsp apple cider vinegar 1 tsp olive/grapeseed oil	6 brussels sprouts 1 grind of salt 1 tbsp freshly grated parmesan

DIRECTIONS and Cooking Time: 10 Minutes
Slice the clean brussels sprouts in half.   Cut thin slices in the opposite direction.   Once sliced, cut the roots off and discard.   Toss together with the apple cider, oil and salt.   Sprinkle with the parmesan cheese, combine and enjoy!

POULTRY RECIPES

123. Mouthwatering Turkey Roll

INGREDIENTS for Servings: 4

1 pound turkey breast fillet, deep slit cut lengthwise with knife	3 tablespoons fresh parsley, chopped finely
1 small red onion, chopped finely	1 teaspoon ground cinnamon
1 garlic clove, crushed	½ teaspoon red chili powder
1½ teaspoons ground cumin	Salt, to taste
	2 tablespoons olive oil

DIRECTIONS and Cooking Time: 40 Minutes
Preheat the Air fryer to 355F and grease an Air fryer basket. Mix garlic, parsley, onion, spices and olive oil in a bowl. Coat the open side of fillet with onion mixture and roll the fillet tightly. Coat the outer side of roll with remaining spice mixture and transfer into the Air fryer. Cook for about 40 minutes and dish out to serve warm.

124. Smoked Chicken Wings

INGREDIENTS for Servings: 8

3 tablespoons paprika	1 teaspoon mustard powder
4 teaspoons salt	4 pounds chicken wings
1 tablespoon chili powder	½ cup barbecue sauce
1 tablespoon garlic powder	1 tablespoon liquid smoke seasoning
1 teaspoon chipotle chili powder	

DIRECTIONS and Cooking Time: 30 Minutes
Place all ingredients in a Ziploc bag. Allow to marinate for at least 2 hours in the fridge. Preheat the air fryer at 375F. Place the grill pan accessory in the air fryer. Grill the chicken for 30 minutes. Flip the chicken every 10 minutes for even grilling. Meanwhile, pour the marinade in a saucepan and heat over medium heat until the sauce thickens. Before serving the chicken, brush with the glaze.

125. Glazed Chicken Wings

INGREDIENTS for Servings: 4

8 chicken wings	1 tablespoon soy sauce
2 tablespoons all-purpose flour	½ teaspoon dried oregano, crushed
1 teaspoon garlic, chopped finely	Salt and freshly ground black pepper, to taste
1 tablespoon fresh lemon juice	

DIRECTIONS and Cooking Time: 19 Minutes
Preheat the Air fryer to 355F and grease an Air fryer basket. Mix all the ingredients except wings in a large bowl. Coat wings generously with the marinade and refrigerate for about 2 hours. Remove the chicken wings from marinade and sprinkle with flour evenly. Transfer the wings in the Air fryer tray and cook for about 6 minutes, flipping once in between. Dish out the chicken wings in a platter and serve hot.

126. Eggs 'n Turkey Bake

INGREDIENTS for Servings: 4

½ teaspoon garlic powder	1 cup coconut milk
½ teaspoon onion powder	2 cups kale, chopped
1-pound leftover turkey, shredded	4 eggs, beaten
	Salt and pepper to taste

DIRECTIONS and Cooking Time: 15 Minutes
Preheat the air fryer for 5 minutes. In a mixing bowl, combine the eggs, coconut milk, garlic powder, and onion powder. Season with salt and pepper to taste. Place the turkey meat and kale in a baking dish. Pour over the egg mixture. Place in the air fryer. Cook for 15 minutes at 350F.

127. Hot Chicken Wings

INGREDIENTS for Servings: 4

1 tablespoon olive oil	2 teaspoons smoked paprika
2 pounds chicken wings	1 teaspoon red pepper flakes, crushed
1 tablespoon lime juice	Salt and black pepper to the taste

DIRECTIONS and Cooking Time: 30 Minutes
In a bowl, mix the chicken wings with all the other ingredients and toss well. Put the chicken wings in your air fryer's basket and cook at 380 degrees F for 15 minutes on each side. Divide between plates and serve with a side salad.

128. Cajun-mustard Turkey Fingers

INGREDIENTS for Servings: 4

½ cup cornmeal mix	1 tsp. soy sauce
½ cup flour	¾ lb. turkey tenderloins, cut into finger-sized strips
1 ½ tbsp. Cajun seasoning	
1 ½ tbsp. whole-grain	

| mustard | Salt and ground black |
| 1 ½ cups buttermilk | pepper to taste |

DIRECTIONS and Cooking Time: 20 Minutes
In a bowl, combine the cornmeal, flour, and Cajun seasoning. In a separate bowl, combine the whole-grain mustard, buttermilk and soy sauce. Sprinkle some salt and pepper on the turkey fingers. Dredge each finger in the buttermilk mixture, before coating them completely with the cornmeal mixture. Place the prepared turkey fingers in the Air Fryer baking pan and cook for 15 minutes at 360°F. Serve immediately, with ketchup if desired.

129. Shishito Pepper Rubbed Wings

INGREDIENTS for Servings: 6

| 1 ½ cups shishito peppers, pureed | 3 pounds chicken wings |
| 2 tablespoons sesame oil | Salt and pepper to taste |

DIRECTIONS and Cooking Time: 30 Minutes
Place all Ingredients in a Ziploc bowl and allow to marinate for at least 2 hours in the fridge. Preheat the air fryer to 390F. Place the grill pan accessory in the air fryer. Grill for at least 30 minutes flipping the chicken every 5 minutes and basting with the remaining sauce.

130. Caesar Marinated Grilled Chicken

INGREDIENTS for Servings: 3

¼ cup crouton	1-pound ground chicken
1 teaspoon lemon zest. Form into ovals, skewer and grill.	2 tablespoons Caesar dressing and more for drizzling
1/2 cup Parmesan	
1/4 cup breadcrumbs	2-4 romaine leaves

DIRECTIONS and Cooking Time: 24 Minutes
In a shallow dish, mix well chicken, 2 tablespoons Caesar dressing, parmesan, and breadcrumbs. Mix well with hands. Form into 1-inch oval patties. Thread chicken pieces in skewers. Place on skewer rack in air fryer. For 12 minutes, cook on 360F. Halfway through cooking time, turnover skewers. If needed, cook in batches. Serve and enjoy on a bed of lettuce and sprinkle with croutons and extra dressing.

131. Turkey Sliders & Chive Mayonnaise

INGREDIENTS for Servings: 6

For the Turkey Sliders:	2 tbsp. chopped scallions
¾ lb. turkey mince	Sea salt and ground black pepper to taste
¼ cup pickled jalapeno, chopped	For the Chive Mayo:
1 tbsp. oyster sauce	1 cup mayonnaise
1 – 2 cloves garlic, minced	1 tbsp. chives
	1 tsp. salt
1 tbsp. chopped fresh cilantro	Zest of 1 lime

DIRECTIONS and Cooking Time: 20 Minutes
In a bowl, combine together all of the ingredients for the turkey sliders. Use your hands to shape 6 equal amounts of the mixture into slider patties. Transfer the patties to the Air Fryer and fry them at 365°F for 15 minutes. In the meantime, prepare the Chive Mayo by combining the rest of the ingredients. Make sandwiches by placing each patty between two burger buns and serve with the mayo.

132. Simple Paprika Duck

INGREDIENTS for Servings: 4

Salt and black pepper to the taste	1 pound duck breasts, skinless, boneless and cubed
1 tablespoon olive oil	¼ cup chicken stock
½ teaspoon sweet paprika	1 teaspoon thyme, chopped

DIRECTIONS and Cooking Time: 25 Minutes
Heat up a pan that fits your air fryer with the oil over medium heat, add the duck pieces, and brown them for 5 minutes. Add the rest of the ingredients, toss, put the pan in the machine and cook at 380 degrees F for 20 minutes. Divide between plates and serve.

133. Asian Chicken Filets With Cheese

INGREDIENTS for Servings: 2

4 rashers smoked bacon	2 chicken filets
1/2 teaspoon coarse sea salt	1 teaspoon black mustard seeds
1/4 teaspoon black pepper, preferably freshly ground	1 teaspoon mild curry powder
1 teaspoon garlic, minced	1/2 cup coconut milk
	1/3 cup tortilla chips, crushed
1 (2-inch) piece ginger, peeled and minced	1/2 cup Pecorino Romano cheese, freshly grated

DIRECTIONS and Cooking Time: 50 Minutes
Start by preheating your Air Fryer to 400 degrees F. Add the smoked bacon and cook in the preheated Air

Fryer for 5 to 7 minutes. Reserve. In a mixing bowl, place the chicken fillets, salt, black pepper, garlic, ginger, mustard seeds, curry powder, and milk. Let it marinate in your refrigerator about 30 minutes. In another bowl, mix the crushed chips and grated Pecorino Romano cheese. Dredge the chicken fillets through the chips mixture and transfer them to the cooking basket. Reduce the temperature to 380 degrees F and cook the chicken for 6 minutes. Turn them over and cook for a further 6 minutes. Repeat the process until you have run out of ingredients. Serve with reserved bacon. Enjoy!

134. Rotisserie Chicken With Herbes De Provence

INGREDIENTS for Servings: 6

3 pounds chicken, whole	2 tablespoons dried herbes de Provence
1 tablespoon salt	

DIRECTIONS and Cooking Time: 1 Hour
Season the whole chicken with dried herbes de Provence and salt. Rub all the seasoning on the chicken including the cavity. Preheat the air fryer at 375F. Place the grill pan accessory in the air fryer. Place the chicken and grill for 1 hour.

135. Hoisin Glazed Turkey Drumsticks

INGREDIENTS for Servings: 4

2 turkey drumsticks	Salt and ground black pepper, to taste
2 tbsp. balsamic vinegar	2 ½ tbsp. butter, melted
2 tbsp. dry white wine	For the Hoisin Glaze:
1 tbsp. extra-virgin olive oil	2 tbsp. hoisin sauce
1 sprig rosemary, chopped	1 tbsp. honey
	1 tbsp. honey mustard

DIRECTIONS and Cooking Time: 40 Minutes + Marinating Time
In a bowl, coat the turkey drumsticks with the vinegar, wine, olive oil, and rosemary. Allow to marinate for 3 hours. Pre-heat the Air Fryer to 350°F. Sprinkle the turkey drumsticks with salt and black pepper. Cover the surface of each drumstick with the butter. Place the turkey in the fryer and cook at 350°F for 30 - 35 minutes, flipping it occasionally through the cooking time. You may have to do this in batches. In the meantime, make the Hoisin glaze by combining all the glaze ingredients. Pour the glaze over the turkey, and roast for another 5 minutes. Allow the drumsticks to rest for about 10 minutes before carving.

136. Cardamom And Almond Duck

INGREDIENTS for Servings: 4

4 duck legs	¼ teaspoon allspice
Juice of ½ lemon	2 tablespoons almonds, toasted and chopped
Zest of ½ lemon, grated	
1 tablespoon cardamom, crushed	2 tablespoons olive oil

DIRECTIONS and Cooking Time: 30 Minutes
In a bowl, mix the duck legs with the remaining ingredients except the almonds and toss. Put the duck legs in your air fryer's basket and cook at 380 degrees F for 15 minutes on each side. Divide the duck legs between plates, sprinkle the almonds on top and serve with a side salad.

137. Paprika Chicken Legs With Turnip

INGREDIENTS for Servings: 3

1 pound chicken legs	1 teaspoon paprika
1 teaspoon Himalayan salt	1 teaspoon butter, melted
1/2 teaspoon ground black pepper	1 turnip, trimmed and sliced

DIRECTIONS and Cooking Time: 30 Minutes
Spritz the sides and bottom of the cooking basket with a nonstick cooking spray. Season the chicken legs with salt, paprika, and ground black pepper. Cook at 370 degrees F for 10 minutes. Increase the temperature to 380 degrees F. Drizzle turnip slices with melted butter and transfer them to the cooking basket with the chicken. Cook the turnips and chicken for 15 minutes more, flipping them halfway through the cooking time. As for the chicken, an instant-read thermometer should read at least 165 degrees F. Serve and enjoy!

138. Air Fried Chicken With Honey & Lemon

INGREDIENTS for Servings: 6

1 whole chicken, 3 lb	1 apple
2 red and peeled onions	Fresh chopped thyme
2 tbsp olive oil	Salt and pepper
2 apricots	Marinade:
1 zucchini	5 oz honey
2 cloves finely chopped garlic	juice from 1 lemon
	2 tbsp olive oil
	Salt and pepper

DIRECTIONS and Cooking Time: 40 Minutes

For the stuffing, chop all ingredients into tiny pieces. Transfer to a large bowl and add the olive oil. Season with salt and pepper. Fill the cavity of the chicken with the stuffing, without packing it tightly. Place the chicken in the air fryer and cook for 10 minutes at 340 F. Warm the honey and the lemon juice in a large pan; season with salt and pepper. Reduce the temperature of the air fryer to 320 F. Brush the chicken with some of the honey-lemon marinade and return it to the fryer. Cook for another 15 minutes; brush the chicken every 5 minutes with the marinade. Serve.

139. Balsamic Duck And Cranberry Sauce

INGREDIENTS for Servings: 4

A pinch of salt and black pepper	4 duck breasts, boneless, skin-on and scored
1 tablespoon olive oil	
¼ cup balsamic vinegar	½ cup dried cranberries

DIRECTIONS and Cooking Time: 25 Minutes
Heat up a pan that fits your air fryer with the oil over medium-high heat, add the duck breasts skin side down and cook for 5 minutes. Add the rest of the ingredients, toss, put the pan in the fryer and cook at 380 degrees F for 20 minutes. Divide between plates and serve.

140. Marrod's Meatballs

INGREDIENTS for Servings: 6

1 lb. ground turkey	1 tsp. crushed red pepper flakes
1 tbsp. fresh mint leaves, finely chopped	¼ cup melted butter
1 tsp. onion powder	¾ tsp. fine sea salt
1 ½ teaspoons garlic paste	¼ cup grated Pecorino Romano

DIRECTIONS and Cooking Time: 15 Minutes
In a bowl, combine all of the ingredients well. Using an ice cream scoop, mold the meat into balls. Air fry the meatballs at 380°F for about 7 minutes, in batches if necessary. Shake the basket frequently throughout the cooking time for even results. Serve with basil leaves and tomato sauce if desired.

141. Crispy 'n Salted Chicken Meatballs

INGREDIENTS for Servings: 6

½ cup almond flour	1 tablespoon coconut milk
¾ pound skinless boneless chicken breasts, ground	2 eggs, beaten
	Salt and pepper to taste

1 ½ teaspoon herbs de Provence	

DIRECTIONS and Cooking Time: 20 Minutes
Mix all ingredient in a bowl. Form small balls using the palms of your hands. Place in the fridge to set for at least 2 hours. Preheat the air fryer for 5 minutes. Place the chicken balls in the fryer basket. Cook for 20 minutes at 325F. Halfway through the cooking time, give the fryer basket a shake to cook evenly on all sides.

142. Honey-balsamic Orange Chicken

INGREDIENTS for Servings: 3

½ cup balsamic vinegar	½ cup honey
1 ½ pounds boneless chicken breasts, pounded	1 teaspoon fresh oregano, chopped
	2 tablespoons extra virgin olive oil
1 tablespoon orange zest	Salt and pepper to taste

DIRECTIONS and Cooking Time: 40 Minutes
Put the chicken in a Ziploc bag and pour over the rest of the Ingredients. Shake to combine everything. Allow to marinate in the fridge for at least 2 hours. Preheat the air fryer to 390F. Place the grill pan accessory in the air fryer. Grill the chicken for 40 minutes.

143. Original Chicken Chilaquiles

INGREDIENTS for Servings: 4

1 (8-ounce) skinless, boneless chicken breast	4 tablespoons feta cheese, crumbled
2 (14½-ounce) can diced tomatoes	3 garlic cloves, chopped
10 corn tortillas, cut into diamond slices	½ of poblano pepper
	Salt, to taste
3 red onions, sliced	1 tablespoon olive oil
	¼ cup sour cream

DIRECTIONS and Cooking Time: 30 Minutes
Preheat the Air fryer to 400F and grease an Air fryer basket. Add half of tortilla slices, half of olive oil in a bowl and salt and toss to coat well. Cook chicken breasts for about 20 minutes in a pan of water. Dish out the chicken and shred with 2 forks. Put onion, garlic, poblano pepper and tomato in a food processor and pulse till smooth. Transfer the onion mixture into a skillet and bring to a boil on medium-high heat. Reduce the heat to medium-low and let it simmer for about 10 minutes. Season with salt and dish out to keep aside. Arrange the tortilla slices in an Air fryer

basket in 2 batches and cook for about 10 minutes. Dish out the tortillas into the serving bowl and top with chicken and onion sauce.

144. Juicy Turkey Breast Tenderloin

INGREDIENTS for Servings: 3

1 turkey breast tenderloin	1/2 tsp sage
	1/2 tsp pepper
1/2 tsp smoked paprika	1/2 tsp thyme
	1/2 tsp salt

DIRECTIONS and Cooking Time: 25 Minutes
Preheat the air fryer to 350 F. Spray air fryer basket with cooking spray. Rub turkey breast tenderloin with paprika, pepper, thyme, sage, and salt and place in the air fryer basket. Cook for 25 minutes. Turn halfway through. Slice and serve.

145. Korean Chicken Tenders

INGREDIENTS for Servings: 3

12 oz chicken tenders, skinless and boneless	2 tsp sesame seeds, toasted
2 tbsp green onion, chopped	1 tbsp ginger, grated
	1/4 cup sesame oil
3 garlic cloves, chopped	1/2 cup soy sauce
	1/4 tsp pepper

DIRECTIONS and Cooking Time: 10 Minutes
Slide chicken tenders onto the skewers. In a large bowl, mix together green onion, garlic, sesame seeds, ginger, sesame oil, soy sauce, and pepper. Add chicken skewers into the bowl and coat well with marinade. Place in refrigerator for overnight. Preheat the air fryer to 390 F. Place marinated chicken skewers into the air fryer basket and cook for 10 minutes.

146. Cheese Herb Chicken Wings

INGREDIENTS for Servings: 4

1 tsp herb de Provence	2 lbs chicken wings
	1 tsp paprika
½ cup parmesan cheese, grated	Salt

DIRECTIONS and Cooking Time: 15 Minutes
Preheat the air fryer to 350 F. In a small bowl, mix together cheese, herb de Provence, paprika, and salt. Spray air fryer basket with cooking spray. Toss chicken wings with cheese mixture and place into the air fryer basket and cook for 15 minutes. Turn halfway through. Serve and enjoy.

147. Duck And Lettuce Salad

INGREDIENTS for Servings: 4

2 duck breasts, boneless and skin on	3 cups lettuce leaves, torn
1 teaspoon coconut oil, melted	12 mint leaves, torn
	For the dressing:
A pinch of salt and black pepper	1 tablespoon lemon juice
2 shallots, sliced	½ tablespoon balsamic vinegar
12 cherry tomatoes, halved	2 and ½ tablespoons olive oil
1 tablespoon balsamic vinegar	½ teaspoon mustard

DIRECTIONS and Cooking Time: 20 Minutes
Heat up a pan that fits your air fryer with the coconut oil over medium heat, add the duck breasts skin side down and cook for 3 minutes. Add salt, pepper, shallots, tomatoes and 1 tablespoon balsamic vinegar, toss, put the pan in the fryer and cook at 370 degrees F for 17 minutes. Cool this mix down, thinly slice the duck breast and put it along with the tomatoes and shallots in a bowl. Add mint and salad leaves and toss. In a separate bowl, mix ½ tablespoon vinegar with lemon juice, oil and mustard and whisk well. Pour this over the duck salad, toss and serve.

148. Tarragon Turkey Tenderloins With Baby Potatoes

INGREDIENTS for Servings: 6

2 pounds turkey tenderloins	2 tablespoons dry white wine
2 teaspoons olive oil	1 tablespoon fresh tarragon leaves, chopped
Salt and ground black pepper, to taste	
1 teaspoon smoked paprika	1 pound baby potatoes, rubbed

DIRECTIONS and Cooking Time: 50 Minutes
Brush the turkey tenderloins with olive oil. Season with salt, black pepper, and paprika. Afterwards, add the white wine and tarragon. Cook the turkey tenderloins at 350 degrees F for 30 minutes, flipping them over halfway through. Let them rest for 5 to 9 minutes before slicing and serving. After that, spritz the sides and bottom of the cooking basket with the remaining 1 teaspoon of olive oil. Then, preheat your Air Fryer to 400 degrees F; cook the baby potatoes for 15 minutes. Serve with the turkey and enjoy!

149. Bacon-wrapped Chicken

INGREDIENTS for Servings: 6

1 chicken breast, cut into 6 pieces	6 rashers back bacon
	1 tbsp. soft cheese

DIRECTIONS and Cooking Time: 20 Minutes
Put the bacon rashers on a flat surface and cover one side with the soft cheese. Lay the chicken pieces on each bacon rasher. Wrap the bacon around the chicken and use a toothpick stick to hold each one in place. Put them in Air Fryer basket. Air fry at 350°F for 15 minutes.

150.   Cajun Chicken Thighs

INGREDIENTS for Servings: 4

½ cup all-purpose flour	1½ tablespoons Cajun seasoning
1 egg	1 teaspoon seasoning salt
4 (4-ounces) skin-on chicken thighs	

DIRECTIONS and Cooking Time: 25 Minutes
Preheat the Air fryer to 355F and grease an Air fryer basket. Mix the flour, Cajun seasoning and salt in a bowl. Whisk the egg in another bowl and coat the chicken thighs with the flour mixture. Dip into the egg and dredge again into the flour mixture. Arrange the chicken thighs into the Air Fryer basket, skin side down and cook for about 25 minutes. Dish out the chicken thighs onto a serving platter and serve hot.

151.   Garlic Paprika Rubbed Chicken Breasts

INGREDIENTS for Servings: 4

1 tablespoon stevia powder	2 tablespoons lemon juice, freshly squeezed
2 tablespoons Spanish paprika	4 boneless chicken breasts
2 teaspoon minced garlic	Salt and pepper to taste
3 tablespoons olive oil	

DIRECTIONS and Cooking Time: 30 Minutes
Preheat the air fryer for 5 minutes. Place all ingredients in a baking dish that will fit in the air fryer. Stir to combine. Place the chicken pieces in the air fryer. Cook for 30 minutes at 325F.

152.   Quick And Crispy Chicken

INGREDIENTS for Servings: 4

2 tbsp butter	1 large egg, whisked
2 oz breadcrumbs	

DIRECTIONS and Cooking Time: 15 Minutes
Preheat air fryer to 380 F. Combine butter the breadcrumbs in a bowl. Keep mixing and stirring until

the mixture gets crumbly. Dip the chicken in the egg wash. Then dip the chicken in the crumbs mix. Cook for 10 minutes. Serve.

153.   Simple Chicken Wings

INGREDIENTS for Servings: 2

Salt and black pepper, to taste	1 pound chicken wings

DIRECTIONS and Cooking Time: 25 Minutes
Preheat the Air fryer to 380F and grease an Air fryer basket. Season the chicken wings evenly with salt and black pepper. Arrange the drumsticks into the Air Fryer basket and cook for about 25 minutes. Dish out the chicken drumsticks onto a serving platter and serve hot.

154.   Turkey With Indian Mint Sauce

INGREDIENTS for Servings: 4

1 1/2 pounds turkey breast, quartered	1/2 cup dry sherry
1/2 teaspoon hot paprika	Freshly cracked pink or green peppercorns, to taste
1 teaspoon kosher salt	For the Indian Mint Sauce:
1/3 teaspoon shallot powder	1/3 cup sour cream
2 cloves garlic, peeled and halved	1 ½ tablespoons fresh roughly chopped mint
	1 cup plain yogurt

DIRECTIONS and Cooking Time: 35 Minutes + Marinating Time
Firstly, rub the garlic halves evenly over the surface of the turkey breast. Add the dry sherry, shallot powder, hot paprika, salt, and cracked peppercorns. Allow it to marinate in your refrigerator for at least 1½ hours. Set your air fryer to cook at 365 degrees F. Roast the turkey for 32 minutes, turning halfway through; roast in batches. Meanwhile, prepare your sauce by mixing all the ingredients. Serve warm the roasted turkey with the sauce. Bon appétit!

155.   Chicken Satay

INGREDIENTS for Servings: 4

4 chicken wings	1 teaspoon dried cilantro
1 teaspoon olive oil	½ teaspoon salt
1 teaspoon keto tomato sauce	

DIRECTIONS and Cooking Time: 14 Minutes
String the chicken wings on the wooden skewers. Then in the shallow bowl mix up olive oil, tomato sauce, dried cilantro, and salt. Spread the chicken

skewers with the tomato mixture. Preheat the air fryer to 390F. Arrange the chicken satay in the air fryer and cook the meal for 10 minutes. Then flip the chicken satay on another side and cook it for 4 minutes more.

156. Red Thai Turkey Drumsticks In Coconut Milk

INGREDIENTS for Servings: 2

1 tablespoon red curry paste 1/2 teaspoon cayenne pepper 1 ½ tablespoons minced ginger 2 turkey drumsticks	1/4 cup coconut milk 1 teaspoon kosher salt, or more to taste 1/3 teaspoon ground pepper, to more to taste

DIRECTIONS and Cooking Time: 25 Minutes
First of all, place turkey drumsticks with all ingredients in your refrigerator; let it marinate overnight. Cook turkey drumsticks at 380 degrees F for 23 minutes; make sure to flip them over at half-time. Serve with the salad on the side.

157. Penne Chicken Sausage Meatballs

INGREDIENTS for Servings: 4

1 cup chicken meat, ground 1 sweet red pepper, minced ¼ cup green onions, chopped 1 green garlic, minced ½ tsp. cumin powder	4 tbsp. friendly bread crumbs 1 tbsp. fresh coriander, minced ½ tsp. sea salt ¼ tsp. mixed peppercorns, ground 1 package penne pasta, cooked

DIRECTIONS and Cooking Time: 20 Minutes
Pre-heat the Air Fryer at 350°F. Put the chicken, red pepper, green onions, and garlic into a mixing bowl and stir together to combine. Throw in the seasoned bread crumbs and all of the seasonings. Combine again. Use your hands to mold equal amounts of the mixture into small balls, each one roughly the size of a golf ball. Put them in the fryer and cook for 15 minutes. Shake once or twice throughout the cooking time for even results. Serve with cooked penne pasta.

158. Lemon & Garlic Chicken

INGREDIENTS for Servings: 1

1 chicken breast 1 tsp. garlic, minced 1 tbsp. chicken	Handful black peppercorns

seasoning 1 lemon juice	Pepper and salt to taste

DIRECTIONS and Cooking Time: 25 Minutes
Pre-heat the Air Fryer to 350°F. Sprinkle the chicken with pepper and salt. Massage the chicken seasoning into the chicken breast, coating it well, and lay the seasoned chicken on a sheet of aluminum foil. Top the chicken with the garlic, lemon juice, and black peppercorns. Wrap the foil to seal the chicken tightly. Cook the chicken in the fryer basket for 15 minutes.

159. Crunchy Chicken Tacos

INGREDIENTS for Servings: 4

1 tbsp taco seasoning Salt and black pepper to taste 1 cup flour 1 egg, beaten ½ cup breadcrumbs	4 taco shells 2 cups shredded white cabbage 3 tbsp Greek yogurt dressing

DIRECTIONS and Cooking Time: 20 Minutes
Preheat your Air Fryer to 380 F. Spray the air fryer basket with cooking spray. Season the chicken with taco seasoning, salt, and black pepper. In 3 separate bowls, add breadcrumbs in one, flour in another, and beaten egg in a third bowl. Dredge chicken in flour, then in egg, and then in the breadcrumbs. Spray with cooking spray and transfer to the cooking basket. Cook for 12 minutes, flipping once halfway through. Fill the taco shells with chicken strips, cabbage, and yogurt dressing to serve.

160. Spicy Chicken Drumsticks With Herbs

INGREDIENTS for Servings: 6

6 chicken drumsticks Sauce: 3 tablespoons olive oil 3 tablespoons tamari sauce	6 ounces hot sauce 1 teaspoon dried thyme 1/2 teaspoon dried oregano

DIRECTIONS and Cooking Time: 40 Minutes
Spritz the sides and bottom of the cooking basket with a nonstick cooking spray. Cook the chicken drumsticks at 380 degrees F for 35 minutes, flipping them over halfway through. Meanwhile, heat the hot sauce, olive oil, tamari sauce, thyme, and oregano in a pan over medium-low heat; reserve. Drizzle the sauce over the prepared chicken drumsticks; toss to coat well and serve. Bon appétit!

161. Crunchy Coconut Chicken

INGREDIENTS for Servings: 4

4 chicken breasts cut into strips	¼ tsp pepper
½ cup cornstarch	¼ tsp salt
	3 eggs, beaten

DIRECTIONS and Cooking Time: 22 Minutes
Preheat air fryer to 350 F. Mix salt, pepper, and cornstarch in a bowl. Line a baking sheet with parchment paper. Dip the chicken first in the cornstarch, then into the eggs, and finally, coat with coconut flakes. Arrange on the air fryer basket and cook for 16 minutes, flipping once until crispy.

162.   Dijon-garlic Thighs

INGREDIENTS for Servings: 6

1 tablespoon cider vinegar	2 tablespoon olive oil
1 tablespoon Dijon mustard	2 teaspoons herbs de Provence
1-pound chicken thighs	Salt and pepper to taste

DIRECTIONS and Cooking Time: 25 Minutes
Place all ingredients in a Ziploc bag. Allow to marinate in the fridge for at least 2 hours. Preheat the air fryer for 5 minutes. Place the chicken in the fryer basket. Cook for 25 minutes at 350F.

163.   Roast Chicken Recipe From Africa

INGREDIENTS for Servings: 6

¼ cup fresh lemon juice	½ cup piri piri sauce
1 large shallots, quartered	3 cloves of garlic, minced
1-inch fresh ginger, peeled and sliced thinly	3 pounds chicken breasts
	Salt and pepper to taste

DIRECTIONS and Cooking Time: 45 Minutes
Preheat the air fryer to 390F. Place the grill pan accessory in the air fryer. On a large foil, place the chicken top with the rest of the Ingredients. Fold the foil and crimp the edges. Grill for 45 minutes.

164.   Sweet And Sour Chicken Thighs

INGREDIENTS for Servings: 2

1 scallion, finely chopped	½ tablespoon soy sauce
2 (4-ounces) skinless, boneless chicken thighs	½ tablespoon rice vinegar
	1 teaspoon sugar

½ cup corn flour	Salt and black pepper, as required
1 garlic clove, minced	

DIRECTIONS and Cooking Time: 20 Minutes
Preheat the Air fryer to 390F and grease an Air fryer basket.   Mix all the ingredients except chicken and corn flour in a bowl.   Place the corn flour in another bowl.   Coat the chicken thighs into the marinade and then dredge into the corn flour.   Arrange the chicken thighs into the Air Fryer basket, skin side down and cook for about 10 minutes.   Set the Air fryer to 355F and cook for 10 more minutes.   Dish out the chicken thighs onto a serving platter and serve hot.

165.   Fajita Style Chicken Breast

INGREDIENTS for Servings: 2

1 green bell pepper, sliced	2 x 6-oz. boneless skinless chicken breasts
¼ medium white onion, sliced	3 tsp. taco seasoning mix
1 tbsp. coconut oil, melted	

DIRECTIONS and Cooking Time: 35 Minutes
Cut each chicken breast in half and place each one between two sheets of cooking parchment. Using a mallet, pound the chicken to flatten to a quarter-inch thick.   Place the chicken on a flat surface, with the short end facing you. Place four slices of pepper and three slices of onion at the end of each piece of chicken. Roll up the chicken tightly, making sure not to let any veggies fall out. Secure with some toothpicks or with butcher's string.   Coat the chicken with coconut oil and then with taco seasoning. Place into your air fryer. Turn the fryer to 350°F and cook the chicken for twenty-five minutes.   Serve the rolls immediately with your favorite dips and sides.

166.   Cracked Chicken Tenders

INGREDIENTS for Servings: 4

2 lb. skinless and boneless chicken tenders	1 cup friendly bread crumbs
3 large eggs	¼ tsp. black pepper
6 tbsp. skimmed milk	1 tsp. salt
½ cup flour	2 tbsp. olive oil

DIRECTIONS and Cooking Time: 30 Minutes
In a large bowl, combine the bread crumbs and olive oil.   In a separate bowl, stir together the eggs and milk using a whisk. Sprinkle in the salt and black pepper.   Put the flour in a third bowl.   Slice up the chicken tenders into 1-inch strips. Coat each piece of chicken in the flour, before dipping it into the egg mixture, followed by the bread crumbs.   Pre-heat the Air Fryer to 380°F.   Cook the coated chicken tenders for about 13 – 15 minutes, shaking the basket a few

times to ensure they turn crispy. Serve hot, with mashed potatoes and a dipping sauce if desired.

167. Chicken And Spinach Salad Recipe

INGREDIENTS for Servings: 2

2 chicken breasts; skinless and boneless	1/2 cup lemon juice
2 tsp. parsley; dried	5 cups baby spinach
1/2 tsp. onion powder	8 strawberries; sliced
1 avocado; pitted, peeled and chopped	1 small red onion; sliced
1/4 cup olive oil	2 tbsp. balsamic vinegar
1 tbsp. tarragon; chopped.	Salt and black pepper to the taste
2 tsp. sweet paprika	

DIRECTIONS and Cooking Time: 22 Minutes
Put chicken in a bowl, add lemon juice, parsley, onion powder and paprika and toss.   Transfer chicken to your air fryer and cook at 360 °F, for 12 minutes.   In a bowl, mix spinach, onion, strawberries and avocado and toss.   In another bowl, mix oil with vinegar, salt, pepper and tarragon, whisk well, add to the salad and toss. Divide chicken on plates, add spinach salad on the side and serve.

168. Chicken With Rice

INGREDIENTS for Servings: 4

1 cup rice	Salt and black pepper
2 cups water	1 onion
2 tomatoes, cubed	3 minced cloves garlic
3 tbsp butter	
1 tbsp tomato paste	

DIRECTIONS and Cooking Time: 40 Minutes
Rub the chicken legs with butter. Sprinkle with salt and pepper and fry in a preheated air fryer for 30 minutes at 380 F. Then, add small onion and a little bit of oil; keep stirring. Add the tomatoes, the tomato paste, and the garlic, and cook for 5 more minutes. Meanwhile, in a pan, boil the rice in 2 cups of water for around 20 minutes. In a baking tray, place the rice and top it with the air fried chicken and cook in the air fryer for 5 minutes. Serve and enjoy!

169. Pizza Stuffed Chicken

INGREDIENTS for Servings: 4

4 small boneless, skinless chicken breasts	16 slices pepperoni
¼ cup pizza sauce	Salt and pepper, to taste
½ cup Colby cheese, shredded	1 ½ tbsp. olive oil
	1 ½ tbsp. dried oregano

DIRECTIONS and Cooking Time: 20 Minutes
Pre-heat your Air Fryer at 370°F.   Flatten the chicken breasts with a rolling pin.   Top the chicken with equal amounts of each ingredients and roll the fillets around the stuffing. Secure with a small skewer or two toothpicks.   Roast in the fryer on the grill pan for 13 - 15 minutes.

170. Turkey With Paprika And Tarragon

INGREDIENTS for Servings: 6

2 pounds turkey tenderloins	Salt and ground black pepper, to taste
2 tablespoons olive oil	1 teaspoon smoked paprika
1 tablespoon fresh tarragon leaves, chopped	2 tablespoons dry white wine

DIRECTIONS and Cooking Time: 40 Minutes
Brush the turkey tenderloins with olive oil. Season with salt, black pepper, and paprika.   Afterwards, add the white wine and tarragon.   Cook the turkey tenderloins at 350 degrees F for 30 minutes, flipping them over halfway through. Let them rest for 5 to 9 minutes before slicing and serving. Enjoy!

171. Peanut Chicken And Pepper Wraps

INGREDIENTS for Servings: 4

1 ½ pounds chicken breast, boneless and skinless	1/4 cup peanut butter
1 tablespoon sesame oil	1 teaspoon fresh garlic, minced
1 tablespoon soy sauce	1 teaspoon brown sugar
2 teaspoons rice vinegar	2 tablespoons lemon juice, freshly squeezed
1 teaspoon fresh ginger, peeled and grated	4 tortillas
	1 bell pepper, julienned

DIRECTIONS and Cooking Time: 25 Minutes
Start by preheating your Air Fryer to 380 degrees F. Cook the chicken breasts in the preheated Air Fryer approximately 6 minutes. Turn them over and cook an additional 6 minutes.   Meanwhile, make the sauce by mixing the peanut butter, sesame oil, soy sauce, vinegar, ginger, garlic, sugar, and lemon juice.   Slice the chicken crosswise across the grain into 1/4-inch strips. Toss the chicken into the sauce.   Decrease temperature to 390 degrees F. Spoon the chicken and sauce onto each tortilla; add bell peppers and wrap

them tightly. Drizzle with a nonstick cooking spray and bake about 7 minutes. Serve warm.

172. Chinese Five Spiced Marinated Chicken

INGREDIENTS for Servings: 4

¼ cup hoisin sauce	2 teaspoons brown sugar
1 ¼ teaspoons sesame oil	3 ½ teaspoon grated ginger
1 ½ teaspoon five spice powder	3 ½ teaspoons honey
2 chicken breasts, halved	3 cucumbers, sliced
2 tablespoons rice vinegar	Salt and pepper to taste

DIRECTIONS and Cooking Time: 40 Minutes
Place all Ingredients except for the cucumber in a Ziploc bag. Allow to rest in the fridge for at least 2 hours. Preheat the air fryer to 390F. Place the grill pan accessory in the air fryer. Grill for 40 minutes and make sure to flip the chicken often for even cooking. Serve chicken with cucumber once cooked.

173. Smoked Duck With Rosemary-infused Gravy

INGREDIENTS for Servings: 4

1 ½ pounds smoked duck breasts, boneless	12 pearl onions peeled
1 tablespoon yellow mustard	1 tablespoon flour
2 tablespoons ketchup	5 ounces chicken broth
1 teaspoon agave syrup	1 teaspoon rosemary, finely chopped

DIRECTIONS and Cooking Time: 30 Minutes
Cook the smoked duck breasts in the preheated Air Fryer at 365 degrees F for 15 minutes. Smear the mustard, ketchup, and agave syrup on the duck breast. Top with pearl onions. Cook for a further 7 minutes or until the skin of the duck breast looks crispy and golden brown. Slice the duck breasts and reserve. Drain off the duck fat from the pan. Then, add the reserved 1 tablespoon of duck fat to the pan and warm it over medium heat; add flour and cook until your roux is dark brown. Add the chicken broth and rosemary to the pan. Reduce the heat to low and cook until the gravy has thickened slightly. Spoon the warm gravy over the reserved duck breasts. Enjoy!

174. Sweet-mustardy Thighs

INGREDIENTS for Servings: 4

3 tbsp honey	Salt and pepper to taste
2 tbsp dijon mustard	
½ tbsp garlic powder	

DIRECTIONS and Cooking Time: 30 Minutes
In a bowl, mix honey, mustard, garlic, salt, and black pepper. Coat the thighs in the mixture and arrange them in your air fryer. Cook for 16 minutes at 400 F, turning once halfway through.

175. Teriyaki Chicken

INGREDIENTS for Servings: 2

2 boneless chicken drumsticks	1 tbsp. cooking wine
1 tsp. ginger, grated	3 tbsp. teriyaki sauce

DIRECTIONS and Cooking Time: 30 Minutes
Combine all of the ingredients in a bowl. Refrigerate for half an hour. Place the chicken in the Air Fryer baking pan and fry at 350°F for 8 minutes. Turn the chicken over and raise the temperature to 380°F. Allow to cook for another 6 minutes. Serve hot.

176. Garlic Chicken Wings

INGREDIENTS for Servings: 4

2 pounds chicken wings	Juice of 2 lemons
¼ cup olive oil	A pinch of salt and black pepper
Zest of 1 lemon, grated	2 garlic cloves, minced

DIRECTIONS and Cooking Time: 30 Minutes
In a bowl, mix the chicken wings with the rest of the ingredients and toss well. Put the chicken wings in your air fryer's basket and cook at 400 degrees F for 30 minutes, shaking halfway. Divide between plates and serve with a side salad.

177. Pizza Spaghetti Casserole

INGREDIENTS for Servings: 4

8 ounces spaghetti	1 tablespoon Italian seasoning mix
1 pound smoked chicken sausage, sliced	3 tablespoons Romano cheese, grated
2 tomatoes, pureed	1 tablespoon fresh basil leaves, chiffonade
1/2 cup Asiago cheese, shredded	

DIRECTIONS and Cooking Time: 30 Minutes
Bring a large pot of lightly salted water to a boil. Cook your spaghetti for 10 minutes or until al dente; drain and reserve, keeping warm. Stir in the chicken sausage, tomato puree, Asiago cheese, and Italian seasoning mix. Then, spritz a baking pan with

cooking spray; add the spaghetti mixture to the pan. Bake in the preheated Air Fryer at 325 degrees F for 11 minutes. Top with the grated Romano cheese. Turn the temperature to 390 degrees F and cook an additional 5 minutes or until everything is thoroughly heated and the cheese is melted. Garnish with fresh basil leaves. Bon appétit!

178.   Air Fried Chicken With Black Beans

INGREDIENTS for Servings: 4

1 can sweet corn	1 can black beans,
1 cup red and green	rinsed and drained
peppers, stripes,	1 tbsp vegetable oil
cooked	2 tbsp chili powder

DIRECTIONS and Cooking Time: 18 Minutes
Coat the chicken with salt, black pepper and a sprinkle of oil; cook for 15 minutes at 380 F. In a deep skillet, pour 1 tbsp. of oil and stir in the chili powder, the corn and the beans. Add a little bit of hot water and keep stirring for 3 more minutes. Transfer the corn, the beans and the chicken to a serving platter.

179.   Pilaf With Chicken And Beer

INGREDIENTS for Servings: 4

1 tablespoon peanut oil	1 cup beer
1 ½ cups white rice	Salt and pepper, to taste
5 cups chicken stock	6 tablespoons grated parmesan
1 pound chicken tenders	

DIRECTIONS and Cooking Time: 45 Minutes
Preheat your Air Fryer to 350 degrees F. Place the peanut oil in the baking pan and heat it for 1 to 2 minutes. Then, add the rice and cook for 3 minutes until the rice is lightly toasted. Pour in the chicken stock and beer; cook for 20 minutes. Add the chicken tenders and cook for a further 10 minutes. Season with salt and pepper. Check the rice for doneness. Top with the grated parmesan and cook an additional 5 minutes. Spoon the warm pilaf into individual bowl and serve warm.

180.   Creamy Chicken Breasts With Crumbled Bacon

INGREDIENTS for Servings: 4

¼ cup olive oil	4 chicken breasts
1 block cream cheese	Salt and pepper to
8 slices of bacon, fried and crumbled	taste

DIRECTIONS and Cooking Time: 25 Minutes
Preheat the air fryer for 5 minutes. Place the chicken breasts in a baking dish that will fit in the air fryer. Add the olive oil and cream cheese. Season with salt and pepper to taste. Place the baking dish with the chicken and cook for 25 minutes at 350F. Sprinkle crumbled bacon after.

181.   Italian Seasoned Chicken Tenders

INGREDIENTS for Servings: 2

2 eggs, lightly beaten	1 tsp Italian seasoning
1 1/2 lbs chicken tenders	2 tbsp ground flax seed
1/2 tsp onion powder	1 cup almond flour
1/2 tsp garlic powder	1/2 tsp pepper
1 tsp paprika	1 tsp sea salt

DIRECTIONS and Cooking Time: 10 Minutes
Preheat the air fryer to 400 F. Season chicken with pepper and salt. In a medium bowl, whisk eggs to combine. In a shallow dish, mix together almond flour, all seasonings, and flaxseed. Dip chicken into the egg then coats with almond flour mixture and place on a plate. Spray air fryer basket with cooking spray. Place half chicken tenders in air fryer basket and cook for 10 minutes. Turn halfway through. Cook remaining chicken tenders using same steps. Serve and enjoy.

182.   Turkey And Sausage Meatloaf With Herbs

INGREDIENTS for Servings: 4

1/2 cup milk	1 teaspoon rosemary
4 bread slices, crustless	1 teaspoon basil
1 tablespoon olive oil	1 teaspoon thyme
1 onion, finely chopped	1 teaspoon cayenne pepper
1 garlic clove, minced	Kosher salt and ground black pepper, to taste
1/2 pound ground turkey	1/2 cup ketchup
1/2 pound ground breakfast sausage	2 tablespoons molasses
1 duck egg, whisked	1 tablespoon brown mustard

DIRECTIONS and Cooking Time: 45 Minutes
In a shallow bowl, pour the milk over the bread and let it soak in for 5 to 6 minutes. Heat 1 tablespoon of oil over medium-high heat in a nonstick pan. Sauté the onions and garlic until tender and fragrant, about 2 minutes. Add the turkey, sausage, egg, rosemary, basil, thyme, cayenne pepper, salt, and ground black

pepper. Stir in the milk-soaked bread. Mix until everything is well incorporated. Shape the mixture into a loaf and transfer it to a pan that is lightly greased with an olive oil mister. Next, lower the pan onto the cooking basket. In a mixing bowl, whisk the ketchup with molasses and mustard. Spread this mixture over the top of your meatloaf. Cook approximately 27 minutes or until the meatloaf is no longer pink in the middle. Allow it to sit 10 minutes before slicing and serving. Bon appétit!

183.   Sweet Chili Chicken Wings

INGREDIENTS for Servings: 4

1 tsp garlic powder 1 tbsp tamarind powder	¼ cup sweet chili sauce

DIRECTIONS and Cooking Time: 20 Minutes

Preheat your Air Fryer to 390 F. Spray the air fryer basket with cooking spray. Rub the chicken wings with tamarind and garlic powders. Spray with cooking spray and place in the cooking basket. Cook for 6 minutes, Slide out the fryer basket and cover with sweet chili sauce; cook for 8 more minutes. Serve cooled.

BEEF, PORK & LAMB RECIPES

184. Sweet & Sour Pork Chops

INGREDIENTS for Servings: 6

6 pork loin chops	2 tablespoons soy sauce
Salt and ground black pepper, as required	1 tablespoon balsamic vinegar
2 garlic cloves, minced	¼ teaspoon ground ginger
2 tablespoons honey	

DIRECTIONS and Cooking Time: 16 Minutes
With a meat tenderizer, tenderize the chops completely and then, sprinkle each with salt and black pepper. In a large bowl, mix the remaining ingredients. Add the chops and generously coat with marinade. Cover and refrigerate for about 2-8 hours. Set the temperature of air fryer to 355 degrees F. Grease an air fryer basket. Arrange chops into the prepared air fryer basket in a single layer. Air fry for about 6-8 minutes per side. Remove from air fryer and transfer the chops onto plates. Serve hot.

185. Creamy Pork Chops

INGREDIENTS for Servings: 4

2 pork chops	½ teaspoon salt
¼ cup coconut flakes	1 egg, beaten
3 tablespoons almond flour	1 tablespoon heavy cream
½ teaspoon dried parsley	1 teaspoon butter, melted

DIRECTIONS and Cooking Time: 10 Minutes
Cut every pork chops into 2 chops. Then sprinkle them with salt and dried parsley. After this, in the mixing bowl mix up coconut flakes and almond flour. In the separated bowl mix up egg, heavy cream, and melted butter. Coat the pork chops in the almond flour mixture and them dip in the egg mixture. Repeat the same steps one more time. Then coat the pork chops in the remaining almond flour mixture. Place the meat in the air fryer basket. Cook the pork chops for 10 minutes at 400F. Flip them on another side after 5 minutes of cooking.

186. Hot Pepper Lamb Mix

INGREDIENTS for Servings: 4

1 pound lamb leg, boneless and sliced	½ cup walnuts, chopped
2 tablespoons olive oil	¼ teaspoon red pepper flakes
A pinch of salt and black pepper	½ teaspoon mustard seeds
2 garlic cloves, minced	½ teaspoon Italian
1 tablespoon rosemary, chopped	seasoning
	1 tablespoon parsley, chopped

DIRECTIONS and Cooking Time: 35 Minutes
In a bowl, mix the lamb with all the ingredients except the walnuts and parsley, rub well, put the slices your air fryer's basket and cook at 370 degrees F for 35 minutes, flipping the meat halfway. Divide between plates, sprinkle the parsley and walnuts on top and serve with a side salad.

187. Festive Teriyaki Beef

INGREDIENTS for Servings: 4

2 heaping tablespoons fresh parsley, roughly chopped	½ cup grapefruit juice
	1/3 cup hoisin sauce
1 pound beef rump steaks	1 tablespoon fresh ginger, grated
2 heaping tablespoons fresh chives, roughly chopped	1 ½ tablespoons mirin
	3 garlic cloves, minced
	2 tablespoon rice bran oil
Salt and black pepper (or mixed peppercorns, to savor	½ cup soy sauce
	1/3 cup brown sugar
For the Sauce:	

DIRECTIONS and Cooking Time: 40 Minutes
Firstly, steam the beef rump steaks for 8 minutes (use the method of steaming that you prefer. Season the beef with salt and black pepper; scatter the chopped parsley and chives over the top. Roast the beef rump steaks in an air fryer basket for 28 minutes at 345 degrees, turning halfway through. While the beef is cooking, combine the ingredients for the teriyaki sauce in a sauté pan. Then, let it simmer over low heat until it has thickened. Toss the beef with the teriyaki sauce until it is well covered and serve.

188. Scallion Sauce On Lemongrass-chili Marinated Tri-tip

INGREDIENTS for Servings: 4

1 cup canned unsweetened coconut milk	1/4 cup fish sauce
	15 scallions, very thinly sliced
2 tablespoons packed light brown sugar	3 tablespoons grapeseed oil
1 tablespoon fresh lime juice	2 tablespoons black vinegar
6 garlic cloves	2 tablespoons toasted sesame seeds
4 red or green Thai chiles, stemmed	1/4 cup fish sauce

2 lemongrass stalks, bottom third only, tough outer layers removed 1-pound tri-tip fat cap left on , cut into 1-inch cubes 1 1 1/2" piece ginger, peeled Scallion Dip Ingredients	Basting Sauce Ingredients 1 1/2 tablespoons fresh lime juice 1/2 cup canned unsweetened coconut milk 2 garlic cloves, crushed 3 tablespoons fish sauce

DIRECTIONS and Cooking Time: 20 Minutes
Except for meat, puree all Ingredients in a blender. Transfer into a bowl and marinate beef at least overnight in the ref. In a medium bowl, mix well all scallion dip Ingredients and set aside. In a separate bowl mix all basting sauce Ingredients. Thread meat into skewers and place on skewer rack in air fryer. Baste with sauce. Cook for 10 minutes at 390F or to desired doneness. Halfway through cooking time, baste and turnover skewers. Serve and enjoy with the dip on the side.

189. Eggs'n Bacon On Biscuit Brekky

INGREDIENTS for Servings: 4

½ of 16-ounces refrigerated breakfast biscuits 1 cup shredded extra sharp cheddar cheese	¼ cup milk 4 scallions, chopped 5 eggs 8 slices cooked center cut bacon

DIRECTIONS and Cooking Time: 28 Minutes
In baking pan cook bacon for 8 minutes at 360F or until crisped. Remove bacon and discard excess fat. Evenly spread biscuits on bottom. For 5 minutes, cook at same temperature. Meanwhile, whisk eggs, milk, and scallions. Remove basket, evenly layer bacon on top of biscuit, sprinkle cheese on top, and pour eggs. Cook for another 15 minutes or until eggs are set. Serve and enjoy.

190. Garlic Lemon-wine On Lamb Steak

INGREDIENTS for Servings: 4

¼ cup extra virgin olive oil 1 tablespoon brown sugar 2 pounds lamb steak, pounded 2 tablespoons lemon juice	½ cup dry white wine 3 tablespoons ancho chili powder 8 cloves of garlic, minced Salt and pepper to taste

DIRECTIONS and Cooking Time: 1 Hour And 30 Minutes
Place all Ingredients in bowl and allow the meat to marinate in the fridge for at least 2 hours. Preheat the air fryer to 390F. Place the grill pan accessory in the air fryer. Grill the meat for 20 minutes per batch. Meanwhile, pour the marinade in a saucepan and allow to simmer for 10 minutes until the sauce thickens.

191. Skirt Steak Bbq Recipe From Korea

INGREDIENTS for Servings: 1

1 skirt steak, halved 3 tablespoons gochujang sauce 3 tablespoons olive oil	3 tablespoons rice vinegar Salt and pepper to taste

DIRECTIONS and Cooking Time: 30 Minutes
Preheat the air fryer to 390F. Place the grill pan accessory in the air fryer. Rub all spices and seasonings on the skirt steak. Place on the grill and cook for 15 minutes per batch. Flip the steak halfway through the cooking time. Serve with more gochujang or kimchi.

192. Cumin'n Chili Rubbed Steak Fajitas

INGREDIENTS for Servings: 2

¼ teaspoon chili powder ¼ teaspoon oregano ½ cup cotija cheese ½ medium red onion, chopped ½ teaspoon ground cumin 1 small bell pepper	1-pound sliced beef, cut into strips 2 chopped serrano peppers 2 tablespoons olive oil Corn tortillas Salt and pepper to taste

DIRECTIONS and Cooking Time: 25 Minutes
Preheat the air fryer to 390F. Place the grill pan accessory in the air fryer. In a mixing bowl, combine the beef and season with salt, pepper, oregano, ground cumin, chili powder, and olive oil. Place on the grill pan and cook for 25 minutes. Halfway through the cooking time, stir the meat to brown evenly. Once cooked, serve the beef with corn tortillas, cheese, and Serrano peppers.

193. Eastern Chunky Shish Kebabs

INGREDIENTS for Servings: 4

1 tablespoon prepared mustard 1 tablespoon Worcestershire sauce 1 clove garlic, minced 1 teaspoon coarsely cracked black pepper 16 mushroom caps 2 green bell peppers, cut into chunks	1 red bell pepper, cut into chunks 1 large onion, cut into large squares 1/2 cup soy sauce 1 1/2 teaspoons salt 1 1/2 pounds lean beef, cut into 1-inch cubes 1/3 cup vegetable oil 1/4 cup lemon juice

DIRECTIONS and Cooking Time: 20 Minutes

In a resealable bag, mix well salt, pepper, garlic, Worcestershire, mustard, lemon juice, soy sauce, and oil. Add beef and toss well to coat. Remove excess air and seal. Marinate for 8 hours. Add mushroom and marinate for an additional 8 hours. Thread mushrooms, bell peppers, onion, and meat in skewers. Pour marinade in saucepan and thicken for 10 minutes and transfer to a bowl for basting. Place skewers on skewer rack in air fryer. If needed, cook in batches. For 10 minutes, cook on 390F. Halfway through cooking time, baste and turnover skewers. Serve and enjoy.

194.   Classic Smoked Pork Chops

INGREDIENTS for Servings: 6

Hickory-smoked salt, to savor Ground black pepper, to savor 1 teaspoon onion powder	6 pork chops 1/2 teaspoon garlic powder 1/2 teaspoon cayenne pepper 1/3 cup almond meal

DIRECTIONS and Cooking Time: 25 Minutes

Simply place all of the above ingredients into a zip-top plastic bag; shake them up to coat well. Spritz the chops with a pan spray (canola spray works well here) and transfer them to the Air Fryer cooking basket. Roast them for 20 minutes at 375 degrees F. Serve with sautéed vegetables. Bon appétit!

195.   Garlic-mustard Rubbed Roast Beef

INGREDIENTS for Servings: 12

¼ cup Dijon mustard ¼ cup freshly parsley, chopped ¼ cup unsalted butter 2 cups almond flour 2 tablespoons olive oil	3 ½ cups beef broth 3 pounds boneless beef eye round roast 4 cloves of garlic, chopped Salt and pepper to taste

DIRECTIONS and Cooking Time: 2 Hours

In a mixing bowl, combine the garlic, almond flour, parsley, salt and pepper. Heat a butter and olive oil in a skillet and brown the beef on all sides. Rub the almond flour mixture all over the beef. Brush with Dijon mustard. Place the crusted beef in a baking dish. Pour slowly the beef broth. Place the baking dish with the bee in the air fryer. Close. Cook for 2 hours at 400F. Baste the beef with the sauce every 30 minutes.

196.   30-minute Hoisin Pork Loin Steak

INGREDIENTS for Servings: 4

2 tablespoons dry white wine 1/3 cup hoisin sauce 2 teaspoons smoked cayenne pepper 3 garlic cloves, pressed	1/2 pound pork loin steak, cut into strips 3 teaspoons fresh lime juice Salt and ground black pepper, to taste

DIRECTIONS and Cooking Time: 30 Minutes

Start by preheating your Air Fryer to 395 degrees F. Toss the pork with other ingredients; let it marinate at least 20 minutes in a fridge. Then, air-fry the pork strips for 5 minutes. Bon appétit!

197.   Creamy Burger & Potato Bake

INGREDIENTS for Servings: 3

salt to taste freshly ground pepper, to taste 1/2 (10.75 ounce) can condensed cream of mushroom soup 1/2-pound lean ground beef	1-1/2 cups peeled and thinly sliced potatoes 1/2 cup shredded Cheddar cheese 1/4 cup chopped onion 1/4 cup and 2 tablespoons milk

DIRECTIONS and Cooking Time: 55 Minutes

Lightly grease baking pan of air fryer with cooking spray. Add ground beef. For 10 minutes, cook on 360F. Stir and crumble halfway through cooking time. Meanwhile, in a bowl, whisk well pepper, salt, milk, onion, and mushroom soup. Mix well. Drain fat off ground beef and transfer beef to a plate. In same air fryer baking pan, layer ½ of potatoes on bottom, then ½ of soup mixture, and then ½ of beef. Repeat process. Cover pan with foil. Cook for 30 minutes. Remove foil and cook for another 15 minutes or until potatoes are tender. Serve and enjoy.

198.   Veggie Stuffed Beef Rolls

INGREDIENTS for Servings: 6

2 pounds beef flank steak, pounded to 1/8-inch thickness 6 Provolone cheese slices 3-ounce roasted red bell peppers	¾ cup fresh baby spinach 3 tablespoons prepared pesto Salt and black pepper, to taste

DIRECTIONS and Cooking Time: 14 Minutes
Preheat the Air fryer to 400F and grease an Air fryer basket. Place the steak onto a smooth surface and spread evenly with pesto. Top with the cheese slices, red peppers and spinach. Roll up the steak tightly around the filling and secure with the toothpicks. Arrange the roll in the Air fryer basket and cook for about 14 minutes, flipping once in between. Dish out in a platter and serve warm.

199. Oregano And Rosemary Lamb Skewers

INGREDIENTS for Servings: 4

2 pounds lamb meat, cubed ¼ cup olive oil 1 tablespoon garlic, minced 1 tablespoon oregano, dried ½ teaspoon rosemary, dried	2 tablespoons lemon juice A pinch of salt and black pepper 1 tablespoon red vinegar 2 red bell peppers, cut into medium pieces

DIRECTIONS and Cooking Time: 20 Minutes
In a bowl, mix all the ingredients and toss them well. Thread the lamb and bell peppers on skewers, place them in your air fryer's basket and cook at 380 degrees F for 10 minutes on each side. Divide between plates and serve with a side salad.

200. Winter Beef With Garlic-mayo Sauce

INGREDIENTS for Servings: 4

1½ pounds beef, cubed ½ cup full fat sour cream 2 teaspoons dried rosemary 1½ tablespoon herb vinegar 1 teaspoon sweet paprika 3 cloves garlic, minced	1/2 cup white wine 2 tablespoons extra-virgin olive oil 2 teaspoons dried basil 1 tablespoon mayonnaise Salt and ground black pepper, to taste

DIRECTIONS and Cooking Time: 1 Hour 22 Minutes

In a large-sized mixing bowl, whisk together the oil, wine, and beef. Now, stir in the seasonings and herb vinegar. Cover and marinate at least 50 minutes. Then, preheat your Air Fryer to 375 degrees F. Roast the marinated beef for about 18 minutes, turning halfway through. Meanwhile, make the sauce by mixing the sour cream with the mayonnaise and garlic. Serve the warm beef with the garlic sauce and enjoy!

201. Mustard'n Pepper Roast Beef

INGREDIENTS for Servings: 9

¼ cup flat-leaf parsley, chopped 1 ½ pounds medium shallots, chopped 1 boneless rib roast 2 tablespoons whole grain mustard	3 tablespoons mixed peppercorns 4 medium shallots, chopped 4 tablespoons olive oil Salt to taste

DIRECTIONS and Cooking Time: 1 Hour And 30 Minutes
Preheat the air fryer for 5 minutes. Place all ingredients in a baking dish that will fit in the air fryer. Place the dish in the air fryer and cook for 1 hour and 30 minutes at 325F.

202. Cilantro Steak

INGREDIENTS for Servings: 4

1-pound flank steak 1 oz fresh cilantro, chopped 1 garlic clove, diced 1 oz fresh parsley, chopped 1 egg, hard-boiled, peeled	½ green bell pepper, chopped 1 tablespoon avocado oil ½ teaspoon salt ½ teaspoon ground black pepper 1 teaspoon peanut oil

DIRECTIONS and Cooking Time: 25 Minutes
In the mixing bowl, mix up fresh cilantro, diced garlic, parsley, and avocado oil. Then slice the flank steak in one big fillet (square) and brush it with a cilantro mixture. Then chop the egg roughly and put it on the steak. Add chopped bell pepper. After this, roll the meat and secure it with the kitchen thread. Carefully rub the meat roll with salt and ground black pepper. Then sprinkle the meat roll with peanut oil. Preheat the air fryer to 400F. Put the meat in the air fryer basket and cook it for 25 minutes.

203. Cinnamon Lamb Meatloaf

INGREDIENTS for Servings: 4

A pinch of salt and black pepper	2 pounds lamb, ground

½ teaspoon hot paprika	¼ teaspoon cinnamon powder
A drizzle of olive oil	1 teaspoon coriander, ground
2 tablespoons parsley, chopped	1 egg
2 tablespoons cilantro, chopped	2 tablespoons keto tomato sauce
1 teaspoon cumin, ground	4 scallions, chopped
	1 teaspoon lemon juice

DIRECTIONS and Cooking Time: 35 Minutes
In a bowl, combine the lamb with the rest of the ingredients except the oil and stir really well. Grease a loaf pan that fits the air fryer with the oil, add the lamb mix and shape the meatloaf. Put the pan in the air fryer and cook at 380 degrees F for 35 minutes. Slice and serve.

204.   Beef & Broccoli

INGREDIENTS for Servings: 4

1 lb. broccoli, cut into florets	1 tbsp. olive oil
¾ lb. round steak, cut into strips	1 tsp. cornstarch
	1 tsp. sugar
1 garlic clove, minced	1 tsp. soy sauce
1 tsp. ginger, minced	⅓ cup sherry wine
	2 tsp. sesame oil
	⅓ cup oyster sauce

DIRECTIONS and Cooking Time: 25 Minutes
In a bowl, combine the sugar, soy sauce, sherry wine, cornstarch, sesame oil, and oyster sauce. Place the steak strips in the bowl, coat each one with the mixture and allow to marinate for 45 minutes. Put the broccoli in the Air Fryer and lay the steak on top. Top with the olive oil, garlic and ginger. Cook at 350°F for 12 minutes. Serve hot with rice if desired.

205.   Beef Fajita Keto Burrito

INGREDIENTS for Servings: 4

1 pound rump steak	1 teaspoon Mexican oregano
1 teaspoon garlic powder	Salt and ground black pepper, to taste
1/2 teaspoon onion powder	1 cup Mexican cheese blend
1/2 teaspoon cayenne pepper	1 head romaine lettuce, separated into leaves
1 teaspoon piri piri powder	

DIRECTIONS and Cooking Time: 20 Minutes
Toss the rump steak with the garlic powder, onion powder, cayenne pepper, piri piri powder, Mexican oregano, salt, and black pepper. Cook in the preheated Air Fryer at 390 degrees F for 10 minutes. Slice against the grain into thin strips. Add the cheese blend and cook for 2 minutes more. Spoon the beef mixture onto romaine lettuce leaves; roll up burrito-style and serve.

206.   Ham And Kale Egg Cups

INGREDIENTS for Servings: 2

2 eggs	½ cup steamed kale
1/4 teaspoon dried or fresh marjoram	1/4 teaspoon dried or fresh rosemary
2 teaspoons chili powder	4 pork ham slices
1/3 teaspoon kosher salt	1/3 teaspoon ground black pepper, or more to taste

DIRECTIONS and Cooking Time: 20 Minutes
Divide the kale and ham among 2 ramekins; crack an egg into each ramekin. Sprinkle with seasonings. Cook for 15 minutes at 335 degrees F or until your eggs reach desired texture.   Serve warm with spicy tomato ketchup and pickles. Bon appétit!

207.   Top Round Roast With Mustard-rosemary-thyme Blend

INGREDIENTS for Servings: 10

1 teaspoon dry mustard	4 teaspoons dried oregano
2 teaspoons dried rosemary	4 teaspoons dried thyme
3 tablespoons olive oil	Salt and pepper to taste
4 pounds beef top round roast	

DIRECTIONS and Cooking Time: 1 Hour
Preheat the air fryer for 5 minutes.   Place all ingredients in a baking dish that will fit in the air fryer. Place the dish in the air fryer and cook for 1 hour at 325F.

208.   Egg Noodles, Ground Beef & Tomato Sauce Bake

INGREDIENTS for Servings: 3

1 (15 ounce) can tomato sauce	1/2 teaspoon garlic salt
4-ounce egg noodles, cooked according to manufacturer's directions	1/2 cup sour cream
	1/2 large white onion, diced
1/2-pound ground beef	1/4 cup shredded sharp Cheddar cheese, or more to taste
1/2 teaspoon white sugar	
1/2 teaspoon salt	1.5-ounce cream cheese

DIRECTIONS and Cooking Time: 45 Minutes
Lightly grease baking pan of air fryer with cooking spray. Add ground beef, for 10 minutes cook on 360F. Halfway through cooking time crumble beef. When done cooking, discard excess fat. Stir in tomato sauce, garlic salt, salt, and sugar. Mix well and cook for another 15 minutes. Transfer to a bowl. In another bowl, whisk well onion, cream cheese, and sour cream. Place half of the egg noodles on bottom of air fryer baking pan. Top with half of the sour cream mixture, then half the tomato sauce mixture. Repeat layering. And then top off with cheese. Cover pan with foil. Cook for another 15 minutes. Uncover and cook for another 5 minutes. Serve and enjoy.

209. Beef Steaks With Mediterranean Herbs

INGREDIENTS for Servings: 4

2 tablespoons soy sauce	2 teaspoons smoked cayenne pepper
3 heaping tablespoons fresh chives	1/2 teaspoon dried basil
2 tablespoons olive oil	1/2 teaspoon dried rosemary
3 tablespoons dry white wine	1 teaspoon freshly ground pepper
4 small-sized beef steaks	1 teaspoon sea salt, or more to taste

DIRECTIONS and Cooking Time: 25 Minutes
Firstly, coat the steaks with the cayenne pepper, black pepper, salt, basil, and rosemary. Drizzle the steaks with olive oil, white wine, soy sauce, and honey. Finally, roast in an Air Fryer basket for 20 minutes at 335 degrees F. Serve garnished with fresh chives. Bon appétit!

210. Pork Sausage Meatloaf With Veggies

INGREDIENTS for Servings: 6

Non-stick cooking spray	3/4 pound spicy ground pork sausage
1 shallot, finely chopped	1/4 pound ground turkey
1 rib celery, finely chopped	2 sprigs rosemary, leaves only, crushed
2 gloves garlic, minced	1/4 cup minced fresh parsley
1 tablespoon Worcestershire sauce	1 egg, lightly whisked
Salt and freshly ground pepper, to your liking	3 tablespoons fresh panko
	1/3 cup tomato paste

DIRECTIONS and Cooking Time: 30 Minutes

Spritz a cast-iron skillet with a cooking spray. Then, sauté the shallots, celery and garlic until just tender and fragrant. Now, add Worcestershire sauce and both kinds of meat to the sautéed mixture. Remove from the heat. Add the rosemary, parsley, egg, fresh panko, salt, and pepper; mix to combine well. Transfer the mixture to the baking pan and shape into a loaf. Cover the prepared meatloaf with tomato paste. Air-fry at 390 degrees F for 25 minutes or until thoroughly warmed.

211. Mustard Chives And Basil Lamb

INGREDIENTS for Servings: 4

8 lamb cutlets	1 tablespoon chives, chopped
A pinch of salt and black pepper	1 tablespoon basil, chopped
A drizzle of olive oil	1 tablespoon oregano, chopped
2 garlic cloves, minced	1 tablespoon mint chopped
¼ cup mustard	

DIRECTIONS and Cooking Time: 30 Minutes
In a bowl, mix the lamb with the rest of the ingredients and rub well. Put the cutlets in your air fryer's basket and cook at 380 degrees F for 15 minutes on each side. Divide between plates and serve with a side salad.

212. Smoked Chili Lamb Chops

INGREDIENTS for Servings: 4

4 garlic cloves, minced	4 lamb chops
½ teaspoon chili powder	2 tablespoons olive oil
¼ teaspoon smoked paprika	A pinch of salt and black pepper

DIRECTIONS and Cooking Time: 20 Minutes
In a bowl, mix the lamb with the rest of the ingredients and toss well. Transfer the chops to your air fryer's basket and cook at 390 degrees F for 10 minutes on each side. Serve with a side salad.

213. Grilled Tri Tip Over Beet Salad

INGREDIENTS for Servings: 6

1 bunch arugula, torn	3 beets, peeled and sliced thinly
1 bunch scallions, chopped	3 tablespoons balsamic vinegar
1-pound tri-tip, sliced	Salt and pepper to taste
2 tablespoons olive oil	

DIRECTIONS and Cooking Time: 45 Minutes

Preheat the air fryer to 390F. Place the grill pan accessory in the air fryer. Season the tri-tip with salt and pepper. Drizzle with oil. Grill for 15 minutes per batch. Meanwhile, prepare the salad by tossing the rest of the ingredients in a salad bowl. Toss in the grilled tri-trip and drizzle with more balsamic vinegar.

214. Shepherd's Pie Made Of Ground Lamb

INGREDIENTS for Servings: 4

1-pound lean ground lamb	1/2 onion, diced
2 tablespoons and 2 teaspoons all-purpose flour	1/2 teaspoon paprika
	1-1/2 teaspoons ketchup
salt and ground black pepper to taste	1-1/2 cloves garlic, minced
1 teaspoon minced fresh rosemary	1/2 (12 ounce) package frozen peas and carrots, thawed
2 tablespoons cream cheese	1-1/2 teaspoons butter
2 ounces Irish cheese (such as Dubliner®), shredded	1/2 pinch ground cayenne pepper
salt and ground black pepper to taste	1/2 egg yolk
1 tablespoon milk	1-1/4 cups water, or as needed
1-1/2 teaspoons olive oil	1-1/4 pounds Yukon Gold potatoes, peeled and halved
1-1/2 teaspoons butter	1/8 teaspoon ground cinnamon

DIRECTIONS and Cooking Time: 50 Minutes
Bring a large pan of salted water to boil and add potatoes. Simmer for 15 minutes until tender. Meanwhile, lightly grease baking pan of air fryer with butter. Melt for 2 minutes at 360F. Add ground lamb and onion. Cook for 10 minutes, stirring and crumbling halfway through cooking time. Add garlic, ketchup, cinnamon, paprika, rosemary, black pepper, salt, and flour. Mix well and cook for 3 minutes. Add water and deglaze pan. Continue cooking for 6 minutes. Stir in carrots and peas. Evenly spread mixture in pan. Once potatoes are done, drain well and transfer potatoes to a bowl. Mash potatoes and stir in Irish cheese, cream cheese, cayenne pepper, and butter. Mix well. Season with pepper and salt to taste. In a small bowl, whisk well milk and egg yolk. Stir into mashed potatoes. Top the ground lamb mixture with mashed potatoes. Cook for another 15 minutes or until tops of potatoes are lightly browned. Serve and enjoy.

215. Classic Cube Steak With Sauce

INGREDIENTS for Servings: 4

1 ½ pounds cube steak	4 ounces butter
Salt, to taste	2 tablespoon fresh parsley, finely chopped
1/4 teaspoon ground black pepper, or more to taste	1 tablespoon fresh horseradish, grated
2 garlic cloves, finely chopped	1 teaspoon cayenne pepper
2 scallions, finely chopped	

DIRECTIONS and Cooking Time: 20 Minutes
Pat dry the cube steak and season it with salt and black pepper. Spritz the Air Fryer basket with cooking oil. Add the meat to the basket. Cook in the preheated Air Fryer at 400 degrees F for 14 minutes. Meanwhile, melt the butter in a skillet over a moderate heat. Add the remaining ingredients and simmer until the sauce has thickened and reduced slightly. Top the warm cube steaks with Cowboy sauce and serve immediately.

216. Scrumptious Lamb Chops

INGREDIENTS for Servings: 4

2 tablespoons fresh mint leaves, minced	1 garlic clove, minced
4 (6-ounce) lamb chops	2 tablespoons dried rosemary
2 carrots, peeled and cubed	3 tablespoons olive oil
1 parsnip, peeled and cubed	Salt and black pepper, to taste
1 fennel bulb, cubed	

DIRECTIONS and Cooking Time: 8 Minutes
Preheat the Air fryer to 390F and grease an Air fryer basket. Mix herbs, garlic and oil in a large bowl and coat chops generously with this mixture. Marinate in the refrigerator for about 3 hours. Soak the vegetables in a large pan of water for about 15 minutes. Arrange the chops in the Air fryer basket and cook for about 2 minutes. Remove the chops and place the vegetables in the Air fryer basket. Top with the chops and cook for about 6 minutes. Dish out and serve warm.

217. Spicy Pork

INGREDIENTS for Servings: 6

2-pound pork shoulder, boneless	1 teaspoon Erythritol
1 teaspoon salt	¼ teaspoon keto tomato sauce
1 teaspoon chili	1 teaspoon ground

powder	black pepper
1 teaspoon five spices powder	2 tablespoons water
1 tablespoon apple cider vinegar	1 tablespoon avocado oil

DIRECTIONS and Cooking Time: 20 Minutes

Pierce the pork shoulder with the help of the knife. Then make the sauce: in the mixing bowl mix up salt, chili powder, five spices powder, apple cider vinegar, Erythritol, tomato sauce, ground black pepper, and water. Whisk the mixture until it is smooth. Then put the pork shoulder in the sauce and coat well. Leave the meat in the sauce for 8 hours. When the time is finished, preheat the air fryer to 390F. Brush the marinated meat with avocado oil and put it in the preheated air fryer. Cook the meat for 15 minutes. Then flip it on another side and cook for 5 minutes more. Let the cooked pork shoulder rest for 10 minutes before serving.

218.   Classic Keto Cheeseburgers

INGREDIENTS for Servings: 4

1 ½ pounds ground chuck	1 envelope onion soup mix
Kosher salt and freshly ground black pepper, to taste	1 teaspoon paprika
	4 slices Monterey-Jack cheese

DIRECTIONS and Cooking Time: 15 Minutes

In a mixing dish, thoroughly combine ground chuck, onion soup mix, salt, black pepper, and paprika. Then, set your Air Fryer to cook at 385 degrees F. Shape the mixture into 4 patties. Air-fry them for 10 minutes.   Next step, place the slices of cheese on the top of the warm burgers. Air-fry for one minute more. Serve with mustard and pickled salad of choice. Bon appétit!

219.   Peppery Pork Roast With Herbs

INGREDIENTS for Servings: 6

1 tablespoon olive oil	1 pound pork loin
1 teaspoon dried basil	1 Pimento chili pepper, deveined and chopped
1/2 teaspoon dried oregano	1 Yellow wax pepper, deveined and chopped
1/4 teaspoon crushed red pepper flakes	1 bell pepper, deveined and chopped
1 teaspoon dried thyme	1 tablespoon peanut butter
1/4 teaspoon freshly grated nutmeg	1/4 cup beef broth
Sea salt flakes and freshly ground black pepper, to taste	1/2 tablespoon whole-grain mustard
	1 bay leaf

DIRECTIONS and Cooking Time: 30 Minutes

Lightly grease the inside of an Air Fryer baking dish with a thin layer of olive oil. Then, cut 8 slit down the center of pork (about 3x3"). Sprinkle with the seasonings and massage them into the meat to evenly distribute   Then, tuck peppers into the slits and transfer the meat to the Air Fryer baking dish. Scatter remaining peppers around the roast.   In a mixing dish, whisk the peanut butter, beef broth, and mustard; now, pour broth mixture around the roast.   Add the bay leaf and roast the meat for 25 minutes at 390 degrees F; turn the pork over halfway through the roasting time. Bon appétit!

220.   Greek Lamb Chops

INGREDIENTS for Servings: 4

1 tablespoon white flour	4 lamb chops
2 tablespoons olive oil	3 garlic cloves, minced
Salt and black pepper to taste	1 teaspoon thyme, dried
1 teaspoon marjoram, dried	½ cup veggie stock
	1 cup green olives, pitted and sliced

DIRECTIONS and Cooking Time: 14 Minutes

Place all ingredients—except the olives—in a bowl and mix well. Then put in the fridge for 10 minutes. Transfer the lamb chops to your air fryer's basket and cook at 390 degrees F for 7 minutes on each side. Divide the lamb chops between plates, sprinkle the olives on top, and serve.

221.   Grilled Mayo Short Loin Steak

INGREDIENTS for Servings: 4

1 cup mayonnaise	Sea salt, to taste
1 tablespoon fresh rosemary, finely chopped	1 teaspoon smoked paprika
2 tablespoons Worcestershire sauce	1 teaspoon garlic, minced
1/2 teaspoon ground black pepper	1 ½ pounds short loin steak

DIRECTIONS and Cooking Time: 20 Minutes

Combine the mayonnaise, rosemary, Worcestershire sauce, salt, pepper, paprika, and garlic; mix to combine well.   Now, brush the mayonnaise mixture over both sides of the steak. Lower the steak onto the grill pan.   Grill in the preheated Air Fryer at 390 degrees F for 8 minutes. Turn the steaks over and grill an additional 7 minutes.   Check for doneness with a meat thermometer. Serve warm and enjoy!

222. Dill Beef And Artichokes

INGREDIENTS for Servings: 4

1 and ½ pounds beef stew meat, cubed A pinch of salt and black pepper 2 tablespoons olive oil 2 shallots, chopped 1 cup beef stock	2 garlic cloves, minced ½ teaspoon dill, chopped 12 ounces artichoke hearts, drained and chopped

DIRECTIONS and Cooking Time: 30 Minutes

Heat up a pan that fits the air fryer with the oil over medium-high heat, add the meat and brown for 5 minutes. Add the rest of the ingredients except the dill, transfer the pan to your air fryer and cook at 380 degrees F for 25 minutes shaking the air fryer halfway. Divide everything into bowls and serve with the dill sprinkled on top.

223. Spicy Lamb Kebabs

INGREDIENTS for Servings: 6

4 eggs, beaten 1 cup pistachios, chopped 4 tablespoons plain flour 4 tablespoons flat-leaf parsley, chopped 2 teaspoons chili flakes 4 garlic cloves, minced 2 tablespoons fresh lemon juice	1 pound ground lamb 2 teaspoons cumin seeds 1 teaspoon fennel seeds 2 teaspoons dried mint 2 teaspoons salt Olive oil 1 teaspoon coriander seeds 1 teaspoon freshly ground black pepper

DIRECTIONS and Cooking Time: 8 Minutes

Preheat the Air fryer to 355F and grease an Air fryer basket. Mix lamb, pistachios, eggs, lemon juice, chili flakes, flour, cumin seeds, fennel seeds, coriander seeds, mint, parsley, salt and black pepper in a large bowl. Thread the lamb mixture onto metal skewers to form sausages and coat with olive oil. Place the skewers in the Air fryer basket and cook for about 8 minutes. Dish out in a platter and serve hot.

224. Beef, Pearl Onions And Cauliflower

INGREDIENTS for Servings: 4

1 ½ pounds New York strip, cut into strips 1 (1-pound) head cauliflower, broken into florets 1 cup pearl onion,	1 tablespoon olive oil 2 cloves garlic, minced 1 teaspoon of ground ginger 1/4 cup tomato paste 1/2 cup red wine

sliced Marinade:	

DIRECTIONS and Cooking Time: 20 Minutes + Marinating Time

Mix all ingredients for the marinade. Add the beef to the marinade and let it sit in your refrigerator for 1 hour. Preheat your Air Fryer to 400 degrees F. Transfer the meat to the Air Fryer basket. Add the cauliflower and onions. Drizzle a few tablespoons of marinade all over the meat and vegetables. Cook for 12 minutes, shaking the basket halfway through the cooking time. Serve warm.

225. Pork Tenderloin With Bacon & Veggies

INGREDIENTS for Servings: 3

3 potatoes ¾ pound frozen green beans 6 bacon slices	3 (6-ounces) pork tenderloins 2 tablespoons olive oil

DIRECTIONS and Cooking Time: 28 Minutes

Set the temperature of air fryer to 390 degrees F. Grease an air fryer basket. With a fork, pierce the potatoes. Place potatoes into the prepared air fryer basket and air fry for about 15 minutes. Wrap one bacon slice around 4-6 green beans. Coat the pork tenderloins with oil After 15 minutes, add the pork tenderloins into air fryer basket with potatoes and air fry for about 5-6 minutes. Remove the pork tenderloins from basket. Place bean rolls into the basket and top with the pork tenderloins. Air fry for another 7 minutes. Remove from air fryer and transfer the pork tenderloins onto a platter. Cut each tenderloin into desired size slices. Serve alongside the potatoes and green beans rolls.

226. Garlicky Buttered Chops

INGREDIENTS for Servings: 4

1 tablespoons butter, melted 2 teaspoons chopped parsley 4 pork chops	2 teaspoons grated garlic Salt and pepper to taste

DIRECTIONS and Cooking Time: 30 Minutes

Preheat the air fryer to 330F. Place the grill pan accessory in the air fryer. Season the pork chops with the remaining Ingredients. Place on the grill pan and cook for 30 minutes. Flip the pork chops halfway through the cooking time.

227. Chives Beef

INGREDIENTS for Servings: 2

2 tablespoons coconut flour	10 oz flank steak
1 teaspoon sunflower oil	1 teaspoon coconut aminos
½ teaspoon garlic powder	4 tablespoons water
2 tablespoons apple cider vinegar	1 tablespoon Erythritol
	1 teaspoon chives, chopped

DIRECTIONS and Cooking Time: 10 Minutes

Slice the flank steak into the long thin strips and sprinkle with coconut flour Shake the meat gently. Preheat the air fryer to 395F. Put the sliced flank steak in the air fryer and cook it for 5 minutes from each side. Meanwhile, pour sunflower oil in the saucepan. Add garlic powder, apple cider vinegar, soy sauce, water, and Erythritol. Bring the liquid to boil and remove from the heat. When the meat is cooked, put it in the hot sauce and mix up well. Leave the meat to soak in the sauce for 5-10 minutes.

228. French-style Pork And Pepper Meatloaf

INGREDIENTS for Servings: 4

1/2 cup parmesan cheese, grated	1 pound pork, ground
1 ½ tablespoons green garlic, minced	1 leek, chopped
1½ tablespoon fresh cilantro, minced	1 serrano pepper, chopped
1/2 tablespoon fish sauce	2 tablespoons tomato puree
1/3 teaspoon dried basil	1/2 teaspoons dried thyme
	Salt and ground black pepper, to taste

DIRECTIONS and Cooking Time: 35 Minutes

Add all ingredients to a large-sized mixing dish and combine everything using your hands.   Then, form a meatloaf using a spatula.   Bake for 23 minutes at 365 degrees F. Afterward, allow your meatloaf to rest for 10 minutes before slicing and serving. Bon appétit!

229. Cheesy Potato Casserole The Amish Way

INGREDIENTS for Servings: 6

5 medium eggs, lightly beaten	2 cups frozen shredded hash brown potatoes, thawed
1 cup shredded Cheddar cheese	1/2 cup and 2 tablespoons shredded Swiss cheese
1/2-pound sliced bacon, diced	
1/2 sweet onion, chopped	3/4 cup small curd cottage cheese

DIRECTIONS and Cooking Time: 45 Minutes

Lightly grease baking pan of air fryer with cooking spray.   For 10 minutes, cook on 330F the onion and bacon. Discard excess fat.   Meanwhile, in a bowl, whisk well Swiss cheese, cottage cheese, cheddar cheese, eggs, and potatoes. Pour into pan of cooked bacon and mix well.   Cook for another 25 minutes. Let it stand in air fryer for another 10 minutes.   Serve and enjoy.

230. Baked Cheese'n Pepperoni Calzone

INGREDIENTS for Servings: 4

1 cup chopped pepperoni	1 loaf (1 pound) frozen bread dough, thawed
1 to 2 tablespoons 2% milk	1/2 teaspoon Italian seasoning, optional
1 tablespoon grated Parmesan cheese	1/4 cup shredded part-skim mozzarella cheese
1/2 cup pasta sauce with meat	

DIRECTIONS and Cooking Time: 25 Minutes

In a bowl mix well mozzarella cheese, pizza sauce, and pepperoni.   On a lightly floured surface, divide dough into four portions. Roll each into a 6-in. circle; top each with a scant 1/3 cup pepperoni mixture. Fold dough over filling; pinch edges to seal.   Lightly grease baking pan of air fryer with cooking spray. Place dough in a single layer and if needed, cook in batches. For 25 minutes, cook on 330F preheated air fryer or until dough is lightly browned.   Serve and enjoy.

231. Ribeye Steak With Classis Garlic Mayonnaise

INGREDIENTS for Servings: 3

1 ½ pounds ribeye, bone-in	1/2 teaspoon garlic powder
1 tablespoon butter, room temperature	1/2 teaspoon onion powder
Salt, to taste	1 teaspoon ground coriander
1/2 teaspoon crushed black pepper	3 tablespoons mayonnaise
1/2 teaspoon dried dill	1 teaspoon garlic, minced
1/2 teaspoon cayenne pepper	

DIRECTIONS and Cooking Time: 20 Minutes

Start by preheating your Air Fryer to 400 degrees F. Pat dry the ribeye and rub it with softened butter on all sides. Sprinkle with seasonings and transfer to the cooking basket. Cook in the preheated Air Fryer for 15 minutes, flipping them halfway through the cooking time. In the meantime, simply mix the mayonnaise with garlic and place in the refrigerator until ready to serve. Bon appétit!

232. Tomato Salsa Topped Grilled Flank Steak

INGREDIENTS for Servings: 4

¼ cup chopped cilantro	1 red onion, chopped
1 ½ pounds flank steak, pounded	2 cups chopped tomatoes
1 teaspoon coriander powder	Salt and pepper to taste

DIRECTIONS and Cooking Time: 40 Minutes
Preheat the air fryer to 390F. Place the grill pan accessory in the air fryer. Season the flank steak with salt and pepper. Grill for 20 minutes per batch and make sure to flip the beef halfway through the cooking time. Meanwhile, prepare the salsa by mixing in a bowl the tomatoes, cilantro, onions, and coriander. Season with more salt and pepper to taste.

233. Beef And Garlic Onions Sauce

INGREDIENTS for Servings: 6

2-pound beef shank	3 tablespoons apple cider vinegar
1 teaspoon ground black pepper	1 garlic clove, diced
1 teaspoon salt	3 tablespoons water
1 oz crushed tomatoes	3 spring onions, chopped
1 teaspoon sesame oil	

DIRECTIONS and Cooking Time: 20 Minutes
Sprinkle the beef shank with ground black pepper and salt and put in the air fryer. Sprinkle the meat with sesame oil. Cook it for 20 minutes at 390F. Flip the meat on another side after 10 minutes of cooking. Meanwhile, make the sauce: put crushed tomatoes in the saucepan. Add apple cider vinegar, garlic clove, water, and spring onions. Bring the liquid to boil and remove it from the heat. When the meat is cooked, chop it into the servings and sprinkle with hot sauce.

234. Lamb With Paprika Cilantro Sauce

INGREDIENTS for Servings: 4

1 pound lamb, cubed	1 cup coconut cream
3 tablespoons sweet paprika	2 tablespoons cilantro, chopped
2 tablespoons olive oil	

	Salt and black pepper to the taste

DIRECTIONS and Cooking Time: 30 Minutes
Heat up a pan that fits your air fryer with the oil over medium-high heat, add the meat and brown for 5 minutes. Add the rest of the ingredients, toss, put the pan in the air fryer and cook at 380 degrees F for 25 minutes. Divide everything into bowls and serve.

235. Balsamic London Broil With Garlic

INGREDIENTS for Servings: 8

2 pounds London broil	2 tablespoons olive oil
3 large garlic cloves, minced	Sea salt and ground black pepper, to taste
3 tablespoons balsamic vinegar	1/2 teaspoon dried hot red pepper flakes
3 tablespoons whole-grain mustard	

DIRECTIONS and Cooking Time: 30 Minutes + Marinating Time
Score both sides of the cleaned London broil. Thoroughly combine the remaining ingredients; massage this mixture into the meat to coat it on all sides. Let it marinate for at least 3 hours. Set the Air Fryer to cook at 400 degrees F; Then cook the London broil for 15 minutes. Flip it over and cook another 10 to 12 minutes. Bon appétit!

236. Peach Puree On Ribeye

INGREDIENTS for Servings: 2

¼ cup balsamic vinegar	1-pound T-bone steak
1 cup peach puree	2 teaspoons lemon pepper seasoning
1 tablespoon paprika	Salt and pepper to taste
1 teaspoon thyme	

DIRECTIONS and Cooking Time: 45 Minutes
Place all ingredients in a Ziploc bag and allow to marinate in the fridge for at least 2 hours. Preheat the air fryer to 390F. Place the grill pan accessory in the air fryer. Grill for 20 minutes and flip the meat halfway through the cooking time.

237. Ground Beef On Deep Dish Pizza

INGREDIENTS for Servings: 4

1 can (10-3/4 ounces) condensed tomato soup, undiluted	1 teaspoon dried rosemary, crushed
	1 teaspoon each dried

1 can (8 ounces) mushroom stems and pieces, drained	basil, oregano and thyme
1 cup shredded part-skim mozzarella cheese	1 teaspoon salt
	1 teaspoon sugar
1 cup warm water (110°F to 115°F)	1/4 teaspoon garlic powder
1 package (1/4 ounce) active dry yeast	1-pound ground beef, cooked and drained
1 small green pepper, julienned	2 tablespoons canola oil
	2-1/2 cups all-purpose flour

DIRECTIONS and Cooking Time: 25 Minutes
In a large bowl, dissolve yeast in warm water. Add the sugar, salt, oil and 2 cups flour. Beat until smooth. Stir in enough remaining flour to form a soft dough. Cover and let rest for 20 minutes. Divide into two and store half in the freezer for future use. On a floured surface, roll into a square the size of your air fryer. Transfer to a greased air fryer baking pan. Sprinkle with beef. Mix well seasonings and soup in a small bowl and pour over beef. Sprinkle top with mushrooms and green pepper. Top with cheese. Cover pan with foil. For 15 minutes, cook on 390F. Remove foil, cook for another 10 minutes or until cheese is melted. Serve and enjoy.

238.   Beef With Tomato Sauce And Fennel

INGREDIENTS for Servings: 4

2 tablespoons olive oil	1 fennel bulb, sliced
1 pound beef, cut into strips	1 teaspoon sweet paprika
Salt and black pepper to the taste	1/4 cup keto tomato sauce

DIRECTIONS and Cooking Time: 20 Minutes
Heat up a pan that fits the air fryer with the oil over medium-high heat, add the beef and brown for 5 minutes. Add the rest of the ingredients, toss, put the pan in the machine and cook at 380 degrees F for 15 minutes. Divide the mix between plates and serve.

239.   Creamy Beef And Mushrooms

INGREDIENTS for Servings: 2

1 pound beef, cut into strips	10 white mushrooms, sliced
2 tablespoons coconut oil, melted	1 tablespoon coconut aminos
A pinch of salt and black pepper	1 tablespoon mustard
1 shallot, chopped	1 cup beef stock
2 garlic cloves, minced	1/4 cup coconut cream

	1/4 cup parsley, chopped

DIRECTIONS and Cooking Time: 25 Minutes
Heat up a pan that fits your air fryer with the oil over medium-high heat, add the meat and brown for 2 minutes. Add the garlic, shallots, mushrooms, salt and pepper, and cook for 3 minutes more. Add the remaining ingredients except the parsley, toss, put the pan in the fryer and cook at 390 degrees F for 20 minutes. Divide the mix into bowls and serve with parsley sprinkled on top.

240.   Sweet Pork Belly

INGREDIENTS for Servings: 6

1-pound pork belly	1 teaspoon butter, softened
1 teaspoon Splenda	1/2 teaspoon onion powder
1 teaspoon salt	
1 teaspoon white pepper	

DIRECTIONS and Cooking Time: 55 Minutes
Sprinkle the pork belly with salt, white pepper, and onion powder. Then preheat the air fryer to 385F. Put the pork belly in the air fryer and cook it for 45 minutes. Then turn the pork belly on another side and spread it with butter. After this, top the pork belly with Splenda and cook it at 400f for 10 minutes.

241.   Bolognese Sauce With A Twist

INGREDIENTS for Servings: 4

1 teaspoon kosher salt	1/3 cup tomato paste
1/3 teaspoon cayenne pepper	1/3 tablespoon fresh cilantro, chopped
1½ pounds ground pork	1/2 tablespoon extra-virgin olive oil
3 cloves garlic, minced	1/3 teaspoon freshly cracked black pepper
1/2 medium-sized white onion, peeled and chopped	1/2 teaspoon grated fresh ginger

DIRECTIONS and Cooking Time: 19 Minutes
Begin by preheating your Air Fryer to 395 degrees F. Then, thoroughly combine all the ingredients until the mixture is uniform. Transfer the meat mixture to the Air Fryer baking dish and cook for about 14 minutes. Serve with zucchini noodles and enjoy.

242.   Beef Casserole Recipe

INGREDIENTS for Servings: 12

1 tbsp. olive oil	2 lbs. beef; ground
2 cups eggplant; chopped.	16 oz. tomato sauce
	Salt and black pepper

2 tsp. gluten free Worcestershire sauce 28 oz. canned tomatoes; chopped. 2 cups mozzarella; grated	to the taste 2 tsp. mustard 2 tbsp. parsley; chopped. 1 tsp. oregano; dried

DIRECTIONS and Cooking Time: 65 Minutes
In a bowl; mix eggplant with salt, pepper and oil and toss to coat. In another bowl, mix beef with salt, pepper, mustard and Worcestershire sauce; stir well and spread on the bottom of a pan that fits your air fryer. Add eggplant mix, tomatoes, tomato sauce, parsley, oregano and sprinkle mozzarella at the end. Introduce in your air fryer and cook at 360 °F, for 35 minutes Divide among plates and serve hot.

243. Cheesy Schnitzel

INGREDIENTS for Servings: 1

1 thin beef schnitzel 1 egg, beaten ½ cup friendly bread crumbs 2 tbsp. olive oil	3 tbsp. pasta sauce ¼ cup parmesan cheese, grated Pepper and salt to taste

DIRECTIONS and Cooking Time: 30 Minutes
Pre-heat the Air Fryer to 350°F. In a shallow dish, combine the bread crumbs, olive oil, pepper, and salt.

In another shallow dish, put the beaten egg. Cover the schnitzel in the egg before press it into the breadcrumb mixture and placing it in the Air Fryer basket. Cook for 15 minutes. Pour the pasta sauce over the schnitzel and top with the grated cheese. Cook for an additional 5 minutes until the cheese melts. Serve hot.

244. Rib Eye Steak Recipe From Hawaii

INGREDIENTS for Servings: 6

½ cup soy sauce ½ cup sugar 2 cups pineapple juice 2 teaspoons sesame oil	1-inch ginger, grated 3 pounds rib eye steaks 5 tablespoon apple cider vinegar

DIRECTIONS and Cooking Time: 45 Minutes
Combine all ingredients in a Ziploc bag and allow to marinate in the fridge for at least 2 hours. Preheat the air fryer to 390F. Place the grill pan accessory in the air fryer. Grill the meat for 15 minutes while flipping the meat every 8 minutes and cook in batches. Meanwhile, pour the marinade in a saucepan and allow to simmer until the sauce thickens. Brush the grilled meat with the glaze before serving.

FISH & SEAFOOD RECIPES

245. Nacho Chips Crusted Prawns

INGREDIENTS for Servings: 2

¾ pound prawns, peeled and deveined 1 large egg	5 ounces Nacho flavored chips, finely crushed

DIRECTIONS and Cooking Time: 8 Minutes
In a shallow bowl, beat the egg. In another bowl, place the nacho chips Dip each prawn into the beaten egg and then, coat with the crushed nacho chips. Set the temperature of air fryer to 350 degrees F. Grease an air fryer basket. Arrange prawns into the prepared air fryer basket. Air fry for about 8 minutes. Remove from air fryer and transfer the prawns onto serving plates. Serve hot.

246. Tartar Sauce 'n Crispy Cod Nuggets

INGREDIENTS for Servings: 3

½ cup flour ½ cup non-fat mayonnaise ½ teaspoon Worcestershire sauce 1 ½ pounds cod fillet 1 cup cracker crumbs 1 egg, beaten 1 tablespoon sweet pickle relish	1 tablespoon vegetable oil 1 teaspoon honey Juice from half a lemon Salt and pepper to taste Zest from half of a lemon

DIRECTIONS and Cooking Time: 10 Minutes
Preheat the air fryer to 390F. Season the cods with salt and pepper. Dredge the fish on flour and dip in the beaten egg before dredging on the cracker crumbs. Brush with oil. Place the fish on the double layer rack and cook for 10 minutes. Meanwhile, prepare the sauce by mixing all ingredients in a bowl. Serve the fish with the sauce.

247. Caribbean Ginger Sea Bass

INGREDIENTS for Servings: 2

¼ habanero, chopped 1 teaspoon Caribbean spices 8 oz sea bass, trimmed ½ teaspoon Erythritol	1 teaspoon smoked paprika ¼ teaspoon minced ginger 1 tablespoon avocado oil

DIRECTIONS and Cooking Time: 10 Minutes

In the mixing bowl mix up Caribbean spices, Erythritol, and smoked paprika. Then rub the sea bass with the spice mixture well. In the shallow bowl, whisk together minced ginger and avocado oil. Brush the fish with the ginger mixture. Preheat the air fryer to 400F. Put the sea bass in the air fryer and cook it for 10 minutes.

248. Lemony Tuna

INGREDIENTS for Servings: 8

4 tablespoons fresh parsley, chopped 4 (6-ounce) cans water packed plain tuna 1 cup breadcrumbs 4 teaspoons Dijon mustard	2 eggs 2 tablespoons fresh lime juice 6 tablespoons canola oil Dash of hot sauce Salt and black pepper, to taste

DIRECTIONS and Cooking Time: 12 Minutes
Preheat the Air fryer to 360F and grease an Air fryer basket. Mix tuna fish, breadcrumbs, mustard, parsley, hot sauce, canola oil, eggs, salt and lime juice in a large bowl. Make equal-sized patties from the mixture and refrigerate for about 3 hours. Transfer the patties into the Air fryer basket and cook for about 12 minutes. Dish out and serve warm.

249. Japanese Flounder With Chives

INGREDIENTS for Servings: 4

4 flounder fillets Sea salt and freshly cracked mixed peppercorns, to taste 1 ½ tablespoons dark sesame oil 2 tablespoons sake	1/4 cup soy sauce 1 tablespoon grated lemon rind 2 garlic cloves, minced 2 tablespoons chopped chives, to serve

DIRECTIONS and Cooking Time: 15 Minutes + Marinating Time
Place all the ingredients, without the chives, in a large-sized mixing dish. Cover and allow it to marinate for about 2 hours in your fridge. Remove the fish from the marinade and cook in the Air Fryer cooking basket at 360 degrees F for 10 to 12 minutes; flip once during cooking. Pour the remaining marinade into a pan that is preheated over a medium-low heat; let it simmer, stirring continuously, until it has thickened. Pour the prepared glaze over flounder and serve garnished with fresh chives.

250. Taco Lobster

INGREDIENTS for Servings: 4

4 lettuce leaves	½ teaspoon chili flakes
½ teaspoon taco seasonings	1 tablespoon ricotta cheese
4 lobster tails	
1 teaspoon Splenda	1 teaspoon avocado oil
½ teaspoon ground cumin	

DIRECTIONS and Cooking Time: 6 Minutes
Peel the lobster tails and sprinkle with ground cumin, taco seasonings, and chili flakes. Arrange the lobster tails in the air fryer basket and sprinkle with avocado oil. Cook them for 6 minutes at 380F. After this, remove the cooked lobster tails from the air fryer and chop them roughly. Transfer the lobster tails into the bowl. Add ricotta cheese and Splenda. Mix them up. Place the lobster mixture on the lettuce leaves and fold them.

251. Fried Tilapia Bites

INGREDIENTS for Servings: 4

½ cup cornflakes	Salt to taste
3 tbsp flour	Lemon wedges for serving
1 egg, beaten	

DIRECTIONS and Cooking Time: 20 Minutes
Preheat your Air Fryer to 390 F. Spray the air fryer basket with cooking spray. Put the flour, egg, and conflakes each into a different bowl, three bowls in total. Add salt egg bowl and mix well. Dip the tilapia first in the flour, then in the egg, and lastly, coat in the cornflakes. Lay on the air fryer basket. Spray with cooking spray and cook for 5 minutes. Slide out the fryer basket and shake the shrimp; cook further for 5 minutes. Serve with lemon wedges.

252. Glazed Halibut Steak

INGREDIENTS for Servings: 3

1 lb. halibut steak	¼ tsp. crushed red pepper flakes
2/3 cup low-sodium soy sauce	¼ cup orange juice
½ cup mirin	1 garlic clove, smashed
2 tbsp. lime juice	
¼ cup sugar	¼ tsp. ginger, ground

DIRECTIONS and Cooking Time: 70 Minutes
1 Make the teriyaki glaze by mixing together all of the ingredients except for the halibut in a saucepan.   2 Bring it to a boil and lower the heat, stirring constantly until the mixture reduces by half. Remove from the heat and leave to cool.   3 Pour half of the cooled glaze into a Ziploc bag. Add in the halibut, making sure to coat it well in the sauce. Place in the refrigerator for 30 minutes.   4 Pre-heat the Air Fryer to 390°F.   5 Put the marinated halibut in the fryer and allow to cook for 10 – 12 minutes.   6 Use any the remaining glaze to lightly brush the halibut steak with.   7 Serve with white rice or shredded vegetables.

253. Tomato 'n Onion Stuffed Grilled Squid

INGREDIENTS for Servings: 4

½ cup green onions, chopped	2 pounds squid, gutted and cleaned
½ cup tomatoes, chopped	2 tablespoons olive oil
1 tablespoon fresh lemon juice	Salt and pepper to taste
5 cloves of garlic	

DIRECTIONS and Cooking Time: 15 Minutes
Preheat the air fryer to 390F.   Place the grill pan accessory in the air fryer.   Season the squid with salt, pepper, and lemon juice.   Stuff the cavity with garlic, tomatoes, and onions.   Brush the squid with olive oil. Place on the grill pan and cook for 15 minutes. Halfway through the cooking time, flip the squid.

254. Chinese Garlic Shrimp

INGREDIENTS for Servings: 5

Juice of 1 lemon	Chopped chili to taste
1 tsp sugar	Salt and black pepper to taste
3 tbsp peanut oil	
2 tbsp cornstarch	4 garlic cloves
2 scallions, chopped	
¼ tsp Chinese powder	

DIRECTIONS and Cooking Time: 15 Minutes
Preheat air fryer to 370 F. In a Ziploc bag, mix lemon juice, sugar, pepper, half of oil, cornstarch, powder, Chinese powder and salt. Add in the shrimp and massage to coat evenly. Let sit for 10 minutes.   Add the remaining peanut oil, garlic, scallions, and chili to a pan, and fry for 5 minutes over medium heat. Place the marinated shrimp in your air fryer's basket and cover with the sauce. Cook for 10 minutes, until nice and crispy. Serve.

255. Grilled Salmon With Butter And Wine

INGREDIENTS for Servings: 4

2 cloves garlic, minced	Sea salt and ground black pepper, to taste
4 tablespoons butter, melted	1 tablespoon lime juice
1 teaspoon smoked paprika	1/4 cup dry white wine
1/2 teaspoon onion powder	4 salmon steaks

DIRECTIONS and Cooking Time: 45 Minutes
Place all ingredients in a large ceramic dish. Cover and let it marinate for 30 minutes in the refrigerator. Arrange the salmon steaks on the grill pan. Bake at 390 degrees for 5 minutes, or until the salmon steaks are easily flaked with a fork. Flip the fish steaks, baste with the reserved marinade, and cook another 5 minutes. Bon appétit!

256. Tilapia With Cheesy Caper Sauce

INGREDIENTS for Servings: 4

4 tilapia fillets	1/2 cup crème fraîche
1 tablespoon extra-virgin olive oil	2 tablespoons mayonnaise
Celery salt, to taste	1/4 cup Cottage
Freshly cracked pink peppercorns, to taste	cheese, at room temperature
For the Creamy Caper Sauce:	1 tablespoon capers, finely chopped

DIRECTIONS and Cooking Time: 15 Minutes
Toss the tilapia fillets with olive oil, celery salt, and cracked peppercorns until they are well coated. Place the fillets in a single layer at the bottom of the Air Fryer cooking basket. Air-fry at 360 degrees F for about 12 minutes; turn them over once during cooking. Meanwhile, prepare the sauce by mixing the remaining items. Lastly, garnish air-fried tilapia fillets with the sauce and serve immediately!

257. Grilled Tilapia With Portobello Mushrooms

INGREDIENTS for Servings: 2

1 tablespoon avocado oil	2 tilapia fillets
1/2 teaspoon red pepper flakes, crushed	1/2 teaspoon sea salt
1/2 teaspoon dried sage, crushed	1 teaspoon dried parsley flakes
1/4 teaspoon lemon pepper	4 medium-sized Portobello mushrooms
	A few drizzles of liquid smoke

DIRECTIONS and Cooking Time: 20 Minutes
Toss all ingredients in a mixing bowl; except for the mushrooms. Transfer the tilapia fillets to a lightly greased grill pan. Preheat your Air Fryer to 400 degrees F and cook the tilapia fillets for 5 minutes. Now, turn the fillets over and add the Portobello mushrooms. Continue to cook for 5 minutes longer or until mushrooms are tender and the fish is opaque. Serve immediately.

258. Ham-wrapped Prawns With Roasted Pepper Chutney

INGREDIENTS for Servings: 4

1 large red bell pepper	1 tablespoon olive oil
8 king prawns, peeled and deveined	½ tablespoon paprika
	Salt and freshly
4 ham slices, halved	ground black pepper,
1 garlic clove, minced	to taste

DIRECTIONS and Cooking Time: 13 Minutes
Preheat the Air fryer to 375F and grease an Air fryer basket. Place the bell pepper in the Air fryer basket and cook for about 10 minutes. Dish out the bell pepper into a bowl and keep aside, covered for about 15 minutes. Now, peel the bell pepper and remove the stems and seeds and chop it. Put the chopped bell pepper, garlic, paprika and olive oil in a blender and pulse until a puree is formed. Wrap each ham slice around each prawn and transfer to the Air fryer basket. Cook for about 3 minutes and serve with roasted pepper chutney.

259. Paprika Snapper Mix

INGREDIENTS for Servings: 4

2 tablespoons sweet paprika	4 snapper fillets, boneless and skin scored
3 tablespoons olive oil	6 spring onions,
A pinch of salt and black pepper	chopped
	Juice of ½ lemon

DIRECTIONS and Cooking Time: 14 Minutes
In a bowl, mix the paprika with the rest of the ingredients except the fish and whisk well. Rub the fish with this mix, place the fillets in your air fryer's basket and cook at 390 degrees F for 7 minutes on each side. Divide between plates and serve with a side salad.

260. Sweet & Sour Glazed Salmon

INGREDIENTS for Servings: 2

1/3 cup soy sauce	1 teaspoon water
1/3 cup honey	4 (3½-ounces) salmon
3 teaspoons rice wine vinegar	fillets

DIRECTIONS and Cooking Time: 12 Minutes
In a small bowl, mix together the soy sauce, honey, vinegar, and water. In another bowl, reserve about half of the mixture. Add salmon fillets in the remaining mixture and coat well. Cover the bowl and refrigerate to marinate for about 2 hours. Set the temperature of air fryer to 355 degrees F. Grease

an air fryer basket. Arrange salmon fillets into the prepared air fryer basket in a single layer. Air fry for about 12 minutes, flipping once halfway through and coating with the reserved marinade after every 3 minutes. Remove from air fryer and place the salmon fillets onto serving plates. Serve hot.

261. Ham Tilapia
INGREDIENTS for Servings: 4

16 oz tilapia fillet	½ teaspoon salt
4 ham slices	1 teaspoon dried
1 teaspoon sunflower oil	rosemary

DIRECTIONS and Cooking Time: 10 Minutes
Cut the tilapia on 4 servings. Sprinkle every fish serving with salt, dried rosemary, and sunflower oil. Then carefully wrap the fish fillets in the ham slices and secure with toothpicks. Preheat the air fryer to 400F. Put the wrapped tilapia in the air fryer basket in one layer and cook them for 10 minutes. Gently flip the fish on another side after 5 minutes of cooking.

262. Pesto Sauce Over Fish Filet
INGREDIENTS for Servings: 3

1 bunch fresh basil	2 tablespoons pine nuts
1 cup olive oil	
1 tablespoon parmesan cheese, grated	3 white fish fillets
	Salt and pepper to taste
2 cloves of garlic,	

DIRECTIONS and Cooking Time: 20 Minutes
In a food processor, combine all ingredients except for the fish fillets. Pulse until smooth. Place the fish in a baking dish and pour over the pesto sauce. Place in the air fryer and cook for 20 minutes at 400F.

263. Char-grilled 'n Herbed Sea Scallops
INGREDIENTS for Servings: 3

1-pound sea scallops, meat only	1 teaspoon dried sage
3 tablespoons olive oil, divided	1 cup grape tomatoes, halved
Salt and pepper to taste	1/3 cup basil leaves, shredded

DIRECTIONS and Cooking Time: 10 Minutes
Preheat the air fryer at 390F. Place the grill pan accessory in the air fryer. Season the scallops with half of the olive oil, sage, salt and pepper. Toss into the air fryer and grill for 10 minutes. Once cooked, serve with tomatoes and basil leaves. Drizzle the remaining olive oil and season with more salt and pepper to taste.

264. Easy Battered Lemony Fillet
INGREDIENTS for Servings: 4

½ cup almond flour	4 tablespoons vegetable oil
1 egg, beaten	
1 lemon	Salt and pepper to taste
4 fish fillets	

DIRECTIONS and Cooking Time: 15 Minutes
Season the fish fillets with lemon, salt, and pepper. Soak in the beaten egg and dredge in almond flour. Place in the air fryer basket. Cook for 15 minutes at 400F.

265. Wild Alaskan Salmon With Parsley Sauce
INGREDIENTS for Servings: 4

4 Alaskan wild salmon fillets, 6 oz each	½ cup heavy cream
2 tsp olive oil	½ cup milk
A pinch of salt	A pinch of salt
For Dill Sauce	2 tbsp chopped parsley

DIRECTIONS and Cooking Time: 20 Minutes
Preheat air fryer to 380 F. In a bowl, add salmon and drizzle 1 tsp of oil. Season with salt and pepper. Place the salmon in your air fryer's cooking basket and cook for 15 minutes, until tender and crispy. In a bowl, mix milk, chopped parsley, salt, and whipped cream. Serve the salmon with the sauce.

266. Stevia Cod
INGREDIENTS for Servings: 4

2 tablespoons coconut aminos	1/3 cup stevia
	A pinch of salt and
4 cod fillets, boneless	black pepper

DIRECTIONS and Cooking Time: 14 Minutes
In a pan that fits the air fryer, combine all the ingredients and toss gently. Introduce the pan in the fryer and cook at 350 degrees F for 14 minutes, flipping the fish halfway. Divide everything between plates and serve.

267. Almond Coconut Shrimp
INGREDIENTS for Servings: 4

16 oz shrimp, peeled	2 egg whites
1/2 cup almond flour	1/2 cup unsweetened

1/4 tsp cayenne pepper	shredded coconut 1/2 tsp salt

DIRECTIONS and Cooking Time: 5 Minutes
Preheat the air fryer to 400 F. Spray air fryer basket with cooking spray. Whisk egg whites in a shallow dish. In a bowl, mix together the shredded coconut, almond flour, and cayenne pepper. Dip shrimp into the egg mixture then coat with coconut mixture. Place coated shrimp into the air fryer basket and cook for 5 minutes. Serve and enjoy.

268. Turmeric Fish Fingers

INGREDIENTS for Servings: 4

1-pound cod fillet ½ cup almond flour 2 eggs, beaten ½ teaspoon ground turmeric	1 tablespoon flax meal 1 teaspoon salt 1 teaspoon avocado oil

DIRECTIONS and Cooking Time: 9 Minutes
Slice the cod fillets into the strips (fingers). In the mixing bowl, mix up eggs, ground turmeric, and salt. Stir the liquid until salt is dissolved. Then in the separated bowl mix up almond flour and flax meal. Dip the cod fingers in the egg mixture and coat in the almond flour mixture. Preheat the air fryer to 400F. Place the fish fingers in the air fryer basket in one layer and sprinkle with avocado oil. Cook the fish fingers for 4 minutes. Then flip them on another side and cook for 5 minutes more or until the fish fingers are golden brown.

269. Calamari

INGREDIENTS for Servings: 2

1 cup club soda ½ lb. calamari tubes [or tentacles], about ¼ inch wide, rinsed and dried ½ cup honey 1 – 2 tbsp. sriracha	1 cup flour Sea salt to taste Red pepper and black pepper to taste Red pepper flakes to taste

DIRECTIONS and Cooking Time: 25 Minutes
1 In a bowl, cover the calamari rings with club soda and mix well. Leave to sit for 10 minutes. 2 In another bowl, combine the flour, salt, red and black pepper. 3 In a third bowl mix together the honey, pepper flakes, and Sriracha to create the sauce. 4 Remove any excess liquid from the calamari and coat each one with the flour mixture. 5 Spritz the fryer basket with the cooking spray. 6 Arrange the calamari in the basket, well-spaced out and in a single layer. 7 Cook at 380°F for 11 minutes, shaking the basket at least two times during the cooking time. 8 Take the calamari out of the fryer, coat it with half of the sauce and return to the fryer. Cook for an additional 2 minutes. 9 Plate up the calamari and pour the rest of the sauce over it.

270. Cajun Seasoned Salmon Filet

INGREDIENTS for Servings: 1

1 teaspoon juice from lemon, freshly squeezed 3 tablespoons extra virgin olive oil	1 salmon fillet A dash of Cajun seasoning mix Salt and pepper to taste

DIRECTIONS and Cooking Time: 15 Minutes
Preheat the air fryer for 5 minutes. Place all ingredients in a bowl and toss to coat. Place the fish fillet in the air fryer basket. Bake for 15 minutes at 325F. Once cooked drizzle with olive oil

271. Mahi Mahi And Broccoli Cakes

INGREDIENTS for Servings: 4

½ cup broccoli, shredded 1 tablespoon flax meal 1 egg, beaten 1 teaspoon ground coriander	1 oz Monterey Jack cheese, shredded ½ teaspoon salt 6 oz Mahi Mahi, chopped Cooking spray

DIRECTIONS and Cooking Time: 11 Minutes
In the mixing bowl mix up flax meal, egg, ground coriander, salt, broccoli, and chopped Mahi Mahi. Stir the ingredients gently with the help of the fork and add shredded Monterey Jack cheese. Stir the mixture until homogenous. Then make 4 cakes. Preheat the air fryer to 390F. Place the Mahi Mahi cakes in the air fryer and spray them gently with cooking spray. Cook the fish cakes for 5 minutes and then flip on another side. Cook the fish cakes for 6 minutes more.

272. Tasty Sockeye Fish

INGREDIENTS for Servings: 2

½ bulb fennel, thinly sliced 4 tbsp melted butter Salt and pepper to taste 1-2 tsp fresh dill	2 sockeye salmon fillets 8 cherry tomatoes, halved ¼ cup fish stock

DIRECTIONS and Cooking Time: 25 Minutes
Preheat air fryer to 400 F. Bring to a boil salted water over medium heat. Add the potatoes and blanch for 2 minutes; drain. Cut 2 large-sized rectangles of parchment paper of 13x15 inch size. In a large bowl, mix potatoes, fennel, pepper, and salt. Divide the

mixture between parchment paper pieces and sprinkle with dill. Top with fillets. Add cherry tomatoes on top and drizzle with butter; pour fish stock on top. Fold the squares and seal them. Cook the packets in the air fryer for 10 minutes.

273. Butterflied Prawns With Garlic-sriracha

INGREDIENTS for Servings: 2

1 tablespoon lime juice	1teaspoon fish sauce
1 tablespoon sriracha	2 tablespoons melted butter
1-pound large prawns, shells removed and cut lengthwise or butterflied	2 tablespoons minced garlic
	Salt and pepper to taste

DIRECTIONS and Cooking Time: 15 Minutes
Preheat the air fryer to 390F. Place the grill pan accessory in the air fryer. Season the prawns with the rest of the ingredients. Place on the grill pan and cook for 15 minutes. Make sure to flip the prawns halfway through the cooking time.

274. Paprika Prawns

INGREDIENTS for Servings: 5

3-pound prawns, peeled	1 tablespoon coconut milk
1 tablespoon ground turmeric	1 teaspoon avocado oil
1 teaspoon smoked paprika	½ teaspoon salt

DIRECTIONS and Cooking Time: 5 Minutes
Put the prawns in the bowl and sprinkle them with ground turmeric, smoked paprika, and salt. Then add coconut milk and leave them for 10 minutes to marinate. Meanwhile, preheat the air fryer to 400F. Put the marinated prawns in the air fryer basket and sprinkle with avocado oil. Cook the prawns for 3 minutes. Then shake them well and cook for 2 minutes more.

275. Miso Sauce Over Grilled Salmon

INGREDIENTS for Servings: 4

1/4 cup yellow miso paste	1 1/4 pounds skinless salmon fillets, thinly sliced
2 tablespoons mirin (Japanese rice wine)	Amaranth leaves (optional), to serve
2 teaspoons dashi powder	Shichimi togarashi, to serve
2 teaspoons superfine sugar	

DIRECTIONS and Cooking Time: 16 Minutes
In a bowl mix well sugar, mirin, dashi powder, and miso. Thread salmon into skewers. Baste with miso glaze. Place on skewer rack in air fryer. If needed, cook in batches. For 8 minutes, cook on 360F. Halfway through cooking time, turnover and baste. Serve and enjoy.

276. Air Fried Fresh Broiled Tilapia

INGREDIENTS for Servings: 4

1 tbsp old bay seasoning	2 tbsp lemon pepper
2 tbsp canola oil	Salt to taste
	2-3 butter buds

DIRECTIONS and Cooking Time: 15 Minutes
Preheat fryer to 400 F. Drizzle oil over tilapia. In a bowl, mix salt, lemon pepper, butter buds, and seasoning; spread on the fish. Place the fillets in the air fryer and cook for 10 minutes until crispy.

277. Best Cod Ever

INGREDIENTS for Servings: 2

2 (4-ounce) skinless codfish fillets, cut into rectangular pieces	3 scallions, chopped finely
½ cup flour	2 garlic cloves, minced
3 eggs	1 teaspoon light soy sauce
1 green chili, chopped finely	Salt and black pepper, to taste

DIRECTIONS and Cooking Time: 7 Minutes
Preheat the Air fryer to 375F and grease an Air fryer basket. Place the flour in a shallow dish and mix remaining ingredients in another shallow dish except cod. Coat each fillet with the flour and then dip into the egg mixture. Place the cod in the Air fryer basket and cook for about 7 minutes. Dish out in a platter and serve warm.

278. Crispy Coconut Covered Shrimps

INGREDIENTS for Servings: 6

½ cup almond flour	1 cup egg white
1 cup dried coconut	4 tablespoons butter
12 large shrimps, peeled and deveined	Salt and pepper to taste

DIRECTIONS and Cooking Time: 6 Minutes
Season the shrimps with salt and pepper. Place all ingredients in a Ziploc bag and shake until well combined. Place the ingredients in the air fryer basket. Close and cook for 6 minutes 400F.

279. Mediterranean Crab Cakes With Capers

INGREDIENTS for Servings: 5

1/3 teaspoon ground black pepper	1/2 teaspoon whole-grain mustard
1/2 tablespoon nonpareil capers	1 1/2 pound backfin blue crabmeat
3 eggs, well whisked	1 cup Romano cheese, grated
½ teaspoon dried dill weed	2 ½ tablespoons mayonnaise
1 1/2 tablespoons softened butter	A pinch of salt

DIRECTIONS and Cooking Time: 20 Minutes
Mix all the ingredients thoroughly. Shape into 4 balls and press each ball to form the cakes. Then, spritz your cakes with cooking oil. Air-fry at 365 degrees F for 12 minutes, turning halfway through. Bon appétit!

280. Avocado Shrimp

INGREDIENTS for Servings: 2

½ cup onion, chopped	1 avocado
2 lb. shrimp	½ cup pecans, chopped
1 tbsp. seasoned salt	

DIRECTIONS and Cooking Time: 20 Minutes
Pre-heat the fryer at 400°F. Put the chopped onion in the basket of the fryer and spritz with some cooking spray. Leave to cook for five minutes. Add the shrimp and set the timer for a further five minutes. Sprinkle with some seasoned salt, then allow to cook for an additional five minutes. During these last five minutes, halve your avocado and remove the pit. Cube each half, then scoop out the flesh. Take care when removing the shrimp from the fryer. Place it on a dish and top with the avocado and the chopped pecans.

281. Citrusy Branzini On The Grill

INGREDIENTS for Servings: 2

Salt and pepper to taste	2 branzini fillets
3 lemons, juice freshly squeezed	2 oranges, juice freshly squeezed

DIRECTIONS and Cooking Time: 15 Minutes
Place all ingredients in a Ziploc bag. Allow to marinate in the fridge for 2 hours. Preheat the air fryer at 390F. Place the grill pan accessory in the air fryer. Place the fish on the grill pan and cook for 15 minutes until the fish is flaky.

282. Quick-fix Seafood Breakfast

INGREDIENTS for Servings: 2

1 tablespoon olive oil	1/2 teaspoon dried basil
2 garlic cloves, minced	Salt and white pepper, to taste
1 small yellow onion, chopped	4 eggs, lightly beaten
1/4 pound tilapia pieces	1 tablespoon dry sherry
1/4 pound rockfish pieces	4 tablespoons cheese, shredded

DIRECTIONS and Cooking Time: 30 Minutes
Start by preheating your Air Fryer to 350 degrees F; add the olive oil to a baking pan. Once hot, cook the garlic and onion for 2 minutes or until fragrant. Add the fish, basil, salt, and pepper. In a mixing dish, thoroughly combine the eggs with sherry and cheese. Pour the mixture into the baking pan. Cook at 360 degrees F approximately 20 minutes. Bon appétit!

283. Lemon Crab Patties

INGREDIENTS for Servings: 4

1 egg	1 tsp old bay seasoning
12 oz crabmeat	1 tsp red pepper flakes
2 green onion, chopped	1 tbsp fresh lemon juice
1/4 cup mayonnaise	
1 cup almond flour	

DIRECTIONS and Cooking Time: 10 Minutes
Preheat the air fryer to 400 F. Spray air fryer basket with cooking spray. Add 1/2 almond flour into the mixing bowl. Add remaining ingredients and mix until well combined. Make patties from mixture and coat with remaining almond flour and place into the air fryer basket. Cook patties for 5 minutes then turn to another side and cook for 5 minutes more. Serve and enjoy.

284. Halibut And Capers Mix

INGREDIENTS for Servings: 4

4 halibut fillets, boneless	1 tablespoon lemon zest, grated
A pinch of salt and black pepper	1 tablespoon capers, drained and chopped
1 shallot, chopped	1 tablespoon lemon juice
2 garlic cloves, minced	1 tablespoon olive oil
1 cup parsley, chopped	1 tablespoon butter, melted
1 tablespoon chives, chopped	

DIRECTIONS and Cooking Time: 18 Minutes

Heat up a pan that fits your air fryer with the oil and the butter over medium-high heat, add the shallot and the garlic and sauté for 2 minutes. Add the rest of the ingredients except the fish, toss and sauté for 3 minutes more. Add the fish, sear for 1 minute on each side, toss it gently with the herbed mix, place the pan in the air fryer and cook at 380 degrees F for 12 minutes. Divide everything between plates and serve.

285. Breadcrumbed Fish

INGREDIENTS for Servings: 2 – 4

4 tbsp. vegetable oil 5 oz. friendly bread crumbs	1 egg 4 medium fish fillets

DIRECTIONS and Cooking Time: 25 Minutes
1 Pre-heat your Air Fryer to 350°F.   2 In a bowl, combine the bread crumbs and oil.   3 In a separate bowl, stir the egg with a whisk. Dredge each fish fillet in the egg before coating it in the crumbs mixture. Put them in Air Fryer basket.   4 Cook for 12 minutes and serve hot.

286. Saltine Fish Fillets

INGREDIENTS for Servings: 4

1 cup crushed saltines ¼ cup extra-virgin olive oil 1 tsp. garlic powder ½ tsp. shallot powder	1 egg, well whisked 4 white fish fillets Salt and ground black pepper to taste Fresh Italian parsley to serve

DIRECTIONS and Cooking Time: 15 Minutes
In a shallow bowl, combine the crushed saltines and olive oil.   In a separate bowl, mix together the garlic powder, shallot powder, and the beaten egg. Sprinkle a good amount of salt and pepper over the fish, before dipping each fillet into the egg mixture. Coat the fillets with the crumb mixture.   Air fry the fish at 370°F for 10 - 12 minutes.   Serve with fresh parsley.

287. Shrimp Scampi

INGREDIENTS for Servings: 4

1 lb shrimp, peeled and deveined 10 garlic cloves, peeled 2 tbsp olive oil	1 fresh lemon, cut into wedges 1/4 cup parmesan cheese, grated 2 tbsp butter, melted

DIRECTIONS and Cooking Time: 10 Minutes
Preheat the air fryer to 370 F.   Mix together shrimp, lemon wedges, olive oil, and garlic cloves in a bowl. Pour shrimp mixture into the air fryer pan and place into the air fryer and cook for 10 minutes.   Drizzle

with melted butter and sprinkle with parmesan cheese.   Serve and enjoy.

288. Saucy Garam Masala Fish

INGREDIENTS for Servings: 2

2 teaspoons olive oil 1/2 teaspoon cayenne pepper 1 teaspoon Garam masala 1/4 teaspoon Kala namak (Indian black salt	1/4 cup coconut milk 1/2 teaspoon fresh ginger, grated 1 garlic clove, minced 2 catfish fillets 1/4 cup coriander, roughly chopped

DIRECTIONS and Cooking Time: 25 Minutes
Preheat your Air Fryer to 390 degrees F. Then, spritz the baking dish with a nonstick cooking spray.   In a mixing bowl, whisk the olive oil, milk, cayenne pepper, Garam masala, Kala namak, ginger, and garlic.   Coat the catfish fillets with the Garam masala mixture. Cook the catfish fillets in the preheated Air Fryer approximately 18 minutes, turning over halfway through the cooking time.   Garnish with fresh coriander and serve over hot noodles if desired.

289. Lemon Garlic Shrimp

INGREDIENTS for Servings: 2

½ lb. medium shrimp, shelled and deveined ½ tsp. Old Bay seasoning	1 medium lemon 2 tbsp. unsalted butter, melted ½ tsp. minced garlic

DIRECTIONS and Cooking Time: 15 Minutes
Grate the rind of the lemon into a bowl. Cut the lemon in half and juice it over the same bowl. Toss in the shrimp, Old Bay, and butter, mixing everything to make sure the shrimp is completely covered. Transfer to a round baking dish roughly six inches wide, then place this dish in your fryer.   Cook at 400°F for six minutes. The shrimp is cooked when it turns a bright pink color.   Serve hot, drizzling any leftover sauce over the shrimp.

290. Fried Crawfish

INGREDIENTS for Servings: 4

1 tablespoon avocado oil 1 teaspoon onion powder	1-pound crawfish 1 tablespoon rosemary, chopped

DIRECTIONS and Cooking Time: 5 Minutes
Preheat the air fryer to 340F. Place the crawfish in the air fryer basket and sprinkle with avocado oil and rosemary. Add the onion powder and stir the crawfish gently. Cook the meal for 5 minutes.

291. Sesame Tuna Steak

INGREDIENTS for Servings: 2

1 tbsp. coconut oil, melted	2 tsp. black sesame seeds
2 x 6-oz. tuna steaks	2 tsp. white sesame seeds
½ tsp. garlic powder	

DIRECTIONS and Cooking Time: 12 Minutes
Apply the coconut oil to the tuna steaks with a brunch, then season with garlic powder. Combine the black and white sesame seeds. Embed them in the tuna steaks, covering the fish all over. Place the tuna into your air fryer. Cook for eight minutes at 400°F, turning the fish halfway through. The tuna steaks are ready when they have reached a temperature of 145°F. Serve straightaway.

292. Sea Bream Mix

INGREDIENTS for Servings: 4

1 tablespoon keto tomato sauce	1 teaspoon ground black pepper
1 tablespoon avocado oil	12 oz sea bream fillet
½ teaspoon salt	

DIRECTIONS and Cooking Time: 8 Minutes
Cut the sea bream fillet on 4 servings. After this, in the mixing bowl mix up tomato sauce, avocado oil, salt, and ground black pepper. Rub the fish fillets with tomato mixture from both sides. Preheat the air fryer to 390F. Line the air fryer basket with foil. Put the sea bream fillets on the foil and cook them for 8 minutes.

293. Sea Bass With Vinaigrette

INGREDIENTS for Servings: 4

4 black sea bass fillets, boneless and skin scored	A pinch of salt and black pepper
2 tablespoons olive oil	3 garlic cloves, minced
3 tablespoons black olives, pitted and chopped	1 tablespoon rosemary, chopped
	Juice of 1 lime

DIRECTIONS and Cooking Time: 12 Minutes
In a bowl, mix the oil with the olives and the rest of the ingredients except the fish and whisk well. Place the fish in a pan that fits the air fryer, spread the rosemary vinaigrette all over, put the pan in the machine and cook at 380 degrees F for 12 minutes, flipping the fish halfway. Divide between plates and serve.

294. Air Fried Catfish

INGREDIENTS for Servings: 4

4 catfish fillets	1 tbsp olive oil
1/4 cup fish seasoning	1 tbsp fresh parsley, chopped

DIRECTIONS and Cooking Time: 20 Minutes
Preheat the air fryer to 400 F. Spray air fryer basket with cooking spray. Seasoned fish with seasoning and place into the air fryer basket. Drizzle fish fillets with oil and cook for 10 minutes. Turn fish to another side and cook for 10 minutes more. Garnish with parsley and serve.

295. Spicy Cod

INGREDIENTS for Servings: 2

2 (6-ounces) (1½-inch thick) cod fillets	1 teaspoon onion powder
1 teaspoon smoked paprika	1 teaspoon garlic powder
1 teaspoon cayenne pepper	Salt and ground black pepper, as required
2 teaspoons olive oil	

DIRECTIONS and Cooking Time: 11 Minutes
Preheat the Air fryer to 390F and grease an Air fryer basket. Drizzle the salmon fillets with olive oil and rub with the all the spices. Arrange the salmon fillets into the Air fryer basket and cook for about 11 minutes. Dish out the salmon fillets in the serving plates and serve hot.

296. Easy Grilled Pesto Scallops

INGREDIENTS for Servings: 3

12 large scallops, side muscles removed	½ cup prepared commercial pesto
Salt and pepper to taste	

DIRECTIONS and Cooking Time: 15 Minutes
Place all ingredients in a Ziploc bag and allow the scallops to marinate in the fridge for at least 2 hours. Preheat the air fryer at 390F. Place the grill pan accessory in the air fryer. Grill the scallops for 15 minutes. Serve on pasta or bread if desired.

297. Paprika Shrimp

INGREDIENTS for Servings: 2

1 pound tiger shrimp	½ teaspoon smoked paprika
2 tablespoons olive oil	Salt, to taste

DIRECTIONS and Cooking Time: 10 Minutes

Preheat the Air fryer to 390F and grease an Air fryer basket. Mix all the ingredients in a large bowl until well combined. Place the shrimp in the Air fryer basket and cook for about 10 minutes. Dish out and serve warm.

298. Jamaican-style Fish And Potato Fritters

INGREDIENTS for Servings: 2

1/2 pound sole fillets 1/2 pound mashed potatoes 1 egg, well beaten 1/2 cup red onion, chopped 2 garlic cloves, minced 2 tablespoons fresh parsley, chopped	1 bell pepper, finely chopped 1/2 teaspoon scotch bonnet pepper, minced 1 tablespoon olive oil 1 tablespoon coconut aminos 1/2 teaspoon paprika Salt and white pepper, to taste

DIRECTIONS and Cooking Time: 30 Minutes
Start by preheating your Air Fryer to 395 degrees F. Spritz the sides and bottom of the cooking basket with cooking spray. Cook the sole fillets in the preheated Air Fryer for 10 minutes, flipping them halfway through the cooking time. In a mixing bowl, mash the sole fillets into flakes. Stir in the remaining ingredients. Shape the fish mixture into patties. Bake in the preheated Air Fryer at 390 degrees F for 14 minutes, flipping them halfway through the cooking time. Bon appétit!

299. Buttermilk Tuna Fillets

INGREDIENTS for Servings: 3

1 pound tuna fillets 1/2 cup buttermilk 1/2 cup tortilla chips, crushed 1/4 cup parmesan cheese, grated Salt and ground black pepper, to taste	1/4 cup cassava flour 1 teaspoon mustard seeds 1 teaspoon paprika 1 teaspoon garlic powder 1/2 teaspoon onion powder

DIRECTIONS and Cooking Time: 50 Minutes
Place the tuna fillets and buttermilk in a bowl; cover and let it sit for 30 minutes. In a shallow bowl, thoroughly combine the remaining ingredients; mix until well combined. Dip the tuna fillets in the parmesan mixture until they are covered on all sides. Cook in the preheated Air Fryer at 380 degrees F for 12 minutes, turning halfway through the cooking time. Bon appétit!

300. Fish Cakes With Horseradish Sauce

INGREDIENTS for Servings: 4

Halibut Cakes: 1 pound halibut 2 tablespoons olive oil 1/2 teaspoon cayenne pepper 1/4 teaspoon black pepper Salt, to taste 2 tablespoons cilantro, chopped 1 shallot, chopped	2 garlic cloves, minced 1 cup Romano cheese, grated 1 egg, whisked 1 tablespoon Worcestershire sauce Mayo Sauce: 1 teaspoon horseradish, grated 1/2 cup mayonnaise

DIRECTIONS and Cooking Time: 20 Minutes
Start by preheating your Air Fryer to 380 degrees F. Spritz the Air Fryer basket with cooking oil. Mix all ingredients for the halibut cakes in a bowl; knead with your hands until everything is well incorporated. Shape the mixture into equally sized patties. Transfer your patties to the Air Fryer basket. Cook the fish patties for 10 minutes, turning them over halfway through. Mix the horseradish and mayonnaise. Serve the halibut cakes with the horseradish mayo. Bon appétit!

301. Sole Fish And Cauliflower Fritters

INGREDIENTS for Servings: 2

1/2 pound sole fillets 1/2 pound mashed cauliflower 1 egg, well beaten 1/2 cup red onion, chopped 2 garlic cloves, minced 2 tablespoons fresh parsley, chopped	1 bell pepper, finely chopped 1/2 teaspoon scotch bonnet pepper, minced 1 tablespoon olive oil 1 tablespoon coconut aminos 1/2 teaspoon paprika Salt and white pepper, to taste

DIRECTIONS and Cooking Time: 30 Minutes
Start by preheating your Air Fryer to 395 degrees F. Spritz the sides and bottom of the cooking basket with cooking spray. Cook the sole fillets in the preheated Air Fryer for 10 minutes, flipping them halfway through the cooking time. In a mixing bowl, mash the sole fillets into flakes. Stir in the remaining ingredients. Shape the fish mixture into patties. Bake in the preheated Air Fryer at 390 degrees F for 14 minutes, flipping them halfway through the cooking time. Bon appétit!

302. Italian Halibut And Asparagus

INGREDIENTS for Servings: 2

2 halibut fillets 4 oz asparagus, trimmed 1 tablespoon avocado oil ½ teaspoon garlic powder	1 teaspoon Italian seasonings 1 teaspoon butter 1 teaspoon salt 1 tablespoon lemon juice

DIRECTIONS and Cooking Time: 7 Minutes

Chop the halibut fillet roughly and sprinkle with garlic powder and Italian seasonings. Preheat the air fryer to 400F. Put the asparagus in the air fryer basket and sprinkle it with salt. Then put the fish over the asparagus and sprinkle it with avocado oil and lemon juice. Cook the meal for 8 minutes. Then transfer it in the serving plates and top with butter.

303. Red Hot Chili Fish Curry

INGREDIENTS for Servings: 4

2 tablespoons sunflower oil 1 pound fish, chopped 2 red chilies, chopped 1 tablespoon coriander powder 1 teaspoon red curry paste	1 cup coconut milk Salt and white pepper, to taste 1/2 teaspoon fenugreek seeds 1 shallot, minced 1 garlic clove, minced 1 ripe tomato, pureed

DIRECTIONS and Cooking Time: 25 Minutes

Preheat your Air Fryer to 380 degrees F; brush the cooking basket with 1 tablespoon of sunflower oil. Cook your fish for 10 minutes on both sides. Transfer to the baking pan that is previously greased with the remaining tablespoon of sunflower oil. Add the remaining ingredients and reduce the heat to 350 degrees F. Continue to cook an additional 10 to 12 minutes or until everything is heated through. Enjoy!

304. Lemony Tuna-parsley Patties

INGREDIENTS for Servings: 4

½ cup panko bread crumbs 1 tablespoon lemon juice 2 cans of tuna in brine 2 tablespoons chopped parsley	1 egg, beaten 2 teaspoons Dijon mustard 3 tablespoons olive oil A drizzle Tabasco sauce

DIRECTIONS and Cooking Time: 10 Minutes

Drain the liquid from the canned tuna and put in a bowl. Mix the tuna and season with mustard, bread crumbs, lemon juice, and parsley. Add the egg and Tabasco sauce. Mix until well combined. Form patties using your hands and place in the fried to set for at least 2 hours. Preheat the air fryer to 390F. Place the grill pan accessory. Brush the patties with olive oil and place on the grill pan. Cook for 10 minutes. Make sure to flip the patties halfway through the cooking time for even browning.

305. Grilled Shellfish With Vegetables

INGREDIENTS for Servings: 8

1 bunch broccolini 8 asparagus spears 8 small carrots, peeled and sliced 4 tomatoes, halved 1 red onion, wedged 2 tablespoons olive oil Salt and pepper to taste	16 small oysters, scrubbed 16 littleneck clams, scrubbed 24 large mussels, scrubbed 2 tablespoons lemon juice 4 basil sprigs

DIRECTIONS and Cooking Time: 30 Minutes

Preheat the air fryer at 390F. Place the grill pan accessory in the air fryer. Place all vegetables in a bowl and drizzle with oil. Season with salt and pepper then toss to coat the vegetables with the seasoning. Place on the grill pan and grill for 15 minutes or until the edges of the vegetables are charred. Set aside   On a large foil, place all the shellfish and season with salt, lemon juice, and basil. Fold the foil and crimp the edges. Place the foil packet on the grill pan and cook for another 15 minutes or until the shellfish have opened. Serve the shellfish with the charred vegetables.

VEGETABLE & SIDE DISHES

306. Cauliflower Mash

INGREDIENTS for Servings: 4

2 pounds cauliflower florets	Juice of ½ lemon
1 teaspoon olive oil	Zest of ½ lemon, grated
3 ounces parmesan, grated	Salt and black pepper to the taste
4 ounces butter, soft	

DIRECTIONS and Cooking Time: 20 Minutes
Preheated you air fryer at 380 degrees F, add the basket inside, add the cauliflower, also add the oil, rub well and cook for 20 minutes. Transfer the cauliflower to a bowl, mash well, add the rest of the ingredients, stir really well, divide between plates and serve as a side dish.

307. Beet Wedges Dish

INGREDIENTS for Servings: 4

4 beets; washed, peeled and cut into large wedges	1 tbsp. olive oil
	1 tsp. lemon juice
2 garlic cloves; minced	Salt and black to the taste

DIRECTIONS and Cooking Time: 25 Minutes
In a bowl; mix beets with oil, salt, pepper, garlic and lemon juice; toss well, transfer to your air fryer's basket and cook them at 400 °F, for 15 minutes. Divide beets wedges on plates and serve as a side dish.

308. Brussels Sprouts With Garlic

INGREDIENTS for Servings: 8

2 lbs Brussels sprouts, trimmed and quartered	5 garlic cloves, sliced
	1/8 tsp pepper
2 tbsp coconut oil, melted	1 tsp salt

DIRECTIONS and Cooking Time: 30 Minutes
Preheat the air fryer to 370 F. In a bowl, mix together Brussels sprouts, coconut oil, and garlic. Transfer Brussels sprouts into the air fryer basket and cooks for 30 minutes. Shake basket halfway through. Season with pepper and salt. Serve and enjoy.

309. Sweet Potato Fries With Avocado Dipping Sauce

INGREDIENTS for Servings: 2

2 large sweet potatoes, peeled and cut into thick strips	1 ripe avocado, flesh scooped out
2 tablespoons olive oil	2 tablespoons sour cream
1 teaspoon paprika	2 tablespoons fresh cilantro, chopped
1 teaspoon garlic powder	Juice from ½ lime
Salt and pepper, to taste	½ teaspoon garlic, minced

DIRECTIONS and Cooking Time: 15 Minutes
Place the sweet potatoes in a bowl and season with oil, paprika, garlic powder, salt, and pepper.   Toss to coat. Place the baking dish in the air fryer and add the sweet potato.   Close the air fryer and cook for 15 minutes at 350F.   Halfway through the cooking time, give the baking dish a shake.   Meanwhile, prepare the avocado dip by combining the rest of the ingredient in a food processor.   Dip the sweet potato fries in the avocado dressing.

310. Beef Meatballs

INGREDIENTS for Servings: 3

1 small finger ginger, crushed	1 ½ tsp lemon juice
1 tbsp hot sauce	2 tbsp sugar
3 tbsp vinegar	¼ tsp dry mustard
½ cup tomato ketchup, reduced sugar	Salt and pepper to taste, if needed

DIRECTIONS and Cooking Time: 25 Minutes
In a bowl, add beef, ginger, hot sauce, vinegar, lemon juice, tomato ketchup, sugar, mustard, pepper, and salt, and mix well using a spoon. Shape 2-inch sized balls, with hands. Add the balls to the fryer without overcrowding. Cook at 370 F for 15 minutes, shaking once. Serve with tomato dip.

311. Bbq Chicken

INGREDIENTS for Servings: 3

1 tsp salt	1 tsp garlic powder
1 tsp smoked paprika	1 cup BBQ sauce

DIRECTIONS and Cooking Time: 35 Minutes
Mix salt, paprika, and garlic powder and coat chicken pieces. Place in the air fryer. Cook for 18 minutes at 400 F. Remove to a plate and brush with barbecue sauce. Wipe fryer out from the chicken fat. Return the chicken to the air fryer, skin-side up, and cook for 5 minutes at 340 F. Serve.

312. Maple Glazed Corn

INGREDIENTS for Servings: 4

4 ears of corn	Black pepper to taste
1 tablespoon maple syrup	1 tablespoon butter, melted

DIRECTIONS and Cooking Time: 6 Minutes
Combine the black pepper, butter, and the maple syrup in a bowl.   Rub the corn with the mixture, and then put it in your air fryer.   Cook at 390 degrees F for 6 minutes.   Divide the corn between plates and serve.

313. Parmesan Cauliflower Gnocchi

INGREDIENTS for Servings: 4

2 cups cauliflower, boiled	1 egg yolk
2 oz parmesan, grated	3 tablespoons coconut flour
1 teaspoon ground black pepper	1 tablespoon butter
1 teaspoon cream cheese	1 teaspoon dried cilantro

DIRECTIONS and Cooking Time: 4 Minutes
Put the boiled cauliflower in the blender and grind it until you get the smooth mixture. Then squeeze the cauliflower to get rid of the water and transfer in the bowl. Add grated Parmesan, egg yolk, ground black pepper, cream cheese, and coconut flour. Knead the dough. Then make the log and cut it into pieces (gnocchi). Preheat the air fryer to 390F. Put the gnocchi in the air fryer in one layer and cook them for 4 minutes. Meanwhile, in the mixing bowl mix up butter and dried cilantro. Microwave the mixture until it is melted. When the gnocchi is cooked, place them in the plate and top with the melted butter mixture.

314. Rosemary Cornbread

INGREDIENTS for Servings: 6

1 cup cornmeal	¼ tsp. garlic powder
1 ½ cups flour	2 tbsp. sugar
½ tsp. baking soda	2 eggs
½ tsp. baking powder	¼ cup melted butter
¼ tsp. kosher salt	1 cup buttermilk
1 tsp. dried rosemary	½ cup corn kernels

DIRECTIONS and Cooking Time: 1 Hr.
In a bowl, combine all the dry ingredients. In a separate bowl, mix together all the wet ingredients. Combine the two.   Fold in the corn kernels and stir vigorously.   Pour the batter into a lightly greased round loaf pan that is lightly greased.   Cook for 1 hour at 380°F.

315. Spinach Salad

INGREDIENTS for Servings: 4

1 pound baby spinach	¼ cup apple cider vinegar
Salt and black pepper to the taste	1 tablespoon chives, chopped
1 tablespoon mustard	
Cooking spray	

DIRECTIONS and Cooking Time: 10 Minutes
Grease a pan that fits your air fryer with cooking spray, combine all the ingredients, introduce the pan in the fryer and cook at 350 degrees F for 10 minutes. Divide between plates and serve as a side dish.

316. Carrot And Oat Balls

INGREDIENTS for Servings: 3

4 carrots, grated	2 tablespoons tomato ketchup
1 cup rolled oats, ground	1 teaspoon cayenne pepper
1 tablespoon butter, room temperature	1/2 teaspoon sea salt
1 tablespoon chia seeds	1/4 teaspoon ground black pepper
1/2 cup scallions, chopped	1/2 teaspoon ancho chili powder
2 cloves garlic, minced	1/4 cup fresh bread crumbs

DIRECTIONS and Cooking Time: 25 Minutes
Start by preheating your Air Fryer to 380 degrees F.   In a bowl, mix all ingredients until everything is well incorporated. Shape the batter into bite-sized balls.   Cook the balls for 15 minutes, shaking the basket halfway through the cooking time. Bon appétit!

317. Cauliflower Falafel

INGREDIENTS for Servings: 4

1 cup cauliflower, shredded	½ teaspoon salt
1 teaspoon almond flour	¼ teaspoon cayenne pepper
½ teaspoon ground cumin	1 egg, beaten
¼ teaspoon ground coriander	1 teaspoon tahini paste
½ teaspoon garlic powder	2 tablespoons flax meal
	½ teaspoon sesame oil

DIRECTIONS and Cooking Time: 12 Minutes
In the mixing bowl mix up shredded cauliflower, almond flour, ground cumin, coriander, garlic powder, salt, and cayenne pepper. Add egg and flax meal and stir the mixture until homogenous with the help of the spoon. After this, make the medium size balls (falafel) and press them gently. Preheat the air fryer to 375F. Put the falafel in the air fryer and sprinkle with

sesame oil. Cook the falafel for 6 minutes from each side. Sprinkle the cooked falafel with tahini paste.

318. Coconut Mushrooms Mix
INGREDIENTS for Servings: 4

1 pound brown mushrooms, sliced 1 pound kale, torn Salt and black pepper to the taste	2 tablespoons olive oil 14 ounces coconut milk

DIRECTIONS and Cooking Time: 15 Minutes
In a pan that fits your air fryer, mix the kale with the rest of the ingredients and toss. Put the pan in the fryer, cook at 380 degrees F for 15 minutes, divide between plates and serve.

319. Paprika Jicama
INGREDIENTS for Servings: 5

15 oz jicama, peeled ½ teaspoon salt ½ teaspoon ground paprika	½ teaspoon chili flakes 1 teaspoon sesame oil

DIRECTIONS and Cooking Time: 7 Minutes
Preheat the air fryer to 400F. Cut Jicama into the small sticks and sprinkle with salt, ground paprika, and chili flakes. Then put the Jicama stick in the air fryer and sprinkle with sesame oil. Cook the vegetables for 4 minutes. Then shake them well and cook for 3 minutes.

320. Lime And Mozzarella Eggplants
INGREDIENTS for Servings: 4

2 tablespoons olive oil 2 eggplants, roughly cubed 8 ounces mozzarella cheese, shredded	3 spring onions, chopped Juice of 1 lime 2 tablespoons butter, melted 4 eggs, whisked

DIRECTIONS and Cooking Time: 15 Minutes
Heat up a pan that fits the air fryer with the oil and the butter over medium-high heat, add the spring onions and the eggplants, stir and cook for 5 minutes. Add the eggs and lime juice and stir well. Sprinkle the cheese on top, introduce the pan in the fryer and cook at 380 degrees F for 10 minutes. Divide between plates and serve as a side dish.

321. Spicy Olives And Tomato Mix
INGREDIENTS for Servings: 4

2 cups kalamata olives, pitted 2 small avocados, pitted, peeled and sliced	¼ cup cherry tomatoes, halved Juice of 1 lime 1 tablespoon coconut oil, melted

DIRECTIONS and Cooking Time: 15 Minutes
In a pan that fits the air fryer, combine the olives with the other ingredients, toss, put the pan in your air fryer and cook at 370 degrees F for 15 minutes. Divide the mix between plates and serve.

322. Parm Squash
INGREDIENTS for Servings: 4

1 medium spaghetti squash 2 oz Mozzarella, shredded 1 oz Parmesan, shredded 1 teaspoon avocado oil	½ teaspoon dried oregano ½ teaspoon dried cilantro ½ teaspoon ground nutmeg 2 teaspoons butter

DIRECTIONS and Cooking Time: 25 Minutes
Cut the spaghetti squash into halves and remove the seeds. Then sprinkle it with avocado oil, dried oregano, dried cilantro, and ground nutmeg. Put 1 teaspoon of butter in every spaghetti squash half and transfer the vegetables in the air fryer. Cook them for 15 minutes at 365F. After this, fill the squash with Mozzarella and Parmesan and cook for 10 minutes more at the same temperature.

323. Crusted Coconut Shrimp
INGREDIENTS for Servings: 5

¾ cup shredded coconut 1 tbsp maple syrup	½ cup breadcrumbs ⅓ cup cornstarch ½ cup milk

DIRECTIONS and Cooking Time: 30 Minutes
Pour the cornstarch and shrimp in a zipper bag and shake vigorously to coat. Mix the syrup and milk in a bowl and set aside. In a separate bowl, mix the breadcrumbs and shredded coconut. Open the zipper bag and remove shrimp while shaking off excess starch. Dip shrimp in the milk mixture and then in the crumb mixture. Place in the fryer. Cook 12 minutes at 350 F, flipping once halfway through. Cook until golden brown. Serve with a coconut-based dip.

324. Balsamic Radishes

INGREDIENTS for Servings: 4

2 bunches red radishes, halved	2 tablespoons parsley, chopped
1 tablespoon olive oil	Salt and black pepper to the taste
2 tablespoons balsamic vinegar	

DIRECTIONS and Cooking Time: 15 Minutes

In a bowl, mix the radishes with the remaining ingredients except the parsley, toss and put them in your air fryer's basket. Cook at 400 degrees F for 15 minutes, divide between plates, sprinkle the parsley on top and serve as a side dish.

325. Cheese-crusted Brussels Sprouts

INGREDIENTS for Servings: 4

2 tbsp canola oil	2 tbsp Grana Padano cheese, grated
3 tbsp breadcrumbs	
1 tbsp paprika	2 tbsp sage, chopped

DIRECTIONS and Cooking Time: 20 Minutes

Preheat the Air fryer to 400 F. Line the air fryer basket with parchment paper. In a bowl, mix breadcrumbs and paprika with Grana Padano cheese. Drizzle the Brussels sprouts with the canola oil and pour in the breadcrumb/cheese mixture; toss to coat. Place in the air fryer basket and cook for 15 minutes, shaking it every 4-5 minutes. Serve sprinkled with chopped sage.

326. Tasty Okra

INGREDIENTS for Servings: 2

1/2 lb okra, ends trimmed and sliced	1/2 tsp ground coriander
1 tsp olive oil	1/2 tsp ground cumin
1/2 tsp mango powder	1/8 tsp pepper
1/2 tsp chili powder	1/4 tsp salt

DIRECTIONS and Cooking Time: 12 Minutes

Preheat the air fryer to 350 F. Add all ingredients into the large bowl and toss well. Spray air fryer basket with cooking spray. Transfer okra mixture into the air fryer basket and cook for 10 minutes. Shake basket halfway through. Toss okra well and cook for 2 minutes more. Serve and enjoy.

327. Green Celery Puree

INGREDIENTS for Servings: 6

1-pound celery stalks, chopped	2 oz Parmesan, grated
	¼ cup chicken broth
½ cup spinach, chopped	½ teaspoon cayenne pepper

DIRECTIONS and Cooking Time: 6 Minutes

In the air fryer pan, mix celery stalk with chopped spinach, chicken broth, and cayenne pepper. Blend the mixture until homogenous. After this, top the puree with Parmesan. Preheat the air fryer to 400F. Put the pan with puree in the air fryer basket and cook the meal for 6 minutes.

328. Spicy Glazed Carrots

INGREDIENTS for Servings: 3

1 pound carrots, cut into matchsticks	1 jalapeño, seeded and minced
2 tablespoons peanut oil	1/4 teaspoon dill
	1/2 teaspoon basil
1 tablespoon agave syrup	Salt and white pepper to taste

DIRECTIONS and Cooking Time: 20 Minutes

Start by preheating your Air Fryer to 380 degrees F. Toss all ingredients together and place them in the Air Fryer basket. Cook for 15 minutes, shaking the basket halfway through the cooking time. Transfer to a serving platter and enjoy!

329. Greek Bread

INGREDIENTS for Servings: 6

1 cup Mozzarella, shredded	½ teaspoon baking powder
2 tablespoons Greek yogurt	½ cup almond flour
1 egg, beaten	1 teaspoon butter, melted

DIRECTIONS and Cooking Time: 4 Minutes

In the glass bowl mix up Mozzarella and yogurt. Microwave the mixture for 2 minutes. After this, mix up baking powder, almond flour, and egg. Combine together the almond flour mixture and melted Mozzarella mixture. Stir it with the help of the spatula until smooth. Refrigerate the dough for 10 minutes. Then cut it on 6 pieces and roll up to get the flatbread pieces. Air fryer the bread for 3 minutes at 400F. Then brush it with melted butter and cook for 1 minute more or until the bread is light brown.

330. Dilled Asparagus With Cheese

INGREDIENTS for Servings: 3

1 bunch of asparagus, trimmed	1/2 teaspoon kosher salt
1 tablespoon olive oil	1/2 teaspoon dried dill weed

1/4 teaspoon cracked black pepper, to taste	1/2 cup goat cheese, crumbled

DIRECTIONS and Cooking Time: 15 Minutes
Place the asparagus spears in the lightly greased cooking basket. Toss the asparagus with the olive oil, salt, black pepper, and dill.   Cook in the preheated Air Fryer at 400 degrees F for 9 minutes.   Serve garnished with goat cheese. Bon appétit!

331.   Garlic Tomatoes Recipe

INGREDIENTS for Servings: 4

4 garlic cloves; crushed 1 lb. mixed cherry tomatoes 1/4 cup olive oil	3 thyme springs; chopped. Salt and black pepper to the taste

DIRECTIONS and Cooking Time: 25 Minutes
In a bowl; mix tomatoes with salt, black pepper, garlic, olive oil and thyme, toss to coat, introduce in your air fryer and cook at 360 °F, for 15 minutes. Divide tomatoes mix on plates and serve

332.   Sweet Potato Boats

INGREDIENTS for Servings: 4

2 tbsp olive oil 1 shallot, chopped 1 cup canned mixed beans	1/4 cup mozzarella cheese, grated Salt and black pepper to taste

DIRECTIONS and Cooking Time: 30 Minutes
Preheat the Air fryer to 400 F. Grease a baking dish with the olive oil. Set aside.   Scoop out the flesh from potatoes, so shells are formed. Chop the potato flesh and put it in a bowl. Add in shallot, mixed beans, salt, and pepper and mix to combine. Fill the potato shells with the mixture and top with the cheese. Arrange on the baking dish. Place in the air fryer and cook for 20 minutes.

333.   Spinach Samosa

INGREDIENTS for Servings: 6

1 teaspoon garlic, diced 1/4 teaspoon ground ginger 1 teaspoon olive oil 1 teaspoon ground turmeric 1/2 teaspoon garam masala 1/2 teaspoon ground coriander	1 cup spinach, chopped 3 spring onions, chopped 1 teaspoon keto tomato sauce 1 cup Mozzarella, shredded 1/2 cup almond flour 1/2 teaspoon baking powder Cooking spray

1/2 teaspoon chili flakes	

DIRECTIONS and Cooking Time: 20 Minutes
Preheat the olive oil in the skillet. Add garlic and ground ginger. Cook the ingredients for 2 minutes over the medium heat. Stir them well. Then add 1 teaspoon of ground turmeric, garam masala, ground coriander, and chili flakes. Add spinach and stir the mixture well. Add spring onions and tomato sauce. Stir the mixture well and cook it with the closed lid for 10 minutes over the low heat. The cooked spinach mixture should be very soft. Cool the spinach mixture. Meanwhile, make the samosa dough: microwave the cheese until it is melted. Then mix it up with almond flour and baking powder. Knead the soft dough and put it on the baking paper. Cover the dough with the second baking paper and roll-up. Then cut the flat dough on the triangles. Place the spinach mixture on every triangle and fold them in the shape of the samosa. Secure the edges of samosa well. Preheat the air fryer to 375F. Spray the air fryer basket with cooking spray. Put the samosa in the air fryer in one layer and cook for 5 minutes. Then flip samosa on another side and cook it for 5 minutes or until the meal is light brown.

334.   Parsley Cauliflower Puree

INGREDIENTS for Servings: 2

1 1/2 cup cauliflower, chopped 1 tablespoon butter, melted 1/2 teaspoon salt	1 tablespoon fresh parsley, chopped 1/4 cup heavy cream Cooking spray

DIRECTIONS and Cooking Time: 8 Minutes
Put the cauliflower in the air fryer and spray with cooking spray. Cook it for 8 minutes at 400F. Stir the vegetables after 4 minutes of cooking. Then preheat the heavy cream until it is hot and pour it in the blender. Add cauliflower, parsley, salt, and butter. Blend the mixture until you get the smooth puree.

335.   Cheese Broccoli

INGREDIENTS for Servings: 4

1 cup broccoli, chopped, boiled 1 teaspoon nut oil 1 teaspoon salt 1 teaspoon dried basil	1/2 cup Cheddar cheese, shredded 1/2 cup of coconut milk 1/2 teaspoon butter, softened

DIRECTIONS and Cooking Time: 7 Minutes
Put broccoli in the air fryer pan. Add nut oil, salt, and dried dill. Stir the vegetables well and add coconut milk. Then add butter and top the meal with Cheddar cheese. Stir the meal gently. Preheat the air fryer to

400F and put the pan with the vegetable mixture inside. Cook it for 7 minutes.

336. Basil Zucchini Noodles

INGREDIENTS for Servings: 4

4 zucchinis, cut with a spiralizer 1 tablespoon olive oil 4 garlic cloves, minced 1 and ½ cups tomatoes, crushed	Salt and black pepper to the taste 1 tablespoon basil, chopped ¼ cup green onions, chopped

DIRECTIONS and Cooking Time: 15 Minutes
In a pan that fits your air fryer, mix zucchini noodles with the other ingredients, toss, introduce in the fryer and cook at 380 degrees F for 15 minutes. Divide between plates and serve as a side dish.

337. Keto Tortillas

INGREDIENTS for Servings: 4

½ teaspoon Psyllium husk powder 1/3 teaspoon baking powder	¼ cup almond flour 1 egg white 4 tablespoons water 1 teaspoon sesame oil

DIRECTIONS and Cooking Time: 16 Minutes
In the mixing bowl mix up Psyllium husk, almond flour, baking powder, egg white, and water. Knead the soft non-sticky dough. Then cut the dough on 4 pieces. Roll them up with the help of the rolling pin in the shape of tortillas. Preheat the air fryer to 400F. Place the first tortilla in the air fryer and gently sprinkle with sesame oil. Cook it for 2 minutes from each side or until it is light brown. Repeat the same steps with all remaining tortillas.

338. Baked Potatoes With Bacon

INGREDIENTS for Servings: 4

Salt and black pepper to taste	1 tbsp olive oil 4 oz bacon, chopped

DIRECTIONS and Cooking Time: 25 Minutes
Preheat the Air Fryer to 390 F. Cut the potatoes in half and brush the potatoes with olive oil; season with salt and pepper. Arrange on the greased air fryer basket and top with bacon. Cook for 40 minutes.

339. Ghee Lemony Endives

INGREDIENTS for Servings: 4

3 tablespoons ghee, melted A pinch of salt and black pepper	12 endives, trimmed 1 tablespoon lemon juice

DIRECTIONS and Cooking Time: 15 Minutes
In a bowl, mix the endives with the ghee, salt, pepper and lemon juice and toss. Put the endives in the fryer's basket and cook at 350 degrees F for 15 minutes. Divide between plates and serve.

340. Parsley Asparagus

INGREDIENTS for Servings: 4

1 pound asparagus, trimmed 1 fennel bulb, quartered A pinch of salt and black pepper 2 cherry tomatoes, chopped 2 chili peppers, chopped	2 tablespoons cilantro, chopped 2 tablespoons parsley, chopped 2 tablespoons olive oil 2 tablespoons lemon juice

DIRECTIONS and Cooking Time: 15 Minutes
Heat up a pan that fits the air fryer with the oil over medium-high heat, add chili peppers and the fennel and sauté for 2 minutes. Add the rest of the ingredients, toss, put the pan in the air fryer and cook at 380 degrees F for 12 minutes. Divide everything between plates and serve.

341. Creamy Cauliflower And Broccoli

INGREDIENTS for Servings: 6

1 pound cauliflower florets 1 pound broccoli florets 2 ½ tablespoons sesame oil 1/2 teaspoon smoked cayenne pepper	3/4 teaspoon sea salt flakes 1 tablespoon lemon zest, grated 1/2 cup Colby cheese, shredded

DIRECTIONS and Cooking Time: 20 Minutes
Prepare the cauliflower and broccoli using your favorite steaming method. Then, drain them well; add the sesame oil, cayenne pepper, and salt flakes. Air-fry at 390 degrees F for approximately 16 minutes; make sure to check the vegetables halfway through the cooking time. Afterwards, stir in the lemon zest and Colby cheese; toss to coat well and serve immediately!

342. Cauliflower Croquettes With Colby Cheese

INGREDIENTS for Servings: 4

1 pound cauliflower florets	2 eggs
1 tablespoon olive oil	1/2 cup parmesan cheese, grated
2 tablespoons scallions, chopped	Sea salt and ground black pepper, to taste
1 garlic clove, minced	1/4 teaspoon dried dill weed
1 cup Colby cheese, shredded	1 teaspoon paprika

DIRECTIONS and Cooking Time: 25 Minutes
Blanch the cauliflower in salted boiling water about 3 to 4 minutes until al dente. Drain well and pulse in a food processor.   Add the remaining ingredients; mix to combine well. Shape the cauliflower mixture into bite-sized tots.   Spritz the Air Fryer basket with cooking spray.   Cook in the preheated Air Fryer at 375 degrees F for 16 minutes, shaking halfway through the cooking time. Serve with your favorite sauce for dipping. Bon appétit!

343.   Tomato Artichokes Mix
INGREDIENTS for Servings: 4

14 ounces artichoke hearts, drained	3 garlic cloves, minced
1 tablespoon olive oil	½ cup keto tomato sauce
2 cups black olives, pitted	1 teaspoon garlic powder

DIRECTIONS and Cooking Time: 15 Minutes
In a pan that fits your air fryer, mix the olives with the artichokes and the other ingredients, toss, put the pan in the fryer and cook at 350 degrees F for 15 minutes. Divide the mix between plates and serve.

344.   Healthy Green Beans
INGREDIENTS for Servings: 4

1 lb green beans, trimmed	Pepper
	Salt

DIRECTIONS and Cooking Time: 6 Minutes
Spray air fryer basket with cooking spray.   Preheat the air fryer to 400 F.   Add green beans in air fryer basket and season with pepper and salt.   Cook green beans for 6 minutes. Turn halfway through.   Serve and enjoy.

345.   Parmesan Spinach Balls
INGREDIENTS for Servings: 4

2 cups spinach, chopped	4 oz Parmesan, grated
½ teaspoon ground nutmeg	1 egg, beaten
½ teaspoon ground black pepper	½ cup coconut flour
	1 teaspoon avocado oil

DIRECTIONS and Cooking Time: 5 Minutes
Put the spinach in the blender and grind it. Then transfer the grinded spinach in the bowl and mix it up with grated Parmesan, ground nutmeg, ground black pepper, and egg. Stir the mixture carefully and add coconut flour. Mix it up with the help of the spoon. Then make the spinach balls with the help of the fingertips. Preheat the air fryer to 400F. Put the spinach balls in the air fryer and sprinkle with avocado oil. Cook the spinach balls bites for 5 minutes.

346.   Garlic Thyme Mushrooms
INGREDIENTS for Servings: 2

10 oz mushrooms, quartered	2 garlic cloves, sliced
1 tsp thyme, chopped	1/4 tsp pepper
2 tbsp olive oil	1/4 tsp salt

DIRECTIONS and Cooking Time: 23 Minutes
Preheat the air fryer to 370 F.   Spray air fryer basket with cooking spray.   In a bowl, combine together mushrooms, pepper, salt, thyme, and oil.   Spread mushrooms into the air fryer basket and cook for 20 minutes. Shake basket halfway through.   Add garlic and stir well and cook for 2-3 minutes.   Serve and enjoy.

347.   Cheesy Green Patties
INGREDIENTS for Servings: 2

1 ½ cup fresh spinach, chopped	1 egg, beaten
3 oz provolone cheese, shredded	¼ cup almond flour
	½ teaspoon salt
	Cooking spray

DIRECTIONS and Cooking Time: 6 Minutes
Put the chopped spinach in the blender and blend it until you get a smooth mixture. After this, transfer the grinded spinach in the big bowl. Add shredded provolone cheese, beaten egg, almond flour, and salt. Stir the spinach mixture with the help of the spoon until it is homogenous. Then make the patties from the spinach mixture. Preheat the air fryer to 400F. Spray the air fryer basket with cooking spray from inside and put the spinach patties. Cook them for 3 minutes and then flip on another side. Cook the patties for 3 minutes more or until they are light brown.

348.   Roasted Broccoli With Sesame Seeds
INGREDIENTS for Servings: 2

1 pound broccoli florets	1/2 teaspoon porcini powder
2 tablespoons sesame oil	1 teaspoon garlic powder

1/2 teaspoon shallot powder Sea salt and ground black pepper, to taste	1/2 teaspoon cumin powder 1/4 teaspoon paprika 2 tablespoons sesame seeds

DIRECTIONS and Cooking Time: 15 Minutes
Start by preheating the Air Fryer to 400 degrees F. Blanch the broccoli in salted boiling water until al dente, about 3 to 4 minutes. Drain well and transfer to the lightly greased Air Fryer basket. Add the sesame oil, shallot powder, porcini powder, garlic powder, salt, black pepper, cumin powder, paprika, and sesame seeds. Cook for 6 minutes, tossing halfway through the cooking time. Bon appétit!

349. Potatoes And Special Tomato Sauce Recipe

INGREDIENTS for Servings: 4

2 lbs. potatoes; cubed 4 garlic cloves; minced 1 yellow onion; chopped. 1 cup tomato sauce	1/2 tsp. oregano; dried 1/2 tsp. parsley; dried 2 tbsp. basil; chopped 2 tbsp. olive oil

DIRECTIONS and Cooking Time: 26 Minutes
Heat up a pan that fits your air fryer with the oil over medium heat, add onion; stir and cook for 1-2 minutes. Add garlic, potatoes, parsley, tomato sauce and oregano; stir, introduce in your air fryer and cook at 370 °F and cook for 16 minutes. Add basil, toss everything, divide among plates and serve

350. Air-fried Spiced Wings

INGREDIENTS for Servings: 8

½ tsp bay leaf powder ½ tsp ground black pepper ½ tsp paprika ¼ tsp dry mustard	¼ tsp cayenne pepper ¼ tsp allspice 2 pounds chicken wings

DIRECTIONS and Cooking Time: 45 Minutes
Grease the air fryer basket and preheat to 340 F. In a bowl, mix celery salt, bay leaf powder, black pepper, paprika, dry mustard, cayenne pepper, and allspice. Coat the wings thoroughly in this mixture. Arrange the wings in an even layer in the basket of the air fryer. Cook the chicken until it's no longer pink around the bone, for 30 minutes. Then, increase the temperature to 380 F and cook for 6 minutes more, until crispy on the outside.

351. Asparagus And Green Beans Salad

INGREDIENTS for Servings: 3

3 oz asparagus, chopped 2 oz green beans, chopped 1 cup arugula, chopped 1 tablespoon hazelnuts, chopped 2 oz Mozzarella, chopped	1 teaspoon flax seeds 1 tablespoon olive oil ½ teaspoon salt ½ teaspoon ground paprika ½ teaspoon ground black pepper Cooking spray

DIRECTIONS and Cooking Time: 6 Minutes
Preheat the air fryer to 400F. Put the asparagus and green beans in the air fryer and spray them with cooking spray. Cook the vegetables for 6 minutes at 400F. Shake the vegetables after 3 minutes of cooking. Then cool them to the room temperature and put in the salad bowl. Add hazelnuts, flax seeds, chopped Mozzarella, salt, ground paprika, and ground black pepper. Sprinkle the salad with olive oil and shake well.

352. Cayenne Pepper Wings With Gorgonzola Dip

INGREDIENTS for Servings: 4

1 tsp cayenne pepper Salt to taste 2 tbsp grapeseed oil 2 tsp chili flakes 1 cup heavy cream	3 oz gorgonzola cheese, crumbled ½ lemon, juiced ½ tsp garlic powder

DIRECTIONS and Cooking Time: 30 Minutes
Preheat air fryer to 380 F. Coat the chicken with cayenne pepper, salt, and oil. Place in the basket and cook for 20 minutes. In a bowl, mix heavy cream, gorgonzola cheese, lemon juice, and garlic powder. Serve with chicken wings.

353. Buttery Cauliflower Mix

INGREDIENTS for Servings: 4

1 pound cauliflower florets, roughly grated 3 tablespoons butter, melted	3 eggs, whisked Salt and black pepper to the taste 1 tablespoon sweet paprika

DIRECTIONS and Cooking Time: 15 Minutes
Heat up a pan that fits the air fryer with the butter over high heat, add the cauliflower and brown for 5 minutes. Add whisked eggs, salt, pepper and the paprika, toss, introduce the pan in the fryer and cook

at 400 degrees F for 10 minutes. Divide between plates and serve.

354. Paprika Green Beans

INGREDIENTS for Servings: 4

6 cups green beans, trimmed	1 tablespoon hot paprika
2 tablespoons olive oil	A pinch of salt and black pepper

DIRECTIONS and Cooking Time: 20 Minutes
In a bowl, mix the green beans with the other ingredients, toss, put them in the air fryer's basket and cook at 370 degrees F for 20 minutes. Divide between plates and serve as a side dish.

355. Bell Peppers With Spicy Mayo

INGREDIENTS for Servings: 2

1 onion, sliced (1-inch pieces)	4 bell peppers, seeded and sliced (1-inch pieces)
1 tablespoon olive oil	Kosher salt, to taste
1/2 teaspoon dried rosemary	1/4 teaspoon ground black pepper
1/2 teaspoon dried basil	1/3 cup mayonnaise
	1/3 teaspoon Sriracha

DIRECTIONS and Cooking Time: 20 Minutes
Toss the bell peppers and onions with the olive oil, rosemary, basil, salt, and black pepper. Place the peppers and onions on an even layer in the cooking basket. Cook at 400 degrees F for 12 to 14 minutes. Meanwhile, make the sauce by whisking the mayonnaise and Sriracha. Serve immediately.

356. Cauliflower Fritters With Mustard And Cheese

INGREDIENTS for Servings: 2

1/2 pound cauliflower florets	Sea salt and ground black pepper, to taste
2 garlic cloves, minced	1/4 teaspoon cumin powder
1/2 cup goat cheese, shredded	1/2 cup sour cream
1/2 teaspoon shallot powder	1 teaspoon Dijon mustard

DIRECTIONS and Cooking Time: 30 Minutes
Place the cauliflower florets in a saucepan of water; bring to the boil; reduce the heat and cook for 10 minutes or until tender. Mash the cauliflower using your blender; add the garlic, cheese, and spices; mix to combine well. Form the cauliflower mixture into croquettes shapes. Cook in the preheated Air Fryer

at 375 degrees F for 16 minutes, shaking halfway through the cooking time. Serve with the sour cream and mustard. Bon appétit!

357. Balsamic Asparagus And Tomatoes

INGREDIENTS for Servings: 4

1 pound asparagus, trimmed	½ cup balsamic vinegar
2 cups cherry tomatoes, halved	2 tablespoons olive oil
¼ cup parmesan, grated	A pinch of salt and black pepper

DIRECTIONS and Cooking Time: 10 Minutes
In a bowl, mix the asparagus with the rest of the ingredients except the parmesan, and toss. Put the asparagus and tomatoes in your air fryer's basket and cook at 400 degrees F for 10 minutes Divide between plates and serve with the parmesan sprinkled on top.

358. Harissa Broccoli Spread

INGREDIENTS for Servings: 4

2 cups broccoli, chopped	1 teaspoon salt
1 teaspoon tahini	1 garlic clove
2 tablespoons sesame oil	1 teaspoon coconut oil, melted
	1 teaspoon harissa

DIRECTIONS and Cooking Time: 6 Minutes
Preheat the air fryer to 400F. Put the broccoli and garlic clove in the air fryer basket and sprinkle with 1 teaspoon of sesame oil. Cook the vegetables for 6 minutes. Then transfer the cooked broccoli and garlic in the blender and grind the ingredients until you get the smooth texture. Add salt, all remaining sesame oil, coconut oil, and harissa. After this, add tahini and blend the mixture for 30 seconds more. Transfer the cooked hummus in the bowl.

359. Basic Pepper French Fries

INGREDIENTS for Servings: 4

1 teaspoon fine sea salt	6 Russet potatoes, cut them into fries
1/2 teaspoon freshly ground black pepper	1/2 teaspoon crushed red pepper flakes
2 ½ tablespoons canola oil	

DIRECTIONS and Cooking Time: 33 Minutes
Start by preheating your air fryer to 340 degrees F. Place the fries in your air fryer and toss them with the oil. Add the seasonings and toss again. Cook for 30

minutes, shaking your fries several times. Taste for doneness and eat warm.

360. Almond Brussels Sprouts

INGREDIENTS for Servings: 4

8 oz Brussels sprouts	2 egg whites
2 tablespoons almonds, grinded	½ teaspoon salt
1 teaspoon coconut flakes	½ teaspoon white pepper
	Cooking spray

DIRECTIONS and Cooking Time: 15 Minutes
Whisk the egg whites and add salt and white pepper. Then cut the Brussels sprouts into halves and put the egg white mixture. Shake the vegetables well and then coat in the grinded almonds and coconut flakes. Preheat the air fryer to 380F. Place the Brussels sprouts in the air fryer basket and cook them for 15 minutes. Shake the vegetables after 8 minutes of cooking.

361. Roasted Vegetables

INGREDIENTS for Servings: 6

1 ⅓ cup small parsnips	2 red onions
1 ⅓ cup celery [3 – 4 stalks]	1 tbsp. fresh thyme needles
1 ⅓ cup small butternut squash	1 tbsp. olive oil
	Salt and pepper to taste

DIRECTIONS and Cooking Time: 30 Minutes
Pre-heat the Air Fryer to 390°F. Peel the parsnips and onions and cut them into 2-cm cubes. Slice the onions into wedges. Do not peel the butternut squash. Cut it in half, de-seed it, and cube. Combine the cut vegetables with the thyme, olive oil, salt and pepper. Put the vegetables in the basket and transfer the basket to the Air Fryer. Cook for 20 minutes, stirring once throughout the cooking time, until the vegetables are nicely browned and cooked through.

362. Cheddar Asparagus

INGREDIENTS for Servings: 4

2 pounds asparagus, trimmed	4 garlic cloves, minced
2 tablespoons olive oil	4 bacon slices, cooked and crumbled
1 cup cheddar cheese, shredded	

DIRECTIONS and Cooking Time: 10 Minutes
In a bowl, mix the asparagus with the other ingredients except the bacon, toss and put in your air fryer's basket. Cook at 400 degrees F for 10 minutes,

divide between plates, sprinkle the bacon on top and serve.

363. Teriyaki Chicken Wings

INGREDIENTS for Servings: 4

1 cup soy sauce, divided	2 tbsp fresh garlic, minced
½ cup brown sugar	1 tsp finely ground black pepper
½ cup apple cider vinegar	2 tbsp cornstarch
2 tbsp fresh ginger, minced	2 tbsp cold water
	1 tsp sesame seeds

DIRECTIONS and Cooking Time: 55 Minutes
In a bowl, add chicken wings, and pour in half cup soy sauce. Refrigerate for 20 minutes; drain and pat dry. Arrange wings on the air fryer and cook for 30 minutes at 380 F, turning once halfway through. In a skillet and over medium heat, stir sugar, half cup soy sauce, vinegar, ginger, garlic, and black pepper. Cook for 4 minutes. Dissolve 2 tbsp of cornstarch in cold water and stir in the sauce until it thickens, 2 minutes. Pour the sauce over wings and sprinkle with sesame seeds.

364. Cinnamon Cauliflower

INGREDIENTS for Servings: 4

1 cauliflower head, florets separated	¼ teaspoon turmeric powder
1 tablespoon butter, melted	½ teaspoon cumin, ground
A pinch of salt and black pepper	¼ teaspoon cinnamon powder
1 tablespoon olive oil	¼ teaspoon cloves, ground

DIRECTIONS and Cooking Time: 15 Minutes
In a bowl, mix cauliflower florets with the rest of the ingredients and toss. Put the cauliflower in your air fryer's basket and cook at 390 degrees F for 15 minutes. Divide between plates and serve as a side dish.

365. Sage Artichoke

INGREDIENTS for Servings: 4

4 artichokes	1 teaspoon chives, chopped
1 tablespoon sage	½ teaspoon salt
4 teaspoons avocado oil	

DIRECTIONS and Cooking Time: 12 Minutes
Cut the artichoke into halves and rub them with sage avocado oil, minced garlic, and salt. Preheat the air fryer to 375F. Place the artichoke halves in the air fryer basket and cook them for 12 minutes.

366. Green Beans And Tomato Sauce

INGREDIENTS for Servings: 4

½ pound green beans, trimmed and halved	1 tablespoon olive oil
1 cup black olives, pitted and halved	¼ cup keto tomato sauce
¼ cup bacon, cooked and crumbled	

DIRECTIONS and Cooking Time: 15 Minutes

In a pan that fits the air fryer, combine all the ingredients, toss, put the pan in the air fryer and cook at 380 degrees F for 15 minutes. Divide between plates and serve.

SNACKS & APPETIZERS RECIPES

367. Scallops And Bacon Kabobs

INGREDIENTS for Servings: 6

1 pound sea scallops	1/2 pound bacon,
1/2 cup coconut milk	diced
1 tablespoon	1 shallot, diced
vermouth	1 teaspoon garlic
Sea salt and ground	powder
black pepper, to taste	1 teaspoon paprika

DIRECTIONS and Cooking Time: 40 Minutes
In a ceramic bowl, place the sea scallops, coconut milk, vermouth, salt, and black pepper; let it marinate for 30 minutes. Assemble the skewers alternating the scallops, bacon, and shallots. Sprinkle garlic powder and paprika all over the skewers. Bake in the preheated air Fryer at 400 degrees F for 6 minutes. Serve warm and enjoy!

368. Veggie Pastries

INGREDIENTS for Servings: 8

2 large potatoes,	½ cup onion, chopped
peeled	2 tablespoons fresh
1 tablespoon olive oil	ginger, minced
½ cup carrot, peeled	½ cup green peas,
and chopped	shelled
2 garlic cloves, minced	Salt and ground black
	pepper, as needed
	3 puff pastry sheets

DIRECTIONS and Cooking Time: 37 Minutes
In the pan of a boiling water, put the potatoes and cook for about 15-20 minutes. Drain the potatoes well and with a potato masher, mash the potatoes. In a skillet, heat the oil over medium heat and sauté the carrot, onion, ginger, and garlic for about 4-5 minutes. Drain all the fat from the skillet. Stir in the mashed potatoes, peas, salt, and black pepper. Cook for about 1-2 minutes. Once done, remove the potato mixture from heat and set aside to cool completely. Put the puff pastry onto a smooth surface. Cut each puff pastry sheet into four pieces and then cut each piece in a round shape. Add about two tablespoons of veggie filling over each pastry round. Moisten the edges using your wet fingers. Fold each pastry round in half to seal the filling. Using a fork, firmly press the edges. Set the temperature of Air Fryer to 390 degrees F. Add the pastries in an Air Fryer basket in a single layer in 2 batches. Air Fry for about 5 minutes. Serve.

369. Fried Green Tomatoes

INGREDIENTS for Servings: 2

2 medium green	1 egg
tomatoes	1/3 cup parmesan
¼ cup blanched finely	cheese, grated
ground flour	

DIRECTIONS and Cooking Time: 10 Minutes
Slice the tomatoes about a half-inch thick. Crack the egg into a bowl and beat it with a whisk. In a separate bowl, mix together the flour and parmesan cheese. Dredge the tomato slices in egg, then dip them into the flour-cheese mixture to coat. Place each slice into the fryer basket. They may need to be cooked in multiple batches. Cook at 400°F for seven minutes, turning them halfway through the cooking time, and then serve warm.

370. Italian Dip

INGREDIENTS for Servings: 8

8 oz cream cheese,	1/2 cup roasted red
softened	peppers
1 cup mozzarella	1/4 cup parmesan
cheese, shredded	cheese, grated
1/3 cup basil pesto	

DIRECTIONS and Cooking Time: 12 Minutes
Add parmesan cheese and cream cheese into the food processor and process until smooth. Transfer cheese mixture into the air fryer pan and spread evenly. Pour basil pesto on top of cheese layer. Sprinkle roasted pepper on top of basil pesto layer. Sprinkle mozzarella cheese on top of pepper layer and place dish in air fryer basket. Cook dip at 250 F for 12 minutes. Serve and enjoy.

371. Mini Pepper Poppers

INGREDIENTS for Servings: 4

8 mini sweet peppers	¼ cup pepper jack
4 slices sugar-free	cheese, shredded
bacon, cooked and	4 oz. full-fat cream
crumbled	cheese, softened

DIRECTIONS and Cooking Time: 10 Minutes
Prepare the peppers by cutting off the tops and halving them lengthwise. Then take out the membrane and the seeds. In a small bowl, combine the pepper jack cheese, bacon, and cream cheese, making sure to incorporate everything well Spoon equal-sized portions of the cheese-bacon mixture into each of the pepper halves. Place the peppers inside your fryer and cook for eight minutes at 400°F. Take care when removing them from the fryer and enjoy warm.

372.   Cheese Cookies

INGREDIENTS for Servings: 10

For Dough:	Salt, as required
3.38 fluid ounces cream	½ teaspoon baking powder
5.30 ounces margarine	For Topping:
6.35 ounces Gruyere cheese, grated	1 tablespoon milk
1 teaspoon paprika	2 egg yolks, beaten
5.30 ounces flour, sifted	2 tablespoons poppy seeds

DIRECTIONS and Cooking Time: 12 Minutes
For cookies: in a bowl, mix together the cream, margarine, cheese, paprika, and salt.   Place the flour, and baking powder onto a smooth surface. Mix them well.   Using your hands, create a well in the center of flour.   Add the cheese mixture and knead until a soft dough forms.   Roll the dough into 1-1½-inch thickness.   Cut the cookies using a cookie cutter.   In another bowl, mix together the milk, and egg yolks. Coat the cookies with milk mixture and then, sprinkle with poppy seeds.   Set the temperature of Air Fryer to 340 degrees F.   Place cookies onto the grill pan of an Air Fryer in a single layer.   Air Fry for about 12 minutes.   Serve.

373.   Baby Corn

INGREDIENTS for Servings: 4

8 oz. baby corns, boiled	½ tsp. carom seeds
1 cup flour	¼ tsp. chili powder
1 tsp. garlic powder	Pinch of baking soda
	Salt to taste

DIRECTIONS and Cooking Time: 20 Minutes
In a bowl, combine the flour, chili powder, garlic powder, cooking soda, salt and carom seed. Add in a little water to create a batter-like consistency.   Coat each baby corn in the batter.   Pre-heat the Air Fryer at 350°F.   Cover the Air Fryer basket with aluminum foil before laying the coated baby corns on top of the foil.   Cook for 10 minutes.

374.   Heirloom Tomato Sandwiches With Pesto

INGREDIENTS for Servings: 4

3 tablespoons pine nuts	8-ounce feta cheese, cut into ½ inch thick slices
½ cup fresh basil, chopped	½ cup plus 2 tablespoons olive oil, divided
½ cup fresh parsley, chopped	Salt, to taste
2 heirloom tomatoes, cut into ½ inch thick slices	1 garlic clove, chopped

DIRECTIONS and Cooking Time: 16 Minutes
Preheat the Air fryer to 390F and grease an Air fryer basket.   Mix together 1 tablespoon of olive oil, pine nuts and pinch of salt in a bowl.   Place pine nuts in the Air fryer and cook for about 2 minutes.   Put the pine nuts, remaining oil, fresh basil, fresh parsley, garlic and salt and pulse until combined.   Dish out the pesto in a bowl, cover and refrigerate.   Spread 1 tablespoon of pesto on each tomato slice and top with a feta slice and onion.   Drizzle with olive oil and arrange the prepared tomato slices in the Air fryer basket.   Cook for about 14 minutes and serve with remaining pesto.

375.   Cheesy Zucchini Sticks

INGREDIENTS for Servings: 2

1 zucchini, slice into strips	Sea salt and black pepper, to your liking
2 tablespoons mayonnaise	1 tablespoon garlic powder
1/4 cup tortilla chips, crushed	1/2 teaspoon red pepper flakes
1/4 cup Romano cheese, shredded	

DIRECTIONS and Cooking Time: 20 Minutes
Coat the zucchini with mayonnaise.   Mix the crushed tortilla chips, cheese and spices in a shallow dish. Then, coat the zucchini sticks with the cheese/chips mixture.   Cook in the preheated Air Fryer at 400 degrees F for 12 minutes, shaking the basket halfway through the cooking time.   Work in batches until the sticks are crispy and golden brown. Bon appétit!

376.   Zesty Cilantro Roasted Cauliflower

INGREDIENTS for Servings: 2

2 cups cauliflower florets, chopped	2 ½ tsp. taco seasoning mix
2 tbsp. coconut oil, melted	2 tbsp. cilantro, chopped
1 medium lime	

DIRECTIONS and Cooking Time: 10 Minutes
Mix the cauliflower with the melted coconut oil and the taco seasoning, ensuring to coat the florets all over. Cook at 350°F for seven minutes, shaking the basket a few times through the cooking time. Then transfer the cauliflower to a bowl.   Squeeze the lime juice over the cauliflower and season with the cilantro. Toss once more to coat and enjoy.

377.　Curly's Cauliflower

INGREDIENTS for Servings: 4

4 cups bite-sized cauliflower florets	1 cup friendly bread crumbs, mixed with 1 tsp. salt
¼ cup melted butter [vegan/other]	Mayo [vegan/other] or creamy dressing for dipping
¼ cup buffalo sauce [vegan/other]	

DIRECTIONS and Cooking Time: 30 Minutes
1 In a bowl, combine the butter and buffalo sauce to create a creamy paste.　2 Completely cover each floret with the sauce.　3 Coat the florets with the bread crumb mixture. Cook the florets in the Air Fryer for approximately 15 minutes at 350°F, shaking the basket occasionally.　4 Serve with a raw vegetable salad, mayo or creamy dressing.

378.　Cheesy Bacon Bread

INGREDIENTS for Servings: 2

4 slices sugar-free bacon, cooked and chopped	2 eggs
¼ cup pickled jalapenos, chopped	¼ cup parmesan cheese, grated
	2 cups mozzarella cheese, shredded

DIRECTIONS and Cooking Time: 25 Minutes
Add all of the ingredients together in a bowl and mix together.　Cut out a piece of parchment paper that will fit the base of your fryer's basket. Place it inside the fryer　With slightly wet hands, roll the mixture into a circle. You may have to form two circles to cook in separate batches, depending on the size of your fryer.　Place the circle on top of the parchment paper inside your fryer. Cook at 320°F for ten minutes. Turn the bread over and cook for another five minutes. The bread is ready when it is golden and cooked all the way through. Slice and serve warm.

379.　Cocktail Wieners With Spicy Sauce

INGREDIENTS for Servings: 4

1 pound pork cocktail sausages	1 teaspoon balsamic vinegar
For the Sauce:	1 garlic clove, finely minced
1/4 cup mayonnaise	
1/4 cup cream cheese	1 teaspoon chili powder
1 whole grain mustard	

DIRECTIONS and Cooking Time: 20 Minutes
Take your sausages, give them a few pricks using a fork and place them on the Air Fryer grill pan.　Set the timer for 15 minutes; after 8 minutes, pause the Air Fryer, turn the sausages over and cook for further 7 minutes.　Check for doneness and take the sausages out of the machine.　In the meantime, thoroughly combine all the ingredients for the sauce. Serve with warm sausages and enjoy!

380.　The Best Calamari Appetizer

INGREDIENTS for Servings: 6

1 ½ pounds calamari tubes, cleaned, cut into rings	2 tablespoons lemon juice
Sea salt and ground black pepper, to taste	1 cup all-purpose flour
1 cup cornmeal	1 teaspoon paprika
	1 egg, whisked
	1/4 cup buttermilk

DIRECTIONS and Cooking Time: 20 Minutes
Preheat your Air Fryer to 390 degrees F. Rinse the calamari and pat it dry. Season with salt and black pepper. Drizzle lemon juice all over the calamari. Now, combine the cornmeal, flour, and paprika in a bowl; add the whisked egg and buttermilk.　Dredge the calamari in the egg/flour mixture.　Arrange them in the cooking basket. Spritz with cooking oil and cook for 9 to 12 minutes, shaking the basket occasionally. Work in batches.　Serve with toothpicks. Bon appétit!

381.　Perfect Crab Dip

INGREDIENTS for Servings: 4

1 cup crabmeat	1/2 cup green onion, sliced
2 tbsp parsley, chopped	2 cups cheese, grated
2 tbsp fresh lemon juice	1/4 cup mayonnaise
	1/4 tsp pepper
2 tbsp hot sauce	1/2 tsp salt

DIRECTIONS and Cooking Time: 7 Minutes
In a 6-inch dish, mix together crabmeat, hot sauce, cheese, mayo, pepper, and salt.　Place dish in air fryer basket and cook dip at 400 F for 7 minutes.　Remove dish from air fryer.　Drizzle dip with lemon juice and garnish with parsley.　Serve and enjoy.

382.　Broccoli

INGREDIENTS for Servings: 4

1 large head broccoli	1 tbsp. white sesame seeds
½ lemon, juiced	
3 cloves garlic, minced	2 tsp. Maggi sauce or other seasonings to taste
1 tbsp. coconut oil	

DIRECTIONS and Cooking Time: 30 Minutes
1 Wash and dry the broccoli. Chop it up into small florets.　2 Place the minced garlic in your Air Fryer basket, along with the coconut oil, lemon juice and

Maggi sauce. 3 Heat for 2 minutes at 320°F and give it a stir. Put the garlic and broccoli in the basket and cook for another 13 minutes. 4 Top the broccoli with the white sesame seeds and resume cooking for 5 more minutes, ensuring the seeds become nice and toasty.

383. Cheese Boats

INGREDIENTS for Servings: 2

1 cup ground chicken	½ tsp. garlic powder
1 zucchini	2 tbsp. butter or olive
1 ½ cups crushed	oil
tomatoes	½ cup cheese, grated
½ tsp. salt	¼ tsp. dried oregano
¼ tsp. pepper	

DIRECTIONS and Cooking Time: 30 Minutes
1 Peel and halve the zucchini. Use a spoon to scoop out the flesh. 2 In a bowl, combine the ground chicken, tomato, garlic powder, butter, cheese, oregano, salt, and pepper. Fill in the hollowed-out zucchini with this mixture. 3 Transfer to the Air Fryer and bake for about 10 minutes at 400°F. Serve warm.

384. Shrimps Cakes

INGREDIENTS for Servings: 4

10 oz shrimps, chopped	1 egg, beaten
1 teaspoon dill, chopped	2 tablespoons almond flour
1 teaspoon Psyllium husk	1 teaspoon olive oil
	1 teaspoon chives

DIRECTIONS and Cooking Time: 5 Minutes
In the mixing bowl mix up shrimps, egg, dill, Psyllium husk, almond flour, and chives. When the mixture is homogenous, make 4 cakes. Preheat the air fryer to 400F. Put the cakes in the air fryer and sprinkle with olive oil. Cook the meal for 5 minutes.

385. Jalapeño Guacamole

INGREDIENTS for Servings: 4

2 Hass avocados, ripe	1 tbsp fresh lime juice
¼ red onion	Sea salt
1 jalapeño	

DIRECTIONS and Cooking Time: 30 Minutes
Spoon the avocado innings into a bowl. Dice the jalapeño and onion. Mash the avocado to the desired consistency. Add in the onion, jalapeño and lime juice. Sprinkle with salt.

386. Mozzarella Sticks

INGREDIENTS for Servings: 4

6 x 1-oz. mozzarella string cheese sticks	1 tsp. dried parsley
½ oz. pork rinds, finely ground	½ cup parmesan cheese, grated
	2 eggs

DIRECTIONS and Cooking Time: 60 Minutes
Halve the mozzarella sticks and freeze for forty-five minutes. Optionally you can leave them longer and place in a Ziploc bag to prevent them from becoming freezer burned. In a small bowl, combine the dried parsley, pork rinds, and parmesan cheese. In a separate bowl, beat the eggs with a fork. Take a frozen mozzarella stick and dip it into the eggs, then into the pork rind mixture, making sure to coat it all over. Proceed with the rest of the cheese sticks, placing each coated stick in the basket of your air fryer. Cook at 400°F for ten minutes, until they are golden brown. Serve hot, with some homemade marinara sauce if desired.

387. Friday's Fries

INGREDIENTS for Servings: 2

1 large eggplant, cut into 3-inch slices	1 tbsp. olive oil
¼ cup water	¼ cup cornstarch
	¼ tsp. salt

DIRECTIONS and Cooking Time: 25 Minutes
Pre-heat the Air Fryer to 400°F. In a bowl, combine the water, olive oil, cornstarch, and salt. Coat the sliced eggplant with the mixture. Put the coated eggplant slices in the Air Fryer basket and cook for 20 minutes.

388. Orange Cauliflower

INGREDIENTS for Servings: 2

½ lemon, juiced	Sea salt to taste
1 head cauliflower	Ground black pepper
½ tbsp. olive oil	to taste
1 tsp. curry powder	

DIRECTIONS and Cooking Time: 30 Minutes
Wash the cauliflower. Cut out the leaves and core. Chop the cauliflower into equally-sized florets. Coat the inside of the Air Fryer with the oil and allow it to warm up for about 2 minutes at 390°F. In a bowl, mix together the fresh lemon juice and curry powder. Add in the cauliflower florets. Sprinkle in the pepper and salt and mix again, coating the florets well. Transfer to the fryer, cook for 20 minutes, and serve warm.

389. Wonton Sausage Appetizers

INGREDIENTS for Servings: 5

1/2 pound ground sausage	1/2 tablespoon fish sauce
2 tablespoons scallions, chopped	1 teaspoon Sriracha sauce
1 garlic clove, minced	1 egg, whisked with 1 tablespoon water
20 wonton wrappers	

DIRECTIONS and Cooking Time: 20 Minutes

In a mixing bowl, thoroughly combine the ground sausage, scallions, garlic, fish sauce, and Sriracha. Divide the mixture between the wonton wrappers. Dip your fingers in the egg wash   Fold the wonton in half. Bring up the 2 ends of the wonton and use the egg wash to stick them together. Pinch the edges and coat each wonton with the egg wash.   Place the folded wontons in the lightly greased cooking basket. Cook at 360 degrees F for 10 minutes. Work in batches and serve warm. Bon appétit!

390. Snack Mix

INGREDIENTS for Servings: 10

½ cup honey	2 cups granola
3 tbsp. butter, melted	1 cup cashews
1 tsp. salt	2 cups crispy corn puff
2 cups sesame sticks	cereal [Kix or Corn Pops]
2 cup pepitas [pumpkin seeds]	2 cup mini pretzel crisps

DIRECTIONS and Cooking Time: 30 Minutes

1 In a bowl, combine the honey, butter, and salt.   2 In another bowl, mix together the sesame sticks, pepitas, granola, cashews, corn puff cereal, and pretzel crisps. 3 Combine the contents of the two bowls.   4 Pre-heat your Air Fryer to 370°F.   5 Put the mixture in the fryer basket and air-fry for 10 - 12 minutes to toast the snack mixture, shaking the basket frequently. You will have to do this in two batches.   6 Place the snack mix on a cookie sheet and allow it to cool fully.   7 Store in an airtight container for up to one week. Makes a great holiday gift!

391. Cajun Cheese Sticks

INGREDIENTS for Servings: 4

1/2 cup all-purpose flour	1 tablespoon Cajun seasonings
2 eggs	8 cheese sticks, kid-friendly
1/2 cup parmesan cheese, grated	1/4 cup ketchup

DIRECTIONS and Cooking Time: 15 Minutes

To begin, set up your breading station. Place the all-purpose flour in a shallow dish. In a separate dish, whisk the eggs.   Finally, mix the parmesan cheese and Cajun seasoning in a third dish.   Start by dredging the cheese sticks in the flour; then, dip them into the egg. Press the cheese sticks into the parmesan mixture, coating evenly.   Place the breaded cheese sticks in the lightly greased Air Fryer basket. Cook at 380 degrees F for 6 minutes.   Serve with ketchup and enjoy!

392. Cajun Spiced Snack

INGREDIENTS for Servings: 5

2 tbsp. Cajun or Creole seasoning	1 tsp. cayenne pepper
½ cup butter, melted	4 cups plain popcorn
2 cups peanut	1 tsp. paprika
2 cups mini wheat thin crackers	1 tsp. garlic
2 cups mini pretzels	½ tsp. thyme
2 tsp. salt	½ tsp. oregano
	1 tsp. black pepper
	½ tsp. onion powder

DIRECTIONS and Cooking Time: 30 Minutes

Pre-heat the Air Fryer to 370°F.   In a bowl, combine the Cajun spice with the melted butter.   In a separate bowl, stir together the peanuts, crackers, popcorn and pretzels. Coat the snacks with the butter mixture. Place in the fryer and fry for 8 - 10 minutes, shaking the basket frequently during the cooking time. You will have to complete this step in two batches.   Put the snack mix on a cookie sheet and leave to cool. The snacks can be kept in an airtight container for up to one week.

393. Parmesan Turnip Slices

INGREDIENTS for Servings: 8

1 lb turnip, peel and cut into slices	1 tbsp olive oil
3 oz parmesan cheese, shredded	1 tsp garlic powder
	1 tsp salt

DIRECTIONS and Cooking Time: 10 Minutes

Preheat the air fryer to 360 F.   Add all ingredients into the mixing bowl and toss to coat.   Transfer turnip slices into the air fryer basket and cook for 10 minutes.   Serve and enjoy.

394. Parmesan & Garlic Cauliflower

INGREDIENTS for Servings: 4

3/4 cup cauliflower florets	2 tbsp butter
1 clove garlic, sliced thinly	2 tbsp shredded parmesan
	1 pinch of salt

DIRECTIONS and Cooking Time: 40 Minutes
Preheat your fryer to 350°F/175°C. On a low heat, melt the butter with the garlic for 5-10 minutes. Strain the garlic in a sieve. Add the cauliflower, parmesan and salt. Bake for 20 minutes or until golden.

395. Feta Triangles

INGREDIENTS for Servings: 5

1 egg yolk, beaten	2 sheets of frozen filo
4 oz. feta cheese	pastry, defrosted
2 tbsp. flat-leafed	2 tbsp. olive oil
parsley, finely	ground black pepper
chopped	to taste
1 scallion, finely	
chopped	

DIRECTIONS and Cooking Time: 55 Minutes
1 In a bowl, combine the beaten egg yolk with the feta, parsley and scallion. Sprinkle on some pepper to taste. 2 Slice each sheet of filo dough into three strips. 3 Place a teaspoonful of the feta mixture on each strip of pastry. 4 Pinch the tip of the pastry and fold it up to enclose the filling and create a triangle. Continue folding the strip in zig-zags until the filling is wrapped in a triangle. Repeat with all of the strips of pastry. 5 Pre-heat the Air Fryer to 390°F. 6 Coat the pastry with a light coating of oil and arrange in the cooking basket. 7 Place the basket in the Air Fryer and cook for 3 minutes. 8 Lower the heat to 360°F and cook for a further 2 minutes or until a golden brown color is achieved

396. Greek-style Squash Chips

INGREDIENTS for Servings: 4

1/2 cup seasoned breadcrumbs	1/4 teaspoon oregano Sauce:
1/2 cup Parmesan cheese, grated	1/2 cup Greek-style yogurt
Sea salt and ground black pepper, to taste	1 tablespoon fresh cilantro, chopped
2 yellow squash, cut into slices	1 garlic clove, minced Freshly ground black
2 tablespoons grapeseed oil	pepper, to your liking

DIRECTIONS and Cooking Time: 25 Minutes
In a shallow bowl, thoroughly combine the seasoned breadcrumbs, Parmesan, salt, black pepper, and oregano. Dip the yellow squash slices in the prepared batter, pressing to adhere. Brush with the grapeseed oil and cook in the preheated Air Fryer at 400 degrees F for 12 minutes. Shake the Air Fryer basket periodically to ensure even cooking. Work in batches. While the chips are baking, whisk the sauce

ingredients; place in your refrigerator until ready to serve. Enjoy!

397. Cabbage Chips

INGREDIENTS for Servings: 6

1 large cabbage head, tear cabbage leaves into pieces	1/4 cup parmesan cheese, grated Pepper
2 tbsp olive oil	Salt

DIRECTIONS and Cooking Time: 30 Minutes
Preheat the air fryer to 250 F. Add all ingredients into the large mixing bowl and toss well. Spray air fryer basket with cooking spray. Divide cabbage in batches. Add one cabbage chips batch in air fryer basket and cook for 25-30 minutes at 250 F or until chips are crispy and lightly golden brown. Serve and enjoy.

398. Tuna Bowls

INGREDIENTS for Servings: 2

3 scallion stalks, minced	1 pound tuna, skinless, boneless and
1 chili pepper, minced	cubed
2 tablespoon olive oil	1 tablespoon coconut
1 tablespoon coconut cream	aminos
	2 tomatoes, cubed
	1 teaspoon sesame seeds

DIRECTIONS and Cooking Time: 10 Minutes
In a pan that fits your air fryer, mix all the ingredients except the sesame seeds, toss, introduce in the fryer and cook at 360 degrees F for 10 minutes. Divide into bowls and serve as an appetizer with sesame seeds sprinkled on top.

399. Fried Mushrooms

INGREDIENTS for Servings: 4

2 lb. button mushrooms	1 tbsp. coconut oil
3 tbsp. white or	2 tsp. herbs of your choice
French vermouth [optional]	½ tsp. garlic powder

DIRECTIONS and Cooking Time: 40 Minutes
1 Wash and dry the mushrooms. Slice them into quarters. 2 Pre-heat your Air Fryer at 320°F and add the coconut oil, garlic powder, and herbs to the basket. 3 Briefly cook the ingredients for 2 minutes and give them a stir. Put the mushrooms in the air fryer and cook for 25 minutes, stirring occasionally throughout. 4 Pour in the white vermouth and mix. Cook for an additional 5 minutes. 5 Serve hot.

400. Potato Chips

INGREDIENTS for Servings: 4

2 large potatoes, peel and sliced 1 tbsp. rosemary	3.5 oz. sour cream ¼ tsp. salt

DIRECTIONS and Cooking Time: 45 Minutes
Place the potato slices in water and allow to absorb for 30 minutes. Drain the potato slices and transfer to a large bowl. Toss with the rosemary, sour cream, and salt. Pre-heat the Air Fryer to 320°F Put the coated potato slices in the fryer's basket and cook for 35 minutes. Serve hot.

401. Sprouts Wraps

INGREDIENTS for Servings: 12

12 bacon strips 12 Brussels sprouts	A drizzle of olive oil

DIRECTIONS and Cooking Time: 20 Minutes
Wrap each Brussels sprouts in a bacon strip, brush them with some oil, put them in your air fryer's basket and cook at 350 degrees F for 20 minutes. Serve as an appetizer.

402. Rutabaga Fries

INGREDIENTS for Servings: 8

1 lb rutabaga, cut into fries shape 2 tsp olive oil	1 tsp garlic powder 1/2 tsp chili pepper 1/2 tsp salt

DIRECTIONS and Cooking Time: 18 Minutes
Add all ingredients into the large mixing bowl and toss to coat. Preheat the air fryer to 365 F. Transfer rutabaga fries into the air fryer basket and cook for 18 minutes. Shake 2-3 times. Serve and enjoy.

403. Roasted Peanuts

INGREDIENTS for Servings: 10

1 tablespoon olive oil	2½ cups raw peanuts Salt, as required

DIRECTIONS and Cooking Time: 14 Minutes
Set the temperature of Air Fryer to 320 degrees F. Add the peanuts in an Air Fryer basket in a single layer. Air Fry for about 9 minutes, tossing twice. Remove the peanuts from Air Fryer basket and transfer into a bowl. Add the oil, and salt and toss to coat well. Return the nuts mixture into Air Fryer basket. Air Fry for about 5 minutes. Once done, transfer the hot nuts in a glass or steel bowl and serve.

404. Cucumber Bites

INGREDIENTS for Servings: 4

1 teaspoon cream cheese ½ teaspoon cumin seeds 1 cucumber	4 oz salmon fillet ¼ teaspoon lemon juice ¼ teaspoon olive oil ¼ teaspoon salt

DIRECTIONS and Cooking Time: 7 Minutes
Sprinkle the salmon fillet with lemon juice, olive oil, and salt, Place it in the air fryer and cook for 7 minutes at 385F. Then chop it and mix up with cumin seeds and cream cheese. Cut the cucumber into 4 slices. Top every cucumber slice with salmon mixture.

405. Hillbilly Cheese Surprise

INGREDIENTS for Servings: 6

4 cups broccoli florets ¼ cup ranch dressing ½ cup sharp cheddar cheese, shredded	¼ cup heavy whipping cream Kosher salt and pepper to taste

DIRECTIONS and Cooking Time: 40 Minutes
Preheat your fryer to 375°F/190°C. In a bowl, combine all of the ingredients until the broccoli is well-covered. In a casserole dish, spread out the broccoli mixture. Bake for 30 minutes. Take out of your fryer and mix. If the florets are not tender, bake for another 5 minutes until tender. Serve!

406. Crust-less Meaty Pizza

INGREDIENTS for Servings: 1

½ cup mozzarella cheese, shredded 2 slices sugar-free bacon, cooked and crumbled	¼ cup ground sausage, cooked 7 slices pepperoni 1 tbsp. parmesan cheese, grated

DIRECTIONS and Cooking Time: 15 Minutes
Spread the mozzarella across the bottom of a six-inch cake pan. Throw on the bacon, sausage, and pepperoni, then add a sprinkle of the parmesan cheese on top. Place the pan inside your air fryer. Cook at 400°F for five minutes. The cheese is ready once brown in color and bubbly. Take care when removing the pan from the fryer and serve.

407. Must-serve Thai Prawns

INGREDIENTS for Servings: 4

16 prawns, cleaned and deveined Salt and ground black pepper, to your liking 1/2 teaspoon cumin	1 medium-sized egg, whisked 1 teaspoon baking powder 1 tablespoon curry

83

powder	powder
1 teaspoon fresh lemon juice	1/2 teaspoon grated fresh ginger
1/3 cup of beer	1/2 cup coconut flour

DIRECTIONS and Cooking Time: 10 Minutes

Toss the prawns with salt, pepper, cumin powder, and lemon juice.   In a mixing dish, place the whisked egg, beer, baking powder, curry, and the ginger; mix to combine well.   In another mixing dish, place the coconut flour.   Now, dip the prawns in the beer mixture; roll your prawns over the coconut flour. Air-fry at 360 degrees F for 5 minutes; turn them over, press the power button again and cook for additional 2 to 3 minutes. Bon appétit!

408.   Vegetable Fritters

INGREDIENTS for Servings: 4

1 cup bell peppers, deveined and chopped	¼ tsp. paprika
1 tsp. sea salt flakes	1 ½ tbsp. fresh chopped cilantro
1 tsp. cumin	1 egg, whisked
½ cup shallots, chopped	¾ cup Cheddar cheese, grated
2 cloves garlic, minced	¼ cup cooked quinoa
	¼ cup flour

DIRECTIONS and Cooking Time: 15 Minutes

In a bowl, combine all of the ingredients well.   Divide the mixture into equal portions and shape each one into a ball. Use your palm to flatten each ball very slightly to form patties.   Lightly coat the patties with a cooking spray.   Put the patties in your Air Fryer cooking basket, taking care not to overlap them. Cook at 340°F for 10 minutes, turning them over halfway through.

409.   Crispy Onion Rings

INGREDIENTS for Servings: 3

1 egg, lightly beaten	1 tbsp baking powder
1 onion, cut into slices	1 1/2 cups almond flour
3/4 cup pork rind, crushed	Pepper
1 cup coconut milk	Salt

DIRECTIONS and Cooking Time: 10 Minutes

Preheat the air fryer to 360 F.   In a bowl, mix together almond flour, baking powder, pepper, and salt.   In another bowl, whisk the egg with milk. Pour egg mixture into the almond flour mixture and stir to combine.   In a shallow dish, add crushed pork rinds. Spray air fryer basket with cooking spray.   Dip onion ring in egg batter and coat with pork rind and place into the air fryer basket.   Cook onion rings for 10 minutes at 360 F.   Serve and enjoy.

410.   Kale Chips With Tahini Sauce

INGREDIENTS for Servings: 4

1 ½ tablespoons sesame oil	5 cups kale leaves, torn into 1-inch pieces
1/2 teaspoon shallot powder	1 teaspoon salt
1 teaspoon garlic powder	1/3 cup tahini (sesame butter
1/4 teaspoon porcini powder	1 tablespoon fresh lemon juice
1/2 teaspoon mustard seeds	2 cloves garlic, minced

DIRECTIONS and Cooking Time: 15 Minutes

Toss the kale with the sesame oil and seasonings. Bake in the preheated Air Fryer at 350 degrees F for 10 minutes, shaking the cooking basket occasionally. Bake until the edges are brown. Work in batches. Meanwhile, make the sauce by whisking all ingredients in a small mixing bowl. Serve and enjoy!

411.   "good As Gold" Veggie Bites

INGREDIENTS for Servings: 10

1½ pound fresh spinach, blanched, drained and chopped	2 bread slices, toasted and processed into breadcrumbs
½ of onion, chopped	1 garlic clove, minced
1 carrot, peeled and chopped	1 teaspoon red chili flakes
2 American cheese slices, cut into tiny pieces	Salt, to taste

DIRECTIONS and Cooking Time: 10 Minutes

Preheat the Air fryer to 395F and grease an Air fryer basket.   Mix all the ingredients in a bowl except breadcrumbs until well combined.   Make small equal-sized balls from mixture and arrange these balls on a baking sheet.   Refrigerate for about half an hour.   Place the bread crumbs in a shallow dish and coat the balls evenly in bread crumbs.   Transfer the balls into the Air fryer basket and cook for about 10 minutes. Dish out and serve warm.

412.   Broccoli Melts With Coriander And Cheese

INGREDIENTS for Servings: 6

2 eggs, well whisked	1/4 teaspoon ground black pepper, or more to taste
2 cups Colby cheese, shredded	
1/2 cup almond meal	1 head broccoli, grated
2 tablespoons sesame	

| seeds | 1 cup parmesan |
| Seasoned salt, to taste | cheese, grated |

DIRECTIONS and Cooking Time: 20 Minutes
Thoroughly combine the eggs, Colby cheese, almond meal, sesame seeds, salt, black pepper, and broccoli to make the consistency of dough. Chill for 1 hour and shape into small balls; roll the patties over parmesan cheese. Spritz them with cooking oil on all sides. Cook at 360 degrees F for 10 minutes. Check for doneness and return to the Air Fryer for 8 to 10 more minutes. Serve with a sauce for dipping. Bon appétit!

413. Crab Mushrooms

INGREDIENTS for Servings: 16

16 mushrooms, clean and chop stems	2 oz crab meat, chopped
1/4 tsp chili powder	8 oz cream cheese, softened
1/4 tsp onion powder	
1/4 cup mozzarella cheese, shredded	2 tsp garlic, minced
	1/4 tsp pepper

DIRECTIONS and Cooking Time: 8 Minutes
In a mixing bowl, mix together stems, chili powder, onion powder, pepper, cheese, crabmeat, cream cheese, and garlic until well combined. Stuff mushrooms with bowl mixture and place into the air fryer basket. Cook mushrooms at 370 F for 8 minutes. Serve and enjoy.

414. Cashew Bowls

INGREDIENTS for Servings: 4

| 1 teaspoon ranch seasoning | 4 oz cashew |
| | 1 teaspoon sesame oil |

DIRECTIONS and Cooking Time: 5 Minutes
Preheat the air fryer to 375F. Mix up cashew with ranch seasoning and sesame oil and put in the preheated air fryer. Cook the cashew for 4 minutes. Then shake well and cook for 1 minute more.

415. Tofu In Sweet And Spicy Sauce

INGREDIENTS for Servings: 2

1 (14-ounces) block firm tofu, pressed and cubed	½ teaspoon sesame oil
	1½ tablespoons chili sauce
½ cup arrowroot flour	1 tablespoon agave nectar
2 scallions (green part), chopped	
4 tablespoons low-sodium soy sauce	2 large garlic cloves, minced
1½ tablespoons rice vinegar	1 teaspoon fresh ginger, peeled and grated

DIRECTIONS and Cooking Time: 6 Minutes
Preheat the Air fryer to 360F and grease an Air fryer basket. Mix together tofu, arrowroot flour, and sesame oil in a bowl. Arrange the tofu into the Air fryer basket and cook for about 20 minutes. Meanwhile, mix together remaining ingredients except scallions in a bowl to make a sauce. Place the tofu and sauce in a skillet and cook for about 3 minutes, stirring occasionally. Garnish with green parts of scallions and serve hot.

416. Avocado Fries With Chipotle Sauce

INGREDIENTS for Servings: 3

2 tablespoons fresh lime juice	1 egg
	1/2 cup breadcrumbs
1 avocado, pitted, peeled, and sliced	1 chipotle chili in adobo sauce
Pink Himalayan salt and ground white pepper, to taste	1/4 cup light mayonnaise
	1/4 cup plain Greek yogurt
1/4 cup flour	

DIRECTIONS and Cooking Time: 20 Minutes
Drizzle lime juice all over the avocado slices and set aside. Then, set up your breading station. Mix the salt, pepper, and all-purpose flour in a shallow dish. In a separate dish, whisk the egg. Finally, place your breadcrumbs in a third dish. Start by dredging the avocado slices in the flour mixture; then, dip them into the egg. Press the avocado slices into the breadcrumbs, coating evenly. Cook in the preheating Air Fryer at 380 degrees F for 11 minutes, shaking the cooking basket halfway through the cooking time. Meanwhile, blend the chipotle chili, mayo, and Greek yogurt in your food processor until the sauce is creamy and uniform. Serve the warm avocado slices with the sauce on the side. Enjoy!

417. Cashew Dip

INGREDIENTS for Servings: 6

½ cup cashews, soaked in water for 4 hours and drained	2 garlic cloves, minced
	A pinch of salt and black pepper
3 tablespoons cilantro, chopped	2 tablespoons coconut milk
1 teaspoon lime juice	

DIRECTIONS and Cooking Time: 8 Minutes
In a blender, combine all the ingredients, pulse well and transfer to a ramekin. Put the ramekin in your air fryer's basket and cook at 350 degrees F for 8 minutes. Serve as a party dip.

418.   Spicy Broccoli Poppers

INGREDIENTS for Servings: 4

2 tablespoons plain yogurt	½ teaspoon red chili powder
1 pound broccoli, cut into small florets	¼ teaspoon ground cumin
2 tablespoons chickpea flour	¼ teaspoon ground turmeric
Salt, to taste	

DIRECTIONS and Cooking Time: 10 Minutes

Preheat the Air fryer to 400F and grease an Air fryer basket.   Mix together the yogurt, red chili powder, cumin, turmeric and salt in a bowl until well combined. Stir in the broccoli and generously coat with marinade. Refrigerate for about 30 minutes and sprinkle the broccoli florets with chickpea flour.   Arrange the broccoli florets in the Air fryer basket and cook for about 10 minutes, flipping once in between.   Dish out and serve warm.

419.   Hot Dogs

INGREDIENTS for Servings: 4

4 hot dogs	½ teaspoon ground turmeric
1 egg, beaten	
1/3 cup coconut flour	

DIRECTIONS and Cooking Time: 5 Minutes

In the bowl mix up egg, coconut flour, and ground turmeric. Then dip the hot dogs in the mixture. Transfer the hot dogs in the freezer and freeze them for 5 minutes. Meanwhile, preheat the air fryer to 400F. Place the frozen hot dogs in the air fryer basket and cook them for 6 minutes or until they are light brown.

420.   Buffalo Cauliflower Wings

INGREDIENTS for Servings: 4

1 cauliflower head, cut into florets	1/2 cup buffalo sauce
	Pepper
1 tbsp butter, melted	Salt

DIRECTIONS and Cooking Time: 14 Minutes

Spray air fryer basket with cooking spray.   In a bowl, mix together buffalo sauce, butter, pepper, and salt. Add cauliflower florets into the air fryer basket and cook at 400 F for 7 minutes.   Transfer cauliflower florets into the buffalo sauce mixture and toss well. Again, add cauliflower florets into the air fryer basket and cook for 7 minutes more at 400 F.   Serve and enjoy.

421.   Cheese Dill Mushrooms

INGREDIENTS for Servings: 6

9 oz mushrooms, cut stems	6 oz cheddar cheese, shredded
1 tsp dried parsley	1 tbsp butter
1 tsp dried dill	1/2 tsp salt

DIRECTIONS and Cooking Time: 5 Minutes

Chop mushrooms stem finely and place into the bowl. Add parsley, dill, cheese, butter, and salt into the bowl and mix until well combined.   Preheat the air fryer to 400 F.   Stuff bowl mixture into the mushroom caps and place into the air fryer basket.   Cook mushrooms for 5 minutes.   Serve and enjoy.

422.   Spinach Chips With Chili Yogurt Dip

INGREDIENTS for Servings: 3

3 cups fresh spinach leaves	1 teaspoon garlic powder
1 tablespoon extra-virgin olive oil	Chili Yogurt Dip:
	1/4 cup yogurt
1 teaspoon sea salt	2 tablespoons mayonnaise
1/2 teaspoon cayenne pepper	1/2 teaspoon chili powder

DIRECTIONS and Cooking Time: 20 Minutes

Toss the spinach leaves with the olive oil and seasonings.   Bake in the preheated Air Fryer at 350 degrees F for 10 minutes, shaking the cooking basket occasionally.   Bake until the edges brown, working in batches.   In the meantime, make the sauce by whisking all ingredients in a mixing dish. Serve immediately.

423.   Roasted Parsnip Sticks With Salted Caramel

INGREDIENTS for Servings: 4

1 pound parsnip, trimmed, scrubbed, cut into sticks	2 tablespoons granulated sugar
	1/4 teaspoon ground allspice
2 tablespoon avocado oil	1/2 teaspoon coarse salt
2 tablespoons butter	

DIRECTIONS and Cooking Time: 25 Minutes

Toss the parsnip with the avocado oil; bake in the preheated Air Fryer at 380 degrees F for 15 minutes, shaking the cooking basket occasionally to ensure even cooking.   Then, heat the sugar and 1 tablespoon of water in a small pan over medium heat. Cook until the sugar has dissolved; bring to a boil.   Keep swirling the pan around until the sugar reaches a rich caramel color. Pour in 2 tablespoons of cold water. Now, add the butter, allspice, and salt. The mixture should be runny. Afterwards, drizzle the salted caramel over the roasted parsnip sticks and enjoy!

424. Bacon Wrapped Shrimp

INGREDIENTS for Servings: 4

1 lb. bacon, thinly sliced, room temperature [16 slices]	1 ¼ lb. tiger shrimp, peeled and deveined [16 pieces]

DIRECTIONS and Cooking Time: 50 Minutes
1 Wrap each bacon slice around a piece of shrimp, from the head to the tail. Refrigerate for 20 minutes. 2 Pre-heat the Air Fryer to 390°F. 3 Place the shrimp in the fryer's basket and cook for 5 – 7 minutes. 4 Allow to dry on a paper towel before serving.

425. Sweet Potato Tots

INGREDIENTS for Servings: 24

2 sweet potatoes, peeled Salt	1/2 tsp cajun seasoning

DIRECTIONS and Cooking Time: 31 Minutes
Add water in large pot and bring to boil. Add sweet potatoes in pot and boil for 15 minutes. Drain well. Grated boil sweet potatoes into a large bowl using a grated. Add cajun seasoning and salt in grated sweet potatoes and mix until well combined. Spray air fryer basket with cooking spray. Make small tot of sweet potato mixture and place in air fryer basket. Cook at 400 F for 8 minutes. Turn tots to another side and cook for 8 minutes more. Serve and enjoy.

426. Crispy Eggplant Slices

INGREDIENTS for Servings: 4

1 medium eggplant, peeled and cut into ½-	Salt, as required 2 eggs, beaten
inch round slices ½ cup all-purpose flour	1 cup Italian-style breadcrumbs ¼ cup olive oil

DIRECTIONS and Cooking Time: 16 Minutes
In a colander, add the eggplant slices and sprinkle with salt. Set aside for about 45 minutes and pat dry the eggplant slices. Add the flour in a shallow dish. Crack the eggs in a second dish and beat well. In a third dish, mix together the oil, and breadcrumbs. Coat each eggplant slice with flour, then dip into beaten eggs and finally, evenly coat with the breadcrumbs mixture. Set the temperature of Air Fryer to 390 degrees F. Arrange the eggplant slices in an Air Fryer basket in a single layer in 2 batches. Air Fry for about 8 minutes. Serve.

427. Ricotta Balls

INGREDIENTS for Servings: 2 – 4

2 cups ricotta, grated	¼ tsp. pepper powder to taste
2 eggs, separated	1 tsp. orange zest, grated
2 tbsp. chives, finely chopped	
2 tbsp. fresh basil, finely chopped	For coating
4 tbsp. flour	¼ cup friendly bread crumbs
¼ tsp. salt to taste	1 tbsp. vegetable oil

DIRECTIONS and Cooking Time: 25 Minutes
Pre-heat your Air Fryer at 390°F. In a bowl, combine the yolks, flour, salt, pepper, chives and orange zest. Throw in the ricotta and incorporate with your hands. Mold equal amounts of the mixture into balls. Mix the oil with the bread crumbs until a crumbly consistency is achieved. Coat the balls in the bread crumbs and transfer each one to the fryer's basket. Put the basket in the fryer. Air fry for 8 minutes or until a golden brown color is achieved. Serve with a sauce of your choosing, such as ketchup.

VEGAN & VEGETARIAN RECIPES

428.   Mediterranean-style Potato Chips With Vegveeta Dip

INGREDIENTS for Servings: 4

1 large potato, cut into 1/8 inch thick slices	Sea salt, to taste
1 tablespoon olive oil	1/2 teaspoon fresh basil
1/2 teaspoon red pepper flakes, crushed	Dipping Sauce:
1 teaspoon fresh rosemary	1/3 cup raw cashews
1/2 teaspoon fresh sage	1 tablespoon tahini
	1 ½ tablespoons olive oil
	1/4 cup raw almonds
	1/4 teaspoon prepared yellow mustard

DIRECTIONS and Cooking Time: 1 Hour
Soak the potatoes in a large bowl of cold water for 20 to 30 minutes. Drain the potatoes and pat them dry with a kitchen towel.   Toss with olive oil and seasonings.   Place in the lightly greased cooking basket and cook at 380 degrees F for 30 minutes. Work in batches.   Meanwhile, puree the sauce ingredients in your food processor until smooth. Serve the potato chips with the Vegveeta sauce for dipping. Bon appétit!

429.   Easy Fry Portobello Mushroom

INGREDIENTS for Servings: 2

1 tablespoon cooking oil	Salt and pepper to taste
1-pound Portobello mushroom, sliced	

DIRECTIONS and Cooking Time: 10 Minutes
Place the grill pan accessory in the air fryer.   In a bowl, place all Ingredients and toss to coat and season the mushrooms.   Place in the grill pan.   Close the air fryer and cook for 10 minutes at 330F.

430.   Spaghetti Squash

INGREDIENTS for Servings: 2

spaghetti squash	4 tbsp. heavy cream
1 tsp. olive oil	1 tsp. butter
Salt and pepper	

DIRECTIONS and Cooking Time: 45 Minutes
Pre-heat your fryer at 360°F.   Cut and de-seed the spaghetti squash. Brush with the olive oil and season with salt and pepper to taste.   Put the squash inside the fryer, placing it cut-side-down. Cook for thirty minutes. Halfway through cooking, fluff the spaghetti inside the squash with a fork.   When the squash is ready, fluff the spaghetti some more, then pour some heavy cream and butter over it and give it a good stir. Serve with the low-carb tomato sauce of your choice.

431.   Crispy 'n Savory Spring Rolls

INGREDIENTS for Servings: 4

½ teaspoon ginger, finely chopped	1 cup shiitake mushroom, sliced thinly
1 celery stalk, chopped	1 teaspoon corn starch + 2 tablespoon water
1 medium carrot, shredded	1 teaspoon nutritional yeast
1 tablespoon soy sauce	8 spring roll wrappers
1 teaspoon coconut sugar	

DIRECTIONS and Cooking Time: 15 Minutes
In a mixing bowl, mix together the celery stalk, carrots, ginger, coconut sugar, soy sauce and nutritional yeast. Get a tablespoon of the vegetable mixture and place at the center of the spring roll wrappers.   Roll and seal the edges of the wrapper with the cornstarch mixture. Cook in a preheated air fryer to 400F for 15 minutes or until the spring roll wrapper is crisp.

432.   Fried Tofu Recipe From Malaysia

INGREDIENTS for Servings: 4

1 block tofu, cut into strips	1 tablespoon soy sauce
1 tablespoon maple syrup	1/2 cup creamy peanut butter
1 teaspoon sriracha sauce	1-2 teaspoons Sriracha sauce to taste
2 cloves of garlic	2 cloves of garlic
2 tablespoons soy sauce	2-inch piece of fresh ginger coarsely chopped
2 teaspoons fresh ginger no need to peel, coarsely chopped	6 tablespoons of water
juice of 1 fresh lime	juice of 1/2 a fresh lemon
Peanut Butter Sauce Ingredients	

DIRECTIONS and Cooking Time: 30 Minutes
In a blender, blend all peanut butter sauce Ingredients until smooth and creamy. Transfer to a medium bowl and set aside for dipping sauce.   In same blender,

blend garlic, sriracha, ginger, maple syrup, lime juice, and soy sauce until smooth. Pour into a bowl and add strips of tofu, Marinate for 30 minutes. With the steel skewer, skewer tofu strips. Place on skewer rack and air fry for 15 minutes at 370F. Serve and enjoy.

433.   Glazed Veggies

INGREDIENTS for Servings: 4

2 ounces cherry tomatoes	6 tablespoons olive oil, divided
1 large parsnip, peeled and chopped	1 teaspoon Dijon mustard
1 large carrot, peeled and chopped	1 teaspoon mixed dried herbs
1 large zucchini, chopped	1 teaspoon garlic paste
1 green bell pepper, seeded and chopped	Salt and black pepper, to taste
3 tablespoons honey	

DIRECTIONS and Cooking Time: 20 Minutes
Preheat the Air fryer to 350F and grease an Air fryer pan.   Arrange cherry tomatoes, parsnip, carrot, zucchini and bell pepper in the Air fryer pan and drizzle with 3 tablespoons of olive oil.   Cook for about 15 minutes and remove from the Air fryer. Mix remaining olive oil, honey, mustard, herbs, garlic, salt, and black pepper in a bowl.   Pour this mixture over the vegetables in the Air fryer pan and set the Air fryer to 390F.   Cook for about 5 minutes and dish out to serve hot.

434.   Crispy Vegetarian Ravioli

INGREDIENTS for Servings: 4

½ cup panko bread crumbs	¼ cup aquafaba
1 teaspoon dried basil	2 teaspoons nutritional yeast
1 teaspoon dried oregano	8-ounces vegan ravioli
1 teaspoon garlic powder	cooking spray
	salt and pepper to taste

DIRECTIONS and Cooking Time: 6 Minutes
Line the air fryer basket with aluminum foil and brush with oil.   Preheat the air fryer to 400F.   Mix together the panko bread crumbs, nutritional yeast, basil, oregano, and garlic powder. Season with salt and pepper to taste.   In another bowl, place the aquafaba.   Dip the ravioli in the aquafaba the dredge in the panko mixture.   Spray with cooking oil and place in the air fryer.   Cook for 6 minutes making sure that you shake the air fryer basket halfway.

435.   Turmeric Crispy Chickpeas

INGREDIENTS for Servings: 4

1 tbsp butter, melted	¼ tsp turmeric
½ tsp dried rosemary	Salt to taste

DIRECTIONS and Cooking Time: 22 Minutes
Preheat the Air fryer to 380 F.   In a bowl, combine together chickpeas, butter, rosemary, turmeric, and salt; toss to coat. Place the prepared chickpeas in your Air Fryer's cooking basket and cook for 6 minutes. Slide out the basket and shake; cook for another 6 minutes until crispy.

436.   Air-fried Veggie Sushi

INGREDIENTS for Servings: 4

4 nori sheets	1 tbsp rice wine vinegar
1 carrot, sliced lengthways	1 cup panko crumbs
1 red bell pepper, seeds removed, sliced	2 tbsp sesame seeds
1 avocado, sliced	Soy sauce, wasabi and pickled ginger to serve
1 tbsp olive oil mixed with	

DIRECTIONS and Cooking Time: 60 Minutes
Prepare a clean working board, a small bowl of lukewarm water and a sushi mat. Wet hands, and lay a nori sheet onto sushi mat and spread half cup sushi rice, leaving a half-inch of nori clear, so you can seal the roll. Place carrot, pepper and avocado sideways to the rice. Roll sushi tightly and rub warm water along the clean nori strip to seal.   In a bowl, mix oil and rice vinegar. In another bowl, mix crumbs and sesame seeds. Roll each sushi log in the vinegar mixture and then straight to the sesame bowl to coat. Arrange sushi onto air fryer and cook for 14 minutes at 360 F, turning once. Slice and serve with soy sauce, pickled ginger and wasabi.

437.   Baked Zucchini Recipe
From Mexico

INGREDIENTS for Servings: 4

1 tablespoon olive oil	1/2 teaspoon cayenne pepper, or to taste
1-1/2 pounds zucchini, cubed	1/2 cup cooked long-grain rice
1/2 cup chopped onion	1/2 cup cooked pinto beans
1/2 teaspoon garlic salt	1-1/4 cups salsa
1/2 teaspoon paprika	3/4 cup shredded Cheddar cheese
1/2 teaspoon dried oregano	

DIRECTIONS and Cooking Time: 30 Minutes

Lightly grease baking pan of air fryer with olive oil. Add onions and zucchini and for 10 minutes, cook on 360F. Halfway through cooking time, stir. Season with cayenne, oregano, paprika, and garlic salt. Mix well. Stir in salsa, beans, and rice. Cook for 5 minutes. Stir in cheddar cheese and mix well. Cover pan with foil. Cook for 15 minutes at 390F until bubbly. Serve and enjoy.

438. Roasted Mushrooms In Herb-garlic Oil

INGREDIENTS for Servings: 4

½ teaspoon minced garlic	3 tablespoons coconut oil
2 pounds mushrooms	Salt and pepper to taste
2 teaspoons herbs de Provence	

DIRECTIONS and Cooking Time: 25 Minutes
Preheat the air fryer for 5 minutes. Place all ingredients in a baking dish that will fit in the air fryer. Mix to combine. Place the baking dish in the air fryer. Cook for 25 minutes at 350F.

439. Minty Green Beans With Shallots

INGREDIENTS for Servings: 6

1 tablespoon fresh mint, chopped	1 teaspoon soy sauce
1 tablespoon sesame seeds, toasted	2 large shallots, sliced
1 tablespoon vegetable oil	2 tablespoons fresh basil, chopped
1-pound fresh green beans, trimmed	2 tablespoons pine nuts

DIRECTIONS and Cooking Time: 25 Minutes
Preheat the air fryer to 330F. Place the grill pan accessory in the air fryer. In a mixing bowl, combine the green beans, shallots, vegetable oil, and soy sauce. Dump in the air fryer and cook for 25 minutes. Once cooked, garnish with basil, mints, sesame seeds, and pine nuts.

440. Cheese Stuffed Zucchini With Scallions

INGREDIENTS for Servings: 4

1 large zucchini, cut into four pieces	1 heaping tablespoon coriander, minced
2 tablespoons olive oil	2 ounces Cheddar cheese, preferably freshly grated
1 cup Ricotta cheese, room temperature	
2 tablespoons	1 teaspoon celery
scallions, chopped	seeds
1 heaping tablespoon fresh parsley, roughly chopped	1/2 teaspoon salt
	1/2 teaspoon garlic pepper

DIRECTIONS and Cooking Time: 20 Minutes
Cook your zucchini in the Air Fryer cooking basket for approximately 10 minutes at 350 degrees F. Check for doneness and cook for 2-3 minutes longer if needed. Meanwhile, make the stuffing by mixing the other items. When your zucchini is thoroughly cooked, open them up. Divide the stuffing among all zucchini pieces and bake an additional 5 minutes.

441. Couscous Stuffed Tomatoes

INGREDIENTS for Servings: 4

4 tomatoes, tops and seeds removed	1½ cups couscous
1 parsnip, peeled and finely chopped	1 teaspoon olive oil
1 cup mushrooms, chopped	1 garlic clove, minced
	1 tablespoon mirin sauce

DIRECTIONS and Cooking Time: 25 Minutes
Preheat the Air fryer to 355F and grease an Air fryer basket. Heat olive oil in a skillet on low heat and add parsnips, mushrooms and garlic. Cook for about 5 minutes and stir in the mirin sauce and couscous. Stuff the couscous mixture into the tomatoes and arrange into the Air fryer basket. Cook for about 20 minutes and dish out to serve warm.

442. Brussel Sprout Salad

INGREDIENTS for Servings: 4

1 pound fresh medium Brussels sprouts, trimmed and halved vertically	2 tablespoons extra-virgin olive oil
2 apples, cored and chopped	2 tablespoons fresh lemon juice
1 red onion, sliced	1 tablespoon apple cider vinegar
4 cups lettuce, torn	1 tablespoon honey
3 teaspoons olive oil	1 teaspoon Dijon mustard
Salt and ground black pepper, as required	Salt and ground black pepper, as required
For Dressing	

DIRECTIONS and Cooking Time: 15 Minutes
Preheat the Air fryer to 360F and grease an Air fryer basket. Mix Brussels sprout, oil, salt, and black pepper in a bowl and toss to coat well. Arrange the Brussels sprouts in the Air fryer basket and cook for about 15 minutes, flipping once in between. Dish out the Brussel sprouts in a serving bowl and keep aside to cool. Add apples, onion, and lettuce and mix well.

Mix all the ingredients for dressing in a bowl and pour over the salad. Toss to coat well and serve immediately.

443. Banana Pepper Stuffed With Tofu 'n Spices

INGREDIENTS for Servings: 8

½ teaspoon red chili powder	1 teaspoon coriander powder
½ teaspoon turmeric powder	3 tablespoons coconut oil
1 onion, finely chopped	8 banana peppers, top end sliced and seeded
1 package firm tofu, crumbled	Salt to taste

DIRECTIONS and Cooking Time: 10 Minutes
Preheat the air fryer for 5 minutes. In a mixing bowl, combine the tofu, onion, coconut oil, turmeric powder, red chili powder, coriander power, and salt. Mix until well-combined. Scoop the tofu mixture into the hollows of the banana peppers. Place the stuffed peppers in the air fryer. Close and cook for 10 minutes at 325F.

444. Ooey-gooey Dessert Quesadilla

INGREDIENTS for Servings: 2

1/4 cup blueberries	1 teaspoon vanilla extract
1/4 cup fresh orange juice	2 (6-inch tortillas
1/2 tablespoon maple syrup	2 teaspoons coconut oil
1/2 cup vegan cream cheese	1/4 cup vegan dark chocolate

DIRECTIONS and Cooking Time: 25 Minutes
Bring the blueberries, orange juice, and maple syrup to a boil in a saucepan. Reduce the heat and let it simmer until the sauce thickens, about 10 minutes. In a mixing dish, combine the cream cheese with the vanilla extract; spread on the tortillas. Add the blueberry filling on top. Fold in half. Place the quesadillas in the greased Air Fryer basket. Cook at 390 degrees F for 10 minutes, until tortillas are golden brown and filling is melted. Make sure to turn them over halfway through the cooking. Heat the coconut oil in a small pan and add the chocolate; whisk to combine well. Drizzle the chocolate sauce over the quesadilla and serve. Enjoy!

445. Roasted Cauliflower And Broccoli Salad

INGREDIENTS for Servings: 4

1/2 pound cauliflower florets	1 teaspoon Dijon mustard
1/3 pound broccoli florets	1 avocado, pitted, peeled and sliced
Sea salt, to taste	1 small sized onion, peeled and sliced
1/2 teaspoon red pepper flakes	1 garlic clove, minced
2 tablespoons cider vinegar	2 cups arugula
2 tablespoons extra-virgin olive oil	2 tablespoons sesame seeds, lightly toasted

DIRECTIONS and Cooking Time: 20 Minutes + Chilling Time
Start by preheating your Air Fryer to 400 degrees F. Brush the cauliflower and broccoli florets with cooking spray. Cook for 12 minutes, shaking the cooking basket halfway through the cooking time. Season with salt and red pepper. In a mixing dish, whisk the vinegar, Dijon mustard, and olive oil. Dress the salad. Add the avocado, onion, garlic, and arugula. Top with sesame seeds. Bon appétit!

446. Cottage And Mayonnaise Stuffed Peppers

INGREDIENTS for Servings: 2

1 red bell pepper, top and seeds removed	Salt and pepper, to taste
1 yellow bell pepper, top and seeds removed	4 tablespoons mayonnaise
1 cup Cottage cheese	2 pickles, chopped

DIRECTIONS and Cooking Time: 20 Minutes
Arrange the peppers in the lightly greased cooking basket. Cook in the preheated Air Fryer at 400 degrees F for 15 minutes, turning them over halfway through the cooking time. Season with salt and pepper. Then, in a mixing bowl, combine the cream cheese with the mayonnaise and chopped pickles. Stuff the pepper with the cream cheese mixture and serve. Enjoy!

447. Sweet & Spicy Cauliflower

INGREDIENTS for Servings: 4

1 head cauliflower, cut into florets	1 tablespoon rice vinegar
¾ cup onion, thinly sliced	1 teaspoon coconut sugar
5 garlic cloves, finely sliced	Pinch of red pepper flakes

1½ tablespoons soy sauce 1 tablespoon hot sauce	Ground black pepper, as required 2 scallions, chopped

DIRECTIONS and Cooking Time: 30 Minutes
Set the temperature of air fryer to 350 degrees F. Grease an air fryer pan. Arrange cauliflower florets into the prepared air fryer pan in a single layer. Air fry for about 10 minutes. Remove from air fryer and stir in the onions. Air fry for another 10 minutes. Remove from air fryer and stir in the garlic. Air fry for 5 more minutes. Meanwhile, in a bowl, mix well soy sauce, hot sauce, vinegar, coconut sugar, red pepper flakes, and black pepper. Remove from the air fryer and stir in the sauce mixture. Air fry for about 5 minutes. Remove from air fryer and transfer the cauliflower mixture onto serving plates. Garnish with scallions and serve.

448. Sautéed Green Beans

INGREDIENTS for Servings: 2

8 ounces fresh green beans, trimmed and cut in half	1 teaspoon sesame oil 1 tablespoon soy sauce

DIRECTIONS and Cooking Time: 10 Minutes
Preheat the Air fryer to 390F and grease an Air fryer basket. Mix green beans, soy sauce, and sesame oil in a bowl and toss to coat well. Arrange green beans into the Air fryer basket and cook for about 10 minutes, tossing once in between. Dish out onto serving plates and serve hot.

449. Vegetable Casserole With Swiss Cheese

INGREDIENTS for Servings: 6

1 tablespoon olive oil 1 shallot, sliced 2 cloves garlic, minced 1 red bell pepper, seeded and sliced 1 yellow bell pepper, seeded and sliced 1 pound broccoli florets, steamed	1 ½ cups kale 6 eggs 1/2 cup milk Sea salt and ground black pepper, to your liking 1 cup Swiss cheese, shredded 4 tablespoons Romano cheese, grated

DIRECTIONS and Cooking Time: 40 Minutes
Heat the olive oil in a saucepan over medium-high heat. Sauté the shallot, garlic, and peppers for 2 to 3 minutes. Add the kale and cook until wilted. Arrange the broccoli florets evenly over the bottom of a lightly greased casserole dish. Spread the sautéed mixture over the top. In a mixing bowl, thoroughly combine the eggs, milk, salt, pepper, and shredded cheese. Pour the mixture into the casserole dish. Lastly, top with Romano cheese. Bake at 330 degrees F for 30 minutes or until top is golden brown. Bon appétit!

450. Rice & Beans Stuffed Bell Peppers

INGREDIENTS for Servings: 5

½ small bell pepper, seeded and chopped 1 (15-ounces) can diced tomatoes with juice 1 (15-ounces) can red kidney beans, rinsed and drained 1 cup cooked rice	1½ teaspoons Italian seasoning 5 large bell peppers, tops removed and seeded ½ cup mozzarella cheese, shredded 1 tablespoon Parmesan cheese, grated

DIRECTIONS and Cooking Time: 15 Minutes
In a bowl, mix well chopped bell pepper, tomatoes with juice, beans, rice, and Italian seasoning. Stuff each bell pepper evenly with the rice mixture. Set the temperature of air fryer to 360 degrees F. Grease an air fryer basket. Arrange bell peppers into the air fryer basket in a single layer. Air fry for about 12 minutes. Meanwhile, in a bowl, mix together the mozzarella and Parmesan cheese. Remove the air fryer basket and top each bell pepper with cheese mixture. Air fry for 3 more minutes. Remove from air fryer and transfer the bell peppers onto a serving platter. Set aside to cool slightly. Serve warm.

451. Curried Cauliflower Florets

INGREDIENTS for Servings: 4

Salt to taste 1 ½ tbsp curry powder	½ cup olive oil ⅓ cup fried pine nuts

DIRECTIONS and Cooking Time: 34 Minutes
Preheat the air fryer to 390 F, and mix the pine nuts and 1 tsp of olive oil, in a medium bowl. Pour them in the air fryer's basket and cook for 2 minutes; remove to cool. Place the cauliflower on a cutting board. Use a knife to cut them into 1-inch florets. Place them in a large mixing bowl. Add the curry powder, salt, and the remaining olive oil; mix well. Place the cauliflower florets in the fryer's basket in 2 batches, and cook each batch for 10 minutes. Remove the curried florets onto a serving platter, sprinkle with the pine nuts, and toss. Serve the florets with tomato sauce or as a side to a meat dish.

452. Crisped Noodle Salad Chinese Style

INGREDIENTS for Servings: 2

1 carrot, sliced thinly	1 sprig coriander, chopped
1 cup cabbage, sliced thinly	1 tablespoon cooking oil
1 green bell pepper, sliced thinly	1 tablespoon lime juice
1 onion, sliced thinly	1 tablespoon red chili sauce
1 package wheat noodles	1 tomato, chopped
1 tablespoon tamari	salt to taste

DIRECTIONS and Cooking Time: 20 Minutes
In a big pot, boil water and add a teaspoon of salt. Bring the water to a boil and add the noodles. Boil the noodles until it is half-cooked. Drain. In a mixing bowl, pour oil over the noodles and mix until the noodles are coated evenly. Place a tin foil on the base of the air fryer basket and place the noodles inside. Cook in a preheated air fryer at 395F for 15 to 20 minutes or until crisp. Meanwhile, mix together the tamari, red chili sauce, and lime juice. Season with salt and pepper to taste. Once the noodles are cooked, assemble the salad by placing the air fried noodles in a bowl. Add the vegetables and pour over sauce.

453. The Best Avocado Fries Ever

INGREDIENTS for Servings: 4

1/2 head garlic (6-7 cloves)	2 eggs
1/2 cup almond meal	2 avocados, cut into wedges
Sea salt and ground black pepper, to taste	Sauce:
1/2 cup parmesan cheese, grated	1/2 cup mayonnaise
	1 teaspoon lemon juice
	1 teaspoon mustard

DIRECTIONS and Cooking Time: 50 Minutes
Place the garlic on a piece of aluminum foil and spritz with cooking spray. Wrap the garlic in the foil. Cook in the preheated Air Fryer at 400 degrees for 12 minutes. Check the garlic, open the top of the foil and continue to cook for 10 minutes more. Let it cool for 10 to 15 minutes; remove the cloves by squeezing them out of the skins; mash the garlic and reserve. In a shallow bowl, combine the almond meal, salt, and black pepper. In another shallow dish, whisk the eggs until frothy. Place the parmesan cheese in a third shallow dish. Dredge the avocado wedges in the almond meal mixture, shaking off the excess. Then, dip in the egg mixture; lastly, dredge in parmesan cheese. Spritz the avocado wedges with cooking oil on all sides. Cook in the preheated Air Fryer at 395 degrees F approximately 8 minutes, turning them over halfway through the cooking time. Meanwhile, combine the sauce ingredients with the smashed roasted garlic. To serve, divide the avocado fries between plates and top with the sauce. Enjoy!

454. Tender Butternut Squash Fry

INGREDIENTS for Servings: 2

1 tablespoon cooking oil	1-pound butternut squash, seeded and sliced
Salt and pepper to taste	

DIRECTIONS and Cooking Time: 10 Minutes
Place the grill pan accessory in the air fryer. In a bowl, place all Ingredients and toss to coat and season the squash. Place in the grill pan. Close the air fryer and cook for 10 minutes at 330F.

455. Mushroom 'n Bell Pepper Pizza

INGREDIENTS for Servings: 10

¼ red bell pepper, chopped	1 shallot, chopped
1 cup oyster mushrooms, chopped	1 vegan pizza dough
	2 tablespoons parsley
	salt and pepper

DIRECTIONS and Cooking Time: 10 Minutes
Preheat the air fryer to 400F. Slice the pizza dough into squares. Set aside. In a mixing bowl, mix together the oyster mushroom, shallot, bell pepper and parsley. Season with salt and pepper to taste. Place the topping on top of the pizza squares. Place inside the air fryer and cook for 10 minutes.

456. Scrumptiously Healthy Chips

INGREDIENTS for Servings: 2

1 bunch kale	2 tablespoons olive oil
1 teaspoon garlic powder	Salt and pepper to taste
2 tablespoons almond flour	

DIRECTIONS and Cooking Time: 10 Minutes
Preheat the air fryer for 5 minutes. In a bowl, combine all ingredients until the kale leaves are coated with the other ingredients. Place in a fryer basket and cook for 10 minutes until crispy.

457. Tomato Sandwiches With Feta And Pesto

INGREDIENTS for Servings: 2

1 (4- oz) block Feta cheese	Salt to taste
1 small red onion, thinly sliced	1 ½ tbsp toasted pine nuts
1 clove garlic	¼ cup chopped parsley
2 tsp + ¼ cup olive oil	¼ cup grated Parmesan cheese
	¼ cup chopped basil

DIRECTIONS and Cooking Time: 60 Minutes
Add basil, pine nuts, garlic and salt to a food processor. Process while adding the ¼ cup of olive oil slowly. Once the oil is finished, pour the basil pesto into a bowl and refrigerate for 30 minutes. Preheat the air fryer to 390 F. Slice the feta cheese and tomato into ½ inch circular slices. Use a kitchen towel to pat the tomatoes dry. Remove the pesto from the fridge and use a tablespoon to spread some pesto on each slice of tomato. Top with a slice of feta cheese. Add the onion and remaining olive oil in a bowl and toss. Spoon on top of feta cheese. Place the tomato in the fryer's basket and cook for 12 minutes. Remove to a serving platter, sprinkle lightly with salt and top with the remaining pesto. Serve with a side of rice or lean meat.

458. Baked Spicy Tortilla Chips

INGREDIENTS for Servings: 3

6 (6-inch) corn tortillas	1 teaspoon salt
1 teaspoon canola oil	1/2 teaspoon ground cumin
1/4 teaspoon ground white pepper	1/2 teaspoon ancho chili powder

DIRECTIONS and Cooking Time: 20 Minutes
Slice the tortillas into quarters. Brush the tortilla pieces with the canola oil until well coated. Toss with the spices and transfer to the Air Fryer basket. Bake at 360 degrees F for 8 minutes or until lightly golden. Work in batches. Bon appétit!

459. Pepper-pineapple With Butter-sugar Glaze

INGREDIENTS for Servings: 2

1 medium-sized pineapple, peeled and sliced	1 teaspoon brown sugar
1 red bell pepper, seeded and julienned	2 teaspoons melted butter
	Salt to taste

DIRECTIONS and Cooking Time: 10 Minutes

Preheat the air fryer to 390F. Place the grill pan accessory in the air fryer. Mix all ingredients in a Ziploc bag and give a good shake. Dump onto the grill pan and cook for 10 minutes making sure that you flip the pineapples every 5 minutes.

460. Crisped Tofu With Paprika

INGREDIENTS for Servings: 4

¼ cup cornstarch	1 tablespoon smoked paprika
1 block extra firm tofu, pressed to remove excess water and cut into cubes	salt and pepper to taste

DIRECTIONS and Cooking Time: 15 Minutes
Line the air fryer basket with aluminum foil and brush with oil. Preheat the air fryer to 370F. Mix all ingredients in a bowl. Toss to combine. Place in the air fryer basket and cook for 12 minutes.

461. Herby Veggie Cornish Pasties

INGREDIENTS for Servings: 4

¼ cup mushrooms, chopped	1 onion, sliced
¾ cup cold coconut oil	1 tablespoon nutritional yeast
1 ½ cups plain flour	1 tablespoon olive oil
1 medium carrot, chopped	1 teaspoon oregano
1 medium potato, diced	a pinch of salt
1 stick celery, chopped	cold water for mixing the dough
	salt and pepper to taste

DIRECTIONS and Cooking Time: 30 Minutes
Preheat the air fryer to 400F. Prepare the dough by mixing the flour, coconut oil, and salt in a bowl. Use a fork and press the flour to combine everything. Gradually add a drop of water to the dough until you achieve a stiff consistency of the dough. Cover the dough with a cling film and let it rest for 30 minutes inside the fridge. Roll the dough out and cut into squares. Set aside. Heat olive oil over medium heat and sauté the onions for 2 minutes. Add the celery, carrots and potatoes. Continue stirring for 3 to 5 minutes before adding the mushrooms and oregano. Season with salt and pepper to taste. Add nutritional yeast last. Let it cool and set aside. Drop a tablespoon of vegetable mixture on to the dough and seal the edges of the dough with water. Place inside the air fryer basket and cook for 20 minutes or until the dough is crispy.

462. Crispy Butternut Squash Fries

INGREDIENTS for Servings: 4

1 cup all-purpose flour Salt and ground black pepper, to taste 3 tablespoons nutritional yeast flakes 1/2 cup almond milk 1/2 cup almond meal	1/2 cup bread crumbs 1 tablespoon herbs (oregano, basil, rosemary, chopped) 1 pound butternut squash, peeled and cut into French fry shapes

DIRECTIONS and Cooking Time: 25 Minutes

In a shallow bowl, combine the flour, salt, and black pepper. In another shallow dish, mix the nutritional yeast flakes with the almond milk until well combined. Mix the almond meal, breadcrumbs, and herbs in a third shallow dish. Dredge the butternut squash in the flour mixture, shaking off the excess. Then, dip in the milk mixture; lastly, dredge in the breadcrumb mixture. Spritz the butternut squash fries with cooking oil on all sides. Cook in the preheated Air Fryer at 400 degrees F approximately 12 minutes, turning them over halfway through the cooking time. Serve with your favorite sauce for dipping. Bon appétit!

463. Elegant Garlic Mushroom

INGREDIENTS for Servings: 3

2 tbsp vermouth ½ tsp garlic powder 1 tbsp olive oil	2 tsp herbs 1 tbsp duck fat

DIRECTIONS and Cooking Time: 20 Minutes

Preheat your air fryer to 350 F, add duck fat, garlic powder and herbs in a blender, and process. Pour the mixture over the mushrooms and cover with vermouth. Place the mushrooms in the cooking basket and cook for 10 minutes. Top with more vermouth and cook for 5 more minutes.

464. Spiced Soy Curls

INGREDIENTS for Servings: 2

3 cups boiling water 4 ounces soy curls ¼ cup nutritional yeast ¼ cup fine ground cornmeal	2 teaspoons Cajun seasoning 1 teaspoon poultry seasoning Salt and ground white pepper, as required

DIRECTIONS and Cooking Time: 10 Minutes

In a heatproof bowl, add the boiling water and soak the soy curls for about 10 minutes. Through a strainer, drain the soy curls and then with a large spoon, press to release the extra water. In a bowl, mix well nutritional yeast, cornmeal, seasonings, salt, and white pepper. Add the soy curls and generously coat with the mixture. Set the temperature of air fryer to 380 degrees F. Grease an air fryer basket. Arrange soy curls into the prepared air fryer basket in a single layer. Air fry for about 10 minutes, shaking once halfway through. Remove from air fryer and transfer the soy curls onto serving plates. Serve warm.

465. Three Veg Bake

INGREDIENTS for Servings: 3

1 large red onion, cut into rings 1 large zucchini, sliced Salt and pepper to taste	2 cloves garlic, crushed 1 bay leaf, cut in 6 pieces 1 tbsp olive oil Cooking spray

DIRECTIONS and Cooking Time: 30 Minutes

Place the turnips, onion, and zucchini in a bowl. Toss with olive oil and season with salt and pepper. Preheat the air fryer to 330 F, and place the veggies into a baking pan that fits in the air fryer. Slip the bay leaves in the different parts of the slices and tuck the garlic cloves in between the slices. Insert the pan in the air fryer's basket and cook for 15 minutes. Serve warm with salad.

466. Cheesy Vegetable Quesadilla

INGREDIENTS for Servings: 1

¼ cup shredded gouda cheese ¼ yellow bell pepper, sliced ¼ zucchini, sliced	½ green onion, sliced 1 tbsp cilantro, chopped 1 tsp olive oil

DIRECTIONS and Cooking Time: 15 Minutes

Preheat the Air fryer to 390 F. Grease the air fryer basket with cooking spray. Place a flour tortilla in the air fryer basket and top with gouda cheese, bell pepper, zucchini, cilantro, and green onion. Cover with the other tortilla and brush with olive oil. Cook for 10 minutes until lightly browned. When ready, cut into 4 wedges to serve.

467. Cheesy Spinach

INGREDIENTS for Servings: 3

1 (10-ounces) package frozen spinach, thawed 2 teaspoons garlic,	½ cup onion, chopped ½ teaspoon ground nutmeg Salt and ground black

| minced | pepper, as required |
| 4 ounces cream cheese, chopped | ¼ cup Parmesan cheese, shredded |

DIRECTIONS and Cooking Time: 15 Minutes
In a bowl, mix well spinach, onion, garlic, cream cheese, nutmeg, salt, and black pepper.   Set the temperature of air fryer to 350 degrees F. Grease an air fryer pan.   Place spinach mixture into the prepared air fryer pan.   Air fry for about 10 minutes. Remove from air fryer and stir the mixture well. Sprinkle the spinach mixture evenly with Parmesan cheese.   Now, set the temperature of air fryer to 400 degrees F and air fry for 5 more minutes.   Remove from air fryer and transfer the spinach mixture onto serving plates.   Serve hot.

468.   Ultra-crispy Tofu

INGREDIENTS for Servings: 4

1 teaspoon chicken bouillon granules	1 teaspoon butter
12-ounce extra-firm tofu, drained and cubed into 1-inch size	2 tablespoons low-sodium soy sauce
	2 tablespoons fish sauce
	1 teaspoon sesame oil

DIRECTIONS and Cooking Time: 30 Minutes
Preheat the Air fryer to 355F and grease an Air fryer basket.   Mix soy sauce, fish sauce, sesame oil and chicken granules in a bowl and toss to coat well.   Stir in the tofu cubes and mix until well combined.   Keep aside to marinate for about 30 minutes and then transfer into Air fryer basket.   Cook for about 30 minutes, flipping every 10 minutes and serve hot.

469.   Loaded Brekky Hash Browns

INGREDIENTS for Servings: 4

3 russet potatoes, peeled and grated	1 teaspoon olive oil
2 garlic cloves chopped	1/4 cup chopped green peppers
1 teaspoon paprika	1/4 cup chopped red peppers
salt and pepper to taste	1/4 cup chopped onions
1 teaspoon canola oil	

DIRECTIONS and Cooking Time: 20 Minutes
For 20 minutes, soak the grated potatoes in a bowl of cold water to make it crunchy and remove the starch. Then drain well and completely dry with paper towels. Lightly grease baking pan of air fryer with cooking spray.   Add grated potatoes in air fryer. Season with garlic, paprika, salt, and pepper. Add canola and olive oil. Toss well to coat.   For 10 minutes, cook on 390F. Remove basket and toss the mixture a bit. Stir in green and red peppers, and onions.   Cook for another 10 minutes.   Serve and enjoy.

470.   Eggplant Caviar

INGREDIENTS for Servings: 3

| ½ red onion, chopped and blended | 2 tbsp balsamic vinegar |
| 1 tbsp olive oil | salt |

DIRECTIONS and Cooking Time: 20 Minutes
Arrange the eggplants in the basket and cook them for 15 minutes at 380 F. Remove them and let them cool. Then cut the eggplants in half, lengthwise, and empty their insides with a spoon.   Blend the onion in a blender. Put the inside of the eggplants in the blender and process everything. Add the vinegar, olive oil and salt, then blend again. Serve cool with bread and tomato sauce or ketchup.

471.   Garden Fresh Veggie Medley

INGREDIENTS for Servings: 4

2 yellow bell peppers seeded and chopped	2 tablespoons herbs de Provence
1 eggplant, chopped	1 tablespoon olive oil
1 zucchini, chopped	1 tablespoon balsamic vinegar
3 tomatoes, chopped	Salt and black pepper, to taste
2 small onions, chopped	
2 garlic cloves, minced	

DIRECTIONS and Cooking Time: 15 Minutes
Preheat the Air fryer to 355F and grease an Air fryer basket.   Mix all the ingredients in a bowl and toss to coat well.   Transfer into the Air fryer basket and cook for about 15 minutes.   Keep in the Air fryer for about 5 minutes and dish out to serve hot.

472.   Easy Glazed Carrots

INGREDIENTS for Servings: 4

3 cups carrots, peeled and cut into large chunks	1 tablespoon olive oil
	Salt and black pepper, to taste
1 tablespoon honey	

DIRECTIONS and Cooking Time: 12 Minutes
Preheat the Air fryer to 390F and grease an Air fryer basket.   Mix all the ingredients in a bowl and toss to coat well.   Transfer into the Air fryer basket and cook for about 12 minutes.   Dish out and serve hot.

473.   Avocado Rolls

INGREDIENTS for Servings: 5

10 egg roll wrappers	¼ tsp pepper
1 tomato, diced	½ tsp salt

DIRECTIONS and Cooking Time: 15 Minutes
Place all filling ingredients in a bowl; mash with a fork until somewhat smooth. There should be chunks left. Divide the feeling between the egg wrappers. Wet your finger and brush along the edges, so the wrappers can seal well. Roll and seal the wrappers. Arrange them on a baking sheet lined dish, and place in the air fryer. Cook at 350 F for 5 minutes. Serve with sweet chili dipping and enjoy.

474. Eggplant Steaks With Garlic & Parsley

INGREDIENTS for Servings: 4

2 cups breadcrumbs	4 eggs
1 tsp Italian seasoning	2 garlic cloves, sliced
1 cup flour	2 tbsp parsley,
Salt to taste	chopped

DIRECTIONS and Cooking Time: 20 Minutes
Preheat the Air fryer to 390 F. Grease the air fryer basket with cooking spray. In a bowl, beat the eggs with salt. In a separate bowl, mix breadcrumbs and Italian seasoning. In a third bowl, pour the flour. Dip eggplant steaks in the flour, followed by a dip in the eggs, and finally, coat with breadcrumbs. Place the prepared steaks in your air fryer's cooking basket and cook for 10 minutes, flipping once. Remove to a platter and sprinkle with garlic and parsley to serve.

475. Italian Seasoned Easy Pasta Chips

INGREDIENTS for Servings: 2

½ teaspoon salt	1 tablespoon olive oil
1 ½ teaspoon Italian seasoning blend	2 cups whole wheat bowtie pasta
1 tablespoon nutritional yeast	

DIRECTIONS and Cooking Time: 10 Minutes
Place the baking dish accessory in the air fryer. Give a good stir. Close the air fryer and cook for 10 minutes at 390F.

476. Hearty Celery Croquettes With Chive Mayo

INGREDIENTS for Servings: 4

2 medium-sized celery stalks, trimmed and grated	1 egg, lightly whisked
	1/4 cup almond flour
	1/2 cup parmesan
1/2 cup of leek, finely	cheese, freshly grated

chopped	1/4 teaspoon baking
1 tablespoon garlic paste	powder
	2 tablespoons fresh
1/4 teaspoon freshly cracked black pepper	chives, chopped
	4 tablespoons
1 teaspoon fine sea salt	mayonnaise
1 tablespoon fresh dill, finely chopped	

DIRECTIONS and Cooking Time: 15 Minutes
Place the celery on a paper towel and squeeze them to remove excess liquid. Combine the vegetables with the other ingredients, except the chives and mayo. Shape the balls using 1 tablespoon of the vegetable mixture. Then, gently flatten each ball with your palm or a wide spatula. Spritz the croquettes with a non - stick cooking oil. Air-fry the vegetable croquettes in a single layer for 6 minutes at 360 degrees F. Meanwhile, mix fresh chives and mayonnaise. Serve warm croquettes with chive mayo. Bon appétit!

477. Crispy Marinated Tofu

INGREDIENTS for Servings: 3

1 (14-ounces) block firm tofu, pressed and cut into 1-inch cubes	2 teaspoons sesame oil, toasted
	1 teaspoon seasoned rice vinegar
2 tablespoons low sodium soy sauce	1 tablespoon cornstarch

DIRECTIONS and Cooking Time: 20 Minutes
In a bowl, mix well tofu, soy sauce, sesame oil, and vinegar. Set aside to marinate for about 25-30 minutes. Coat the tofu cubes evenly with cornstarch. Set the temperature of air fryer to 370 degrees F. Grease an air fryer basket. Arrange tofu pieces into the prepared air fryer basket in a single layer. Air fry for about 20 minutes, shaking once halfway through. Remove from air fryer and transfer the tofu onto serving plates. Serve warm.

478. Buttered Carrot-zucchini With Mayo

INGREDIENTS for Servings: 4

1 tablespoon grated onion	1/4 cup mayonnaise
	1/4 teaspoon
2 tablespoons butter, melted	prepared horseradish
	1/4 teaspoon salt
1/2-pound carrots, sliced	1/4 teaspoon ground black pepper
1-1/2 zucchinis, sliced	1/4 cup Italian bread
1/4 cup water	crumbs

DIRECTIONS and Cooking Time: 25 Minutes

Lightly grease baking pan of air fryer with cooking spray. Add carrots. For 8 minutes, cook on 360F. Add zucchini and continue cooking for another 5 minutes. Meanwhile, in a bowl whisk well pepper, salt, horseradish, onion, mayonnaise, and water. Pour into pan of veggies. Toss well to coat. In a small bowl mix melted butter and bread crumbs. Sprinkle over veggies. Cook for 10 minutes at 390F until tops are lightly browned. Serve and enjoy.

479.   Garlic 'n Basil Crackers

INGREDIENTS for Servings: 6

¼ teaspoon dried basil powder	3 tablespoons coconut oil
½ teaspoon baking powder	A pinch of cayenne pepper powder
1 ¼ cups almond flour	Salt and pepper to taste
1 clove of garlic, minced	

DIRECTIONS and Cooking Time: 15 Minutes
Preheat the air fryer for 5 minutes. Mix everything in a mixing bowl to create a dough. Transfer the dough on a clean and flat working surface and spread out until 2mm thick. Cut into squares. Place gently in the air fryer basket. Do this in batches if possible. Cook for 15 minutes at 325F.

480.   Herby Zucchini 'n Eggplant Bake

INGREDIENTS for Servings: 4

½ lemon, juiced	2 red onions, chopped
1 fennel bulb, sliced crosswise	2 teaspoons herb de Provence
1 sprig flat-leaf parsley	3 large zucchinis, sliced crosswise
1 sprig mint	4 cloves of garlic, minced
1 sprig of basil	4 large tomatoes, chopped
1 tablespoon coriander powder	5 tablespoons olive oil
1 teaspoon capers	salt and pepper to taste
2 eggplants, sliced crosswise	
2 red peppers, sliced crosswise	

DIRECTIONS and Cooking Time: 25 Minutes
In a blender, combine basil, parsley, mint, coriander, capers and lemon juice. Season with salt and pepper to taste. Pulse until well combined. Preheat the air fryer to 400F. Toss the eggplant, onions, garlic, peppers, fennel, and zucchini with olive oil. In a baking dish that can fit in the air fryer, arrange the vegetables and pour over the tomatoes and the herb puree. Season with more salt and pepper and sprinkle with herbs de Provence. Place inside the air fryer and cook for 25 minutes.

481.   Authentic Churros With Hot Chocolate

INGREDIENTS for Servings: 3

1/2 cup water	2 ounces dark chocolate
2 tablespoons granulated sugar	1 cup milk
1/4 teaspoon sea salt	1 tablespoon cornstarch
1 teaspoon lemon zest	1/3 cup sugar
1 tablespoon canola oil	1 teaspoon ground cinnamon
1 cup all-purpose flour	

DIRECTIONS and Cooking Time: 25 Minutes
To make the churro dough, boil the water in a pan over medium-high heat; now, add the sugar, salt and lemon zest; cook until dissolved. Add the canola oil and remove the pan from the heat. Gradually stir in the flour, whisking continuously until the mixture forms a ball. Pour the mixture into a piping bag with a large star tip. Squeeze 4-inch strips of dough into the greased Air Fryer pan. Cook at 410 degrees F for 6 minutes. Meanwhile, prepare the hot chocolate for dipping. Melt the chocolate and 1/2 cup of milk in a pan over low heat. Dissolve the cornstarch in the remaining 1/2 cup of milk; stir into the hot chocolate mixture. Cook on low heat approximately 5 minutes. Mix the sugar and cinnamon; roll the churros in this mixture. Serve with the hot chocolate on the side. Enjoy!

482.   Sweet And Spicy Parsnips

INGREDIENTS for Servings: 6

2 pounds parsnip, peeled and cut into 1-inch chunks	1 tablespoon butter, melted
2 tablespoons honey	¼ teaspoon red pepper flakes, crushed
1 tablespoon dried parsley flakes, crushed	Salt and ground black pepper, to taste

DIRECTIONS and Cooking Time: 44 Minutes
Preheat the Air fryer to 355F and grease an Air fryer basket. Mix the parsnips and butter in a bowl and toss to coat well. Arrange the parsnip chunks in the Air fryer basket and cook for about 40 minutes. Mix the remaining ingredients in another large bowl and stir in the parsnip chunks. Transfer the parsnip chunks in the Air fryer basket and cook for about 4 minutes. Dish out the parsnip chunks onto serving plates and serve hot.

483. Roasted Brussels Sprouts

INGREDIENTS for Servings: 4

½ tsp garlic, chopped	Salt and black pepper
2 tbsp olive oil	to taste

DIRECTIONS and Cooking Time: 25 Minutes
Wash the Brussels sprouts thoroughly under cold water and trim off the outer leaves, keeping only the head of the sprouts. In a bowl, mix oil, garlic, salt, and pepper. Add sprouts to this mixture and let rest for 5 minutes. Place the coated sprouts in your air fryer's cooking basket and cook for 15 minutes.

484. Parmesan Asparagus

INGREDIENTS for Servings: 3

1 pound fresh asparagus, trimmed	1 teaspoon garlic powder
1 tablespoon Parmesan cheese, grated	Salt and black pepper, to taste
1 tablespoon butter, melted	

DIRECTIONS and Cooking Time: 10 Minutes
Preheat the Air fryer to 400F and grease an Air fryer basket. Mix the asparagus, cheese, butter, garlic powder, salt, and black pepper in a bowl and toss to coat well. Arrange the asparagus into the Air fryer basket and cook for about 10 minutes. Dish out in a serving plate and serve hot.

485. Bell Pepper-corn Wrapped In Tortilla

INGREDIENTS for Servings: 4

1 small red bell pepper, chopped	4 large tortillas
1 small yellow onion, diced	4 pieces commercial vegan nuggets, chopped
1 tablespoon water	mixed greens for garnish
2 cobs grilled corn kernels	

DIRECTIONS and Cooking Time: 15 Minutes
Preheat the air fryer to 400F. In a skillet heated over medium heat, water sauté the vegan nuggets together with the onions, bell peppers, and corn kernels. Set aside. Place filling inside the corn tortillas. Fold the tortillas and place inside the air fryer and cook for 15 minutes until the tortilla wraps are crispy. Serve with mix greens on top.

486. Veggie Fajitas With Simple Guacamole

INGREDIENTS for Servings: 4

1 tablespoon canola oil	1 tablespoon yellow mustard
1/2 cup scallions, thinly sliced	1/2 teaspoon Mexican oregano
2 bell peppers, seeded and sliced into strips	1 medium ripe avocado, peeled, pitted and mashed
1 habanero pepper, seeded and minced	1 tablespoon fresh lemon juice
1 garlic clove, minced	1/2 teaspoon onion powder
4 large Portobello mushrooms, thinly sliced	1/2 teaspoon garlic powder
1/4 cup salsa	1 teaspoon red pepper flakes
Kosher salt and ground black pepper, to taste	4 (8-inch) flour tortillas

DIRECTIONS and Cooking Time: 25 Minutes
Brush the sides and bottom of the cooking basket with canola oil. Add the scallions and cook for 1 to 2 minutes or until aromatic. Then, add the peppers, garlic, and mushrooms to the cooking basket. Cook for 2 to 3 minutes or until tender. Stir in the salsa, mustard, salt, black pepper, and oregano. Cook in the preheated Air Fryer at 380 degrees F for 15 minutes, stirring occasionally. In the meantime, make your guacamole by mixing mashed avocado together with the lemon juice, garlic powder, onion powder, and red pepper flakes. Divide between the tortillas and garnish with guacamole. Roll up your tortillas and enjoy!

487. Thai Zucchini Balls

INGREDIENTS for Servings: 4

1 pound zucchini, grated	1/4 teaspoon ground cloves
1 tablespoon orange juice	1/2 cup almond meal
1/2 teaspoon ground cinnamon	1 teaspoon baking powder
	1 cup coconut flakes

DIRECTIONS and Cooking Time: 30 Minutes
In a mixing bowl, thoroughly combine all ingredients, except for coconut flakes. Roll the balls in the coconut flakes. Bake in the preheated Air Fryer at 360 degrees F for 15 minutes or until thoroughly cooked and crispy. Repeat the process until you run out of ingredients. Bon appétit!

488. Spices Stuffed Eggplants

INGREDIENTS for Servings: 4

8 baby eggplants	½ teaspoon ground cumin
4 teaspoons olive oil, divided	½ teaspoon ground turmeric
¾ tablespoon dry mango powder	½ teaspoon garlic powder
¾ tablespoon ground coriander	Salt, to taste

DIRECTIONS and Cooking Time: 12 Minutes

Preheat the Air fryer to 370F and grease an Air fryer basket. Make 2 slits from the bottom of each eggplant leaving the stems intact. Mix one teaspoon of oil and spices in a bowl and fill each slit of eggplants with this mixture. Brush the outer side of each eggplant with remaining oil and arrange in the Air fryer basket. Cook for about 12 minutes and dish out in a serving plate to serve hot.

DESSERTS RECIPES

489.   Avocado Walnut Bread

INGREDIENTS for Servings: 6

¾ cup (3 oz.) almond flour, white	1 teaspoon cinnamon ground
¼ teaspoon baking soda	½ teaspoon kosher salt
2 ripe avocados, cored, peeled and mashed	2 tablespoons vegetable oil
2 large eggs, beaten	½ cup granulated swerve
2 tablespoons (3/4 oz.) Toasted walnuts, chopped roughly	1 teaspoon vanilla extract

DIRECTIONS and Cooking Time: 35 Minutes
Preheat the Air fryer to 310F and line a 6-inch baking pan with parchment paper.   Mix almond flour, salt, baking soda, and cinnamon in a bowl.   Whisk eggs with avocado mash, yogurt, swerve, oil, and vanilla in a bowl.   Stir in the almond flour mixture and mix until well combined.   Pour the batter evenly into the pan and top with the walnuts.   Place the baking pan into the Air fryer basket and cook for about 35 minutes.   Dish out in a platter and cut into slices to serve.

490.   Quick Blueberry Muffins

INGREDIENTS for Servings: 2

1 egg	2/3 cup almond flour
1 tsp baking powder	2 tbsp erythritol
3 tbsp butter, melted	1/3 cup unsweetened almond milk
¾ cup blueberries	

DIRECTIONS and Cooking Time: 14 Minutes
Spray silicone muffins molds with cooking spray and set aside.   Add all ingredients into the bowl and mix until well combined.   Pour batter into the prepared molds and place into the air fryer basket.   Cook at 320 F for 14 minutes.   Serve and enjoy.

491.   Chocolate Molten Lava Cake

INGREDIENTS for Servings: 4

3 ½ oz. butter, melted	3 ½ tbsp. sugar
3 ½ oz. chocolate, melted	1 ½ tbsp. flour
	2 eggs

DIRECTIONS and Cooking Time: 25 Minutes
Pre-heat the Air Fryer to 375°F.   Grease four ramekins with a little butter.   Rigorously combine the eggs and butter before stirring in the melted chocolate.   Slowly fold in the flour.   Spoon an equal amount of the mixture into each ramekin.   Put them in the Air Fryer and cook for 10 minutes   Place the ramekins upside-down on plates and let the cakes fall out. Serve hot.

492.   Double Chocolate Whiskey Brownies

INGREDIENTS for Servings: 10

3 tablespoons whiskey	1/2 cup coconut oil
8 ounces white chocolate	3/4 cup monk fruit
3/4 cup almond flour	2 tablespoons cocoa powder, unsweetened
1/4 cup coconut flakes	1/4 teaspoon ground cardamom
2 eggs plus an egg yolk, whisked	1 teaspoon pure rum extract

DIRECTIONS and Cooking Time: 55 Minutes
Microwave white chocolate and coconut oil until everything's melted; allow the mixture to cool at room temperature.   After that, thoroughly whisk the eggs, monk fruit, rum extract, cocoa powder and cardamom.   Next step, add the rum/egg mixture to the chocolate mixture. Stir in the flour and coconut flakes; mix to combine.   Mix cranberries with whiskey and let them soak for 15 minutes. Fold them into the batter. Press the batter into a lightly buttered cake pan.   Air-fry for 35 minutes at 340 degrees F. Allow them to cool slightly on a wire rack before slicing and serving.

493.   Blackberries Cake

INGREDIENTS for Servings: 4

2 eggs, whisked	¼ cup almond milk
4 tablespoons swerve	½ teaspoon baking powder
2 tablespoons ghee, melted	
1 and ½ cups almond flour	1 teaspoon lemon zest, grated
1 cup blackberries, chopped	1 teaspoon lemon juice

DIRECTIONS and Cooking Time: 25 Minutes
In a bowl, mix all the ingredients and whisk well. Pour this into a cake pan that fits the air fryer lined with parchment paper, put the pan in your air fryer and cook at 340 degrees F for 25 minutes. Cool the cake down, slice and serve.

494.   Air Fryer Chocolate Cake

INGREDIENTS for Servings: 6

3 eggs	1½ teaspoons baking
1 cup almond flour	powder
1 stick butter, room	½ cup sour cream
temperature	2/3 cup swerve
1/3 cup cocoa powder	2 teaspoons vanilla

DIRECTIONS and Cooking Time: 25 Minutes
Preheat the Air fryer to 360F and grease a cake pan lightly. Mix all the ingredients in a bowl and beat well. Pour the batter in the cake pan and transfer into the Air fryer basket. Cook for about 25 minutes and cut into slices to serve.

495.   Baked Pears With Chocolate

INGREDIENTS for Servings: 4

1/3 cup turbinado	4 firm ripe pears,
sugar	peeled, cored and
1/2 teaspoon ground	sliced
anise star	1/2 stick butter, cold
1 teaspoon pure	1/2 cup chocolate
vanilla extract	chips, for garnish
1 teaspoon pure	
orange extract	

DIRECTIONS and Cooking Time: 45 Minutes
Grease the baking dish with a pan spray; lay the pear slices on the bottom of the prepared dish. In a mixing dish, combine the sugar, anise star, vanilla, and orange extract. Then, sprinkle this mixture over the fruit layer. Cut in butter and scatter evenly over the top of the pear layer. Air-fryer at 380 degrees F for 35 minutes. Serve sprinkled with chocolate chips. Enjoy!

496.   Chocolate Lover's Muffins

INGREDIENTS for Servings: 8

1½ cups all-purpose	1 cup yogurt
flour	¼ cup sugar
2 teaspoons baking	Salt, to taste
powder	1/3 cup vegetable oil
1 egg	2 teaspoons vanilla
½ cup mini chocolate	extract
chips	

DIRECTIONS and Cooking Time: 10 Minutes
Preheat the Air fryer to 355F and grease 8 muffin cups lightly. Mix flour, baking powder, sugar and salt in a bowl. Whisk egg, oil, yogurt and vanilla extract in another bowl. Combine the flour and egg mixtures and mix until a smooth mixture is formed. Fold in the chocolate chips and divide this mixture into the prepared muffin cups. Transfer into the Air fryer basket and cook for about 10 minutes. Refrigerate for 2 hours and serve chilled.

497.   Heavenly Tasty Lava Cake

INGREDIENTS for Servings: 6

2/3 cup unsalted	2 eggs
butter	1/3 cup fresh
2/3 cup all-purpose	raspberries
flour	5 tablespoons sugar
1 cup chocolate chips,	Salt, to taste
melted	

DIRECTIONS and Cooking Time: 3 Minutes
Preheat the Air fryer to 355F and grease 6 ramekins lightly. Mix sugar, butter, eggs, chocolate mixture, flour and salt in a bowl until well combined. Fold in the melted chocolate chips and divide this mixture into the prepared ramekins. Transfer into the Air fryer basket and cook for about 3 minutes. Garnish with raspberries and serve immediately.

498.   Banana Walnut Bread

INGREDIENTS for Servings: 1 Loaf

7 oz. flour	14 oz. bananas, peeled
¼ tsp. baking powder	2.8 oz. chopped
2.5 oz. butter	walnuts
5.5 oz. sugar	
2 medium eggs	

DIRECTIONS and Cooking Time: 40 Minutes
Pre-heat the Air Fryer to 350°F. Take a baking tin small enough to fit inside the Air Fryer and grease the inside with butter. Mix together the flour and the baking powder in a bowl. In a separate bowl, beat together the sugar and butter until fluffy and pale. Gradually add in the flour and egg. Stir. Throw in the walnuts and combine again. Mash the bananas using a fork and transfer to the bowl. Mix once more, until everything is incorporated. Pour the mixture into the tin, place inside the fryer and cook for 10 minutes.

499.   Chocolate Brownie

INGREDIENTS for Servings: 4

1 cup bananas,	2 tbsp unsweetened
overripe	cocoa powder
1 scoop protein	1/2 cup almond
powder	butter, melted

DIRECTIONS and Cooking Time: 16 Minutes
Preheat the air fryer to 325 F. Spray air fryer baking pan with cooking spray. Add all ingredients into the blender and blend until smooth. Pour batter into the prepared pan and place in the air fryer basket. Cook brownie for 16 minutes. Serve and enjoy.

500.   Boozy Baileys Fudge Brownies

INGREDIENTS for Servings: 8

1 cup granulated swerve	2 eggs room temperature
2 tablespoons unsweetened cocoa powder, sifted	1 teaspoon vanilla
	2 tablespoons Baileys
1/2 cup almond flour	2 ounces unsweetened chocolate chips
1/2 cup coconut flour	1/2 cup sour cream
1/4 teaspoon salt	1/3 cup powdered erythritol
1/4 teaspoon baking powder	
1/2 cup butter, melted then cooled	3 ounces Ricotta cheese, room temperature

DIRECTIONS and Cooking Time: 35 Minutes
In a mixing bowl, thoroughly combine granulated swerve, cocoa powder, flour, salt, and baking powder. Mix in butter, eggs, and vanilla. Add the batter to a lightly-greased baking pan.   Air-fry for 25 minutes at 355 degrees F. Allow them to cool slightly on a wire rack.   Microwave the chocolate chips until everything's melted; allow the mixture to cool at room temperature.   After that, add Ricotta cheese, Baileys, sour cream, and powdered erythritol; mix until everything is blended.   Spread this mixture onto the top of your brownie. Serve well chilled.

501.   Cinnamon Fried Plums

INGREDIENTS for Servings: 6

6 plums, cut into wedges	½ teaspoon cinnamon powder
1 teaspoon ginger, ground	Zest of 1 lemon, grated
2 tablespoons water	10 drops stevia

DIRECTIONS and Cooking Time: 20 Minutes
In a pan that fits the air fryer, combine the plums with the rest of the ingredients, toss gently, put the pan in the air fryer and cook at 360 degrees F for 20 minutes. Serve cold.

502.   Crispy Banana Split

INGREDIENTS for Servings: 8

3 tablespoons coconut oil	2 eggs
1 cup panko breadcrumbs	3 tablespoons sugar
½ cup corn flour	¼ teaspoon ground cinnamon
4 bananas, peeled and halved lengthwise	2 tablespoons walnuts, chopped

DIRECTIONS and Cooking Time: 14 Minutes

In a medium skillet, heat the oil over medium heat and cook breadcrumbs for about 3-4 minutes or until golden browned and crumbled, stirring continuously. Transfer the breadcrumbs into a shallow bowl and set aside to cool.   In a second bowl, place the corn flour. In a third bowl, whisk the eggs.   Coat the banana slices with flour and then, dip into eggs and finally, coat evenly with the breadcrumbs.   In a small bowl, mix together the sugar and cinnamon   Set the temperature of air fryer to 280 degrees F. Grease an air fryer basket.   Arrange banana slices into the prepared air fryer basket in a single layer and sprinkle with cinnamon sugar   Air fry for about 10 minutes. Remove from air fryer and transfer the banana slices onto plates to cool slightly   Sprinkle with chopped walnuts and serve.

503.   Cinnamon And Sugar Sweet Potato Fries

INGREDIENTS for Servings: 2

1 large sweet potato, peeled and sliced into sticks	1/4 teaspoon ground cardamom
	1/4 cup sugar
1 teaspoon ghee	1 tablespoon ground cinnamon
1 tablespoon cornstarch	

DIRECTIONS and Cooking Time: 30 Minutes
Toss the sweet potato sticks with the melted ghee and cornstarch.   Cook in the preheated Air Fryer at 380 degrees F for 20 minutes, shaking the basket halfway through the cooking time.   Sprinkle the cardamom, sugar, and cinnamon all over the sweet potato fries and serve. Bon appétit!

504.   Seeds And Almond Cookies

INGREDIENTS for Servings: 6

1 teaspoon chia seeds	2 tablespoons Splenda
1 teaspoon sesame seeds	1 tablespoon butter
1 tablespoon pumpkin seeds, crushed	4 tablespoons almond flour
	¼ teaspoon ground cloves
1 egg, beaten	
1 teaspoon vanilla extract	1 teaspoon avocado oil

DIRECTIONS and Cooking Time: 9 Minutes
Put the chia seeds, sesame seeds, and pumpkin seeds in the bowl. Add egg, Splenda, vanilla extract, butter, avocado oil, and ground cloves. Then add almond flour and mix up the mixture until homogenous. Preheat the air fryer to 375F. Line the air fryer basket with baking paper. With the help of the scooper make the cookies and flatten them gently. Place the cookies in the air fryer. Arrange them in one layer. Cook the seeds cookies for 9 minutes.

505.   Grape Stew

INGREDIENTS for Servings: 4

Juice and zest of 1 lemon	1 pound red grapes
	26 ounces grape juice

DIRECTIONS and Cooking Time: 14 Minutes
In a pan that fits your air fryer, add all ingredients and toss.   Place the pan in the fryer and cook at 320 degrees F for 14 minutes.   Divide into cups, refrigerate, and serve cold.

506.   Easy Spanish Churros

INGREDIENTS for Servings: 4

3/4 cup water	1/4 teaspoon ground cloves
1 tablespoon swerve	
1/4 teaspoon sea salt	6 tablespoons butter
1/4 teaspoon grated nutmeg	3/4 cup almond flour
	2 eggs

DIRECTIONS and Cooking Time: 20 Minutes
To make the dough, boil the water in a pan over medium-high heat; now, add the swerve, salt, nutmeg, and cloves; cook until dissolved.   Add the butter and turn the heat to low. Gradually stir in the almond flour, whisking continuously, until the mixture forms a ball. Remove from the heat; fold in the eggs one at a time, stirring to combine well.   Pour the mixture into a piping bag with a large star tip. Squeeze 4-inch strips of dough into the greased Air Fryer pan.   Cook at 410 degrees F for 6 minutes, working in batches. Bon appétit!

507.   Strawberry Pop Tarts

INGREDIENTS for Servings: 6

1 oz reduced-fat Philadelphia cream cheese	1 tsp sugar sprinkles
	1/3 cup low-sugar strawberry preserves
1 tsp cornstarch	2 refrigerated pie crusts
1 tsp stevia	
1/2 cup plain, non-fat vanilla Greek yogurt	olive oil or coconut oil spray

DIRECTIONS and Cooking Time: 25 Minutes
Cut pie crusts into 6 equal rectangles.   In a bowl, mix cornstarch and preserves. Add preserves in middle of crust. Fold over crust. Crimp edges with fork to seal. Repeat process for remaining crusts.   Lightly grease baking pan of air fryer with cooking spray. Add pop tarts in single layer. Cook in batches for 8 minutes at 370F.   Meanwhile, make the frosting by mixing stevia, cream cheese, and yogurt in a bowl. Spread on top of cooked pop tart and add sugar sprinkles. Serve and enjoy.

508.   Favorite New York Cheesecake

INGREDIENTS for Servings: 8

1 ½ cups digestive biscuits crumbs	1/2 cup heavy cream
2 ounces white sugar	1 ¼ cups caster sugar
1 ounce demerara sugar	3 eggs, at room temperature
1/2 stick butter, melted	1 tablespoon vanilla essence
32 ounces full-fat cream cheese	1 teaspoon grated lemon zest

DIRECTIONS and Cooking Time: 40 Minutes + Chilling Time
Coat the sides and bottom of a baking pan with a little flour.   In a mixing bowl, combine the digestive biscuits, white sugar, and demerara sugar. Add the melted butter and mix until your mixture looks like breadcrumbs.   Press the mixture into the bottom of the prepared pan to form an even layer. Bake at 330 degrees F for 7 minutes until golden brown. Allow it to cool completely on a wire rack.   Meanwhile, in a mixer fitted with the paddle attachment, prepare the filling by mixing the soft cheese, heavy cream, and caster sugar; beat until creamy and fluffy.   Crack the eggs into the mixing bowl, one at a time; add the vanilla and lemon zest and continue to mix until fully combined.   Pour the prepared topping over the cooled crust and spread evenly.   Bake in the preheated Air Fryer at 330 degrees F for 25 to 30 minutes; leave it in the Air Fryer to keep warm for another 30 minutes.   Cover your cheesecake with plastic wrap. Place in your refrigerator and allow it to cool at least 6 hours or overnight. Serve well chilled.

509.   Espresso Cinnamon Cookies

INGREDIENTS for Servings: 12

8 tablespoons ghee, melted	½ tablespoon cinnamon powder
1 cup almond flour	2 teaspoons baking powder
¼ cup brewed espresso	2 eggs, whisked
¼ cup swerve	

DIRECTIONS and Cooking Time: 15 Minutes
In a bowl, mix all the ingredients and whisk well. Spread medium balls on a cookie sheet lined parchment paper, flatten them, put the cookie sheet in your air fryer and cook at 350 degrees F for 15 minutes. Serve the cookies cold.

510.   Mixed Berry Puffed Pastry

INGREDIENTS for Servings: 3

3 pastry dough sheets ½ cup mixed berries, mashed 1 tbsp. honey 2 tbsp. cream cheese	3 tbsp. chopped walnuts ¼ tsp. vanilla extract

DIRECTIONS and Cooking Time: 20 Minutes
Pre-heat your Air Fryer to 375°F. Roll out the pastry sheets and spread the cream cheese over each one. In a bowl, combine the berries, vanilla extract and honey. Cover a baking sheet with parchment paper. Spoon equal amounts of the berry mixture into the center of each sheet of pastry. Scatter the chopped walnuts on top. Fold up the pastry around the filling and press down the edges with the back of a fork to seal them. Transfer the baking sheet to the Air Fryer and cook for approximately 15 minutes.

511.   Roasted Pumpkin Seeds & Cinnamon

INGREDIENTS for Servings: 2

1 cup pumpkin raw seeds 1 tbsp. ground cinnamon	2 tbsp. sugar 1 cup water 1 tbsp. olive oil

DIRECTIONS and Cooking Time: 35 Minutes
In a frying pan, combine the pumpkin seeds, cinnamon and water. Boil the mixture over a high heat for 2 - 3 minutes. Pour out the water and place the seeds on a clean kitchen towel, allowing them to dry for 20 - 30 minutes. In a bowl, mix together the sugar, dried seeds, a pinch of cinnamon and one tablespoon of olive oil. Pre-heat the Air Fryer to 340°F. Place the seed mixture in the fryer basket and allow to cook for 15 minutes, shaking the basket periodically throughout.

512.   Berry Cobbler

INGREDIENTS for Servings: 6

1 egg, lightly beaten 1 tbsp butter, melted 2 tsp swerve ½ tsp vanilla 1 cup almond flour	½ cup raspberries, sliced ½ cup strawberries, sliced

DIRECTIONS and Cooking Time: 10 Minutes
Preheat the air fryer to 360 F. Add sliced strawberries and raspberries into the air fryer baking dish. Sprinkle sweetener over berries. Mix together almond flour, vanilla, and butter in the bowl. Add egg in almond flour mixture and stir well to combine. Spread almond flour mixture over sliced berries. Cover dish with foil and place into the air fryer and cook for 10 minutes. Serve and enjoy.

513.   Peppermint Chocolate Cheesecake

INGREDIENTS for Servings: 6

1 cup powdered sugar 1/2 cup all-purpose flour 1/2 cup butter 1 cup mascarpone cheese, at room temperature	4 ounces semisweet chocolate, melted 1 teaspoon vanilla extract 2 drops peppermint extract

DIRECTIONS and Cooking Time: 40 Minutes
Beat the sugar, flour, and butter in a mixing bowl. Press the mixture into the bottom of a lightly greased baking pan. Bake at 350 degrees F for 18 minutes. Place it in your freezer for 20 minutes. Then, make the cheesecake topping by mixing the remaining ingredients. Place this topping over the crust and allow it to cool in your freezer for a further 15 minutes. Serve well chilled.

514.   Old-fashioned Plum Dumplings

INGREDIENTS for Servings: 4

1 (14-ounce) box pie crusts 2 cups plums, pitted 2 tablespoons granulated sugar 2 tablespoons coconut oil	1/4 teaspoon ground cardamom 1/2 teaspoon ground cinnamon 1 egg white, slightly beaten

DIRECTIONS and Cooking Time: 40 Minutes
Place the pie crust on a work surface. Roll into a circle and cut into quarters. Place 1 plum on each crust piece. Add the sugar, coconut oil, cardamom, and cinnamon. Roll up the sides into a circular shape around the plums. Repeat with the remaining ingredients. Brush the edges with the egg white. Place in the lightly greased Air Fryer basket. Bake in the preheated Air Fryer at 360 degrees F for 20 minutes, flipping them halfway through the cooking time. Work in two batches, decorate and serve at room temperature. Bon appétit!

515.   Lemony Cheesecake

INGREDIENTS for Servings: 8

4 oz butter, melted 16 oz plain cream cheese 3 eggs	3 tbsp sugar 1 tbsp vanilla extract Zest of 2 lemons

DIRECTIONS and Cooking Time: 60 Minutes

Line a cake tin, that fits in your air fryer, with baking paper. Mix together the crackers and butter, and press at the bottom of the tin. In a bowl, add cream cheese, eggs, sugar, vanilla and lemon zest and beat with a hand mixer until well combined and smooth. Pour the mixture into the tin, on top of the cracker's base. Cook for 40-45 minutes at 350 F, checking it to ensure it's set but still a bit wobbly. Let cool, then refrigerate overnight.

516.   Hazelnut Brownie Cups

INGREDIENTS for Servings: 12

6 oz. semisweet chocolate chips	¼ cup red wine
1 stick butter, at room temperature	1 tsp. pure vanilla extract
1 cup sugar	¾ cup flour
2 large eggs	2 tbsp. cocoa powder
¼ tsp. hazelnut extract	½ cup ground hazelnuts
	Pinch of kosher salt

DIRECTIONS and Cooking Time: 30 Minutes
Melt the butter and chocolate chips in the microwave. In a large bowl, combine the sugar, eggs, red wine, hazelnut and vanilla extract with a whisk. Pour in the chocolate mix.   Add in the flour, cocoa powder, ground hazelnuts, and a pinch of kosher salt, continuing to stir until a creamy, smooth consistency is achieved.   Take a muffin tin and place a cupcake liner in each cup. Spoon an equal amount of the batter into each one.   Air bake at 360°F for 28 - 30 minutes, cooking in batches if necessary.   Serve with a topping of ganache if desired.

517.   Ninja Pop-tarts

INGREDIENTS for Servings: 6

Pop-tarts:	2 tablespoons swerve
1 cup coconut flour	Lemon Glaze:
1 cup almond flour	1¼ cups powdered swerve
½ cup of ice-cold water	2 tablespoons lemon juice
Pop-tarts:	zest of 1 lemon
¼ teaspoon salt	1 teaspoon coconut oil, melted
2/3 cup very cold coconut oil	¼ teaspoon vanilla extract
½ teaspoon vanilla extract	

DIRECTIONS and Cooking Time: 1 Hour
Pop-tarts: Preheat the Air fryer to 375F and grease an Air fryer basket.   Mix all the flours, swerve, and salt in a bowl and stir in the coconut oil.   Mix well with a fork until an almond meal mixture is formed. Stir in vanilla and 1 tablespoon of cold water and mix until a firm dough is formed.   Cut the dough into two equal pieces and spread in a thin sheet.   Cut each sheet into 12 equal sized rectangles and transfer 4 rectangles in the Air fryer basket.   Cook for about 10 minutes and repeat with the remaining rectangles. Lemon Glaze: Meanwhile, mix all the ingredients for the lemon glaze and pour over the cooked tarts.   Top with sprinkles and serve.

518.   Chocolate And Raspberry Cake

INGREDIENTS for Servings: 8

⅓ cup cocoa powder	1 cup milk
2 tsp baking powder	1 tsp baking soda
¾ cup white sugar	2 eggs
¼ cup brown sugar	1 cup freeze-dried raspberries
⅔ cup butter	1 cup chocolate chips
2 tsp vanilla extract	

DIRECTIONS and Cooking Time: 40 Minutes
Line a cake tin with baking powder. In a bowl, sift flour, cocoa and baking powder. Place the sugars, butter, vanilla, milk and baking soda into a microwave-safe bowl and heat for 60 seconds until the butter melts and the ingredients incorporate; let cool slightly. Whisk the eggs into the mixture.   Pour the wet ingredients into the dry ones, and fold to combine. Add in the raspberries and chocolate chips into the batter. Pour the batter into the tin and cook for 30 minutes at 350 F.

519.   Chocolate Soufflé

INGREDIENTS for Servings: 2

¼ cup butter, melted	3 oz chocolate, melted
2 tbsp flour	½ tsp vanilla extract
3 tbsp sugar	

DIRECTIONS and Cooking Time: 25 Minutes
Preheat the air fryer to 330 F.   Beat the yolks along with the sugar and vanilla extract; stir in butter, chocolate, and flour. and whisk the whites until a stiff peak forms.   Working in batches, gently combine the egg whites with the chocolate mixture. Divide the batter between two greased ramekins. Cook for 14 minutes.

520.   Fruity Oreo Muffins

INGREDIENTS for Servings: 6

1 pack Oreo biscuits, crushed	1 cup milk
¾ teaspoon baking powder	1 teaspoon cocoa powder
1 banana, peeled and chopped	1 teaspoon honey
1 apple, peeled, cored and chopped	1 teaspoon fresh lemon juice
	A pinch of ground cinnamon

DIRECTIONS and Cooking Time: 10 Minutes
Preheat the Air fryer to 320F and grease 6 muffin cups lightly. Mix milk, biscuits, cocoa powder, baking soda, and baking powder in a bowl until well combined. Transfer the mixture into the muffin cups and cook for about 10 minutes. Remove from the Air fryer and invert the muffin cups onto a wire rack to cool. Meanwhile, mix the banana, apple, honey, lemon juice, and cinnamon in another bowl. Scoop some portion of muffins from the center and fill with fruit mixture to serve.

521. Apple-toffee Upside-down Cake

INGREDIENTS for Servings: 9

¼ cup almond butter	¾ cup water
¼ cup sunflower oil	1 cup plain flour
½ cup walnuts, chopped	1 lemon, zest
¾ cup + 3 tablespoon coconut sugar	1 teaspoon baking soda
1 ½ teaspoon mixed spice	1 teaspoon vinegar
	3 baking apples, cored and sliced

DIRECTIONS and Cooking Time: 30 Minutes
Preheat the air fryer to 390F. In a skillet, melt the almond butter and 3 tablespoons sugar. Pour the mixture over a baking dish that will fit in the air fryer. Arrange the slices of apples on top. Set aside. In a mixing bowl, combine flour, ¾ cup sugar, and baking soda. Add the mixed spice. In another bowl, mix the oil, water, vinegar, and lemon zest. Stir in the chopped walnuts. Combine the wet ingredients to the dry ingredients until well combined. Pour over the tin with apple slices. Bake for 30 minutes or until a toothpick inserted comes out clean.

522. Mini Almond Cakes

INGREDIENTS for Servings: 4

3 ounces dark chocolate, melted	¼ teaspoon vanilla extract
¼ cup coconut oil, melted	1 tablespoon almond flour
2 tablespoons swerve	Cooking spray
2 eggs, whisked	

DIRECTIONS and Cooking Time: 20 Minutes
In bowl, combine all the ingredients except the cooking spray and whisk really well. Divide this into 4 ramekins greased with cooking spray, put them in the fryer and cook at 360 degrees F for 20 minutes. Serve warm.

523. Crusty

INGREDIENTS for Servings: 3

2 cups flour	2 large eggs
4 tsp melted butter	½ tsp salt

DIRECTIONS and Cooking Time: 60 Minutes
Mix together the flour and butter. Add in the eggs and salt and combine well to form a dough ball. Place the dough between two pieces of parchment paper. Roll out to 10" by 16" and ¼ inch thick. Serve!

524. Raspberry Wontons

INGREDIENTS for Servings: 12

For Wonton Wrappers:	For Raspberry Syrup:
½ cup powdered sugar	¼ cup water
18 ounces cream cheese, softened	¼ cup sugar
1 teaspoon vanilla extract	1 (12-ounces) package frozen raspberries
1 package of wonton wrappers	1 teaspoon vanilla extract

DIRECTIONS and Cooking Time: 16 Minutes
For wrappers: in a bowl, add the sugar, cream cheese, and vanilla extract and whisk until smooth. Place a wonton wrapper onto a smooth surface. Place one tablespoon of cream cheese mixture in the center of each wrapper. With wet fingers, fold wrappers around the filling and then, pinch the edges to seal. Set the temperature of air fryer to 350 degrees F. Lightly, grease an air fryer basket. Arrange wonton wrappers into the prepared air fryer basket in 2 batches. Air fry for about 8 minutes. Meanwhile, for the syrup: in a medium skillet, add water, sugar, raspberries, and vanilla extract over medium heat and cook for about 5 minutes, stirring continuously. Remove from the heat and set aside to cool slightly. Transfer the mixture into food processor and blend until smooth. Remove the wontons from air fryer and transfer onto a platter. Serve the wontons with topping of raspberry syrup.

525. Yummy Banana Cookies

INGREDIENTS for Servings: 6

1 cup dates, pitted and chopped	1/3 cup vegetable oil
	2 cups rolled oats
1 teaspoon vanilla	3 ripe bananas

DIRECTIONS and Cooking Time: 10 Minutes
Preheat the air fryer to 350F. In a bowl, mash the bananas and add in the rest of the ingredients. Let it rest inside the fridge for 10 minutes. Drop a teaspoonful on cut parchment paper. Place the cookies on parchment paper inside the air fryer

basket. Make sure that the cookies do not overlap. Cook for 20 minutes or until the edges are crispy. Serve with almond milk.

526. Tasty Lemony Biscuits

INGREDIENTS for Servings: 10

8½ ounce self-rising flour	1 small egg
3½-ounce cold butter	3½-ounce caster sugar
1 teaspoon fresh lemon zest, grated finely	2 tablespoons fresh lemon juice
	1 teaspoon vanilla extract

DIRECTIONS and Cooking Time: 5 Minutes
Preheat the Air fryer to 355F and grease a baking sheet lightly. Mix flour and sugar in a large bowl. Add cold butter and mix until a coarse crumb is formed. Stir in the egg, lemon zest and lemon juice and mix until a dough is formed. Press the dough into ½ inch thickness onto a floured surface and cut dough into medium-sized biscuits. Arrange the biscuits on a baking sheet in a single layer and transfer into the Air fryer. Cook for about 5 minutes until golden brown and serve with tea.

527. English-style Scones With Raisins

INGREDIENTS for Servings: 6

1 ½ cups all-purpose flour	1 teaspoon ground cinnamon
1/4 cup brown sugar	1/2 cup raisins
1 teaspoon baking powder	6 tablespoons butter, cooled and sliced
1/4 teaspoon sea salt	1/2 cup double cream
1/4 teaspoon ground cloves	2 eggs, lightly whisked
1/2 teaspoon ground cardamom	1/2 teaspoon vanilla essence

DIRECTIONS and Cooking Time: 20 Minutes
In a mixing bowl, thoroughly combine the flour, sugar, baking powder, salt, cloves, cardamom cinnamon, and raisins. Mix until everything is combined well. Add the butter and mix again. In another mixing bowl, combine the double cream with the eggs and vanilla; beat until creamy and smooth. Stir the wet ingredients into the dry mixture. Roll your dough out into a circle and cut into wedges. Bake in the preheated Air Fryer at 360 degrees for 11 minutes, rotating the pan halfway through the cooking time. Bon appétit!

528. Super Moist Chocolate Cake

INGREDIENTS for Servings: 9

1/3 cup plain flour	1½-ounce castor sugar, divided
1/4 teaspoon baking powder	2 tablespoon vegetable oil
1½ tablespoons unsweetened cocoa powder	1 teaspoon vanilla extract
2 eggs, yolks and whites separated	1/8 teaspoon cream of tartar
3¾ tablespoons milk	

DIRECTIONS and Cooking Time: 40 Minutes
Preheat the Air fryer to 330F and grease a chiffon pan lightly. Mix flour, baking powder and cocoa powder in a bowl. Combine the remaining ingredients in another bowl until well combined. Stir in the flour mixture slowly and pour this mixture into the chiffon pan. Cover with the foil paper and poke some holes in the foil paper. Transfer the baking pan into the Air fryer basket and cook for about 30 minutes. Remove the foil and set the Air fryer to 285F. Cook for 10 more minutes and cut into slices to serve.

529. Baked Coconut Doughnuts

INGREDIENTS for Servings: 6

1 ½ cups all-purpose flour	2 tablespoons coconut oil, melted
1 teaspoon baking powder	1/4 teaspoon ground cardamom
A pinch of kosher salt	1/4 teaspoon ground cinnamon
A pinch of freshly grated nutmeg	1 teaspoon coconut essence
1/2 cup white sugar	1/2 teaspoon vanilla essence
2 eggs	
2 tablespoons full-fat coconut milk	1 cup coconut flakes

DIRECTIONS and Cooking Time: 20 Minutes
In a mixing bowl, thoroughly combine the all-purpose flour with the baking powder, salt, nutmeg, and sugar. In a separate bowl, beat the eggs until frothy using a hand mixer; add the coconut milk and oil and beat again; lastly, stir in the spices and mix again until everything is well combined. Then, stir the egg mixture into the flour mixture and continue mixing until a dough ball forms. Try not to over-mix your dough. Transfer to a lightly floured surface. Roll out your dough to a 1/4-inch thickness using a rolling pin. Cut out the doughnuts using a 3-inch round cutter; now, use a 1-inch round cutter to remove the center.

530. English Lemon Tarts

INGREDIENTS for Servings: 4

½ cup butter ½ lb. flour 1 large lemon, juiced and zested	2 tbsp. sugar 2 tbsp. lemon curd Pinch of nutmeg

DIRECTIONS and Cooking Time: 30 Minutes
In a large bowl, combine the butter, flour and sugar until a crumbly consistency is achieved. Add in the lemon zest and juice, followed by a pinch of nutmeg. Continue to combine. If necessary, add a couple tablespoons of water to soften the dough. Sprinkle the insides of a few small pastry tins with flour. Pour equal portions of the dough into each one and add sugar or lemon zest on top. Pre-heat the Air Fryer to 360°F. Place the lemon tarts inside the fryer and allow to cook for 15 minutes.

531. Lemon Berries Stew
INGREDIENTS for Servings: 4

1 pound strawberries, halved	1 tablespoon lemon juice
4 tablespoons stevia	1 and ½ cups water

DIRECTIONS and Cooking Time: 20 Minutes
In a pan that fits your air fryer, mix all the ingredients, toss, put it in the fryer and cook at 340 degrees F for 20 minutes. Divide the stew into cups and serve cold.

532. Pear Fritters With Cinnamon And Ginger
INGREDIENTS for Servings: 4

2 pears, peeled, cored and sliced 1 tablespoon coconut oil, melted 1 ½ cups all-purpose flour 1 teaspoon baking powder	A pinch of fine sea salt A pinch of freshly grated nutmeg 1/2 teaspoon ginger 1 teaspoon cinnamon 2 eggs 4 tablespoons milk

DIRECTIONS and Cooking Time: 20 Minutes
Mix all ingredients, except for the pears, in a shallow bowl. Dip each slice of the pears in the batter until well coated. Cook in the preheated Air Fryer at 360 degrees for 4 minutes, flipping them halfway through the cooking time. Repeat with the remaining ingredients. Dust with powdered sugar if desired. Bon appétit!

533. Raspberry Muffins
INGREDIENTS for Servings: 10

1 egg 1 cup frozen raspberries, coated	⅓ cup vegetable oil 2 tsp. baking powder Yogurt, as needed

with some flour 1 ½ cups flour ½ cup sugar	1 tsp. lemon zest 2 tbsp. lemon juice Pinch of sea salt

DIRECTIONS and Cooking Time: 35 Minutes
Pre-heat the Air Fryer to 350°F Place all of the dry ingredients in a bowl and combine well. Beat the egg and pour it into a cup. Mix it with the oil and lemon juice. Add in the yogurt, to taste. Mix together the dry and wet ingredients. Add in the lemon zest and raspberries. Coat the insides of 10 muffin tins with a little butter. Spoon an equal amount of the mixture into each muffin tin. Transfer to the fryer, and cook for 10 minutes, in batches if necessary.

534. Cherry Pie
INGREDIENTS for Servings: 8

1 tbsp. milk 2 ready-made pie crusts	21 oz. cherry pie filling 1 egg yolk

DIRECTIONS and Cooking Time: 35 Minutes
Pre-heat the Air Fryer to 310°F. Coat the inside of a pie pan with a little oil or butter and lay one of the pie crusts inside. Use a fork to pierce a few holes in the pastry. Spread the pie filling evenly over the crust. Slice the other crust into strips and place them on top of the pie filling to make the pie look more homemade. Place in the Air Fryer and cook for 15 minutes.

535. Cranberry Cream Surprise
INGREDIENTS for Servings: 1

1 cup mashed cranberries ½ cup Confectioner's Style Swerve 2 tsp natural cherry flavoring	2 tsp natural rum flavoring 1 cup organic heavy cream

DIRECTIONS and Cooking Time: 30 Minutes
Combine the mashed cranberries, sweetener, cherry and rum flavorings. Cover and refrigerate for 20 minutes. Whip the heavy cream until soft peaks form. Layer the whipped cream and cranberry mixture. Top with fresh cranberries, mint leaves or grated dark chocolate. Serve!

536. Citric Chocolate Pudding
INGREDIENTS for Servings: 4

½ cup butter 2/3 cup dark chocolate, chopped 2 teaspoons fresh orange rind, grated finely	2 medium eggs 2 tablespoon self-rising flour ¼ cup caster sugar ¼ cup fresh orange juice

DIRECTIONS and Cooking Time: 14 Minutes
Preheat the Air fryer to 355F and grease 4 ramekins lightly. Microwave butter and chocolate in a bowl on high for about 2 minutes. Add sugar, eggs, orange rind and juice and mix until well combined. Stir in the flour and mix well. Divide this mixture into the ramekins and cook for about 12 minutes. Dish out and serve chilled.

537.   Coconut Brownies

INGREDIENTS for Servings: 8

½ cup coconut oil	¼ tsp. coconut extract
2 oz. dark chocolate	½ tsp. vanilla extract
1 cup sugar	1 tbsp. honey
2 ½ tbsp. water	½ cup flour
4 whisked eggs	½ cup desiccated
¼ tsp. ground cinnamon	coconut
½ tsp. ground anise star	sugar, to dust

DIRECTIONS and Cooking Time: 15 Minutes
Melt the coconut oil and dark chocolate in the microwave. Combine with the sugar, water, eggs, cinnamon, anise, coconut extract, vanilla, and honey in a large bowl. Stir in the flour and desiccated coconut. Incorporate everything well. Lightly grease a baking dish with butter. Transfer the mixture to the dish. Place the dish in the Air Fryer and bake at 355°F for 15 minutes. Remove from the fryer and allow to cool slightly. Take care when taking it out of the baking dish. Slice it into squares. Dust with sugar before serving.

538.   Sponge Cake

INGREDIENTS for Servings: 8

For the Cake:	1 tsp. baking powder
9 oz. sugar	For the Frosting
9 oz. butter	Juice of 1 lemon
3 eggs	Zest of 1 lemon
9 oz. flour	1 tsp. yellow food
1 tsp. vanilla extract	coloring
Zest of 1 lemon	7 oz. sugar
	4 egg whites

DIRECTIONS and Cooking Time: 50 Minutes
Pre-heat your Air Fryer to 320°F. Use an electric mixer to combine all of the cake ingredients. Grease the insides of two round cake pans. Pour an equal amount of the batter into each pan. Place one pan in the fryer and cook for 15 minutes, before repeating with the second pan. In the meantime, mix together all of the frosting ingredients. Allow the cakes to cool. Spread the frosting on top of one cake and stack the other cake on top.

539.   Pumpkin Muffins

INGREDIENTS for Servings: 10

4 large eggs	1 tsp vanilla
1/2 cup pumpkin puree	1/3 cup coconut oil, melted
1 tbsp pumpkin pie spice	1/2 cup almond flour
1 tbsp baking powder, gluten-free	1/2 cup coconut flour
2/3 cup erythritol	1/2 tsp sea salt

DIRECTIONS and Cooking Time: 20 Minutes
Preheat the air fryer to 325 F. In a large bowl, stir together coconut flour, pumpkin pie spice, baking powder, erythritol, almond flour, and sea salt. Stir in eggs, vanilla, coconut oil, and pumpkin puree until well combined. Pour batter into the silicone muffin molds and place into the air fryer basket in batches. Cook muffins for 20 minutes. Serve and enjoy.

540.   Perfectly Puffy Coconut Cookies

INGREDIENTS for Servings: 12

1 cup butter, melted	1 cup coconut flour
1 ¾ cups granulated swerve	1 ¼ cups almond flour
3 eggs	1/2 teaspoon baking powder
2 tablespoons coconut milk	1/2 teaspoon baking soda
1 teaspoon coconut extract	1/2 teaspoon fine table salt
1 teaspoon vanilla extract	1/2 cups coconut chips, unsweetened

DIRECTIONS and Cooking Time: 20 Minutes
Begin by preheating your Air Fryer to 350 degrees F. In the bowl of an electric mixer, beat the butter and swerve until well combined. Now, add the eggs one at a time, and mix well; add the coconut milk, coconut extract, and vanilla; beat until creamy and uniform. Mix the flour with baking powder, baking soda, and salt. Then, stir the flour mixture into the butter mixture and stir until everything is well incorporated. Finally, fold in the coconut chips and mix again. Scoop out 1 tablespoon size balls of the batter on a cookie pan, leaving 2 inches between each cookie. Bake for 10 minutes or until golden brown, rotating the pan once or twice through the cooking time. Let your cookies cool on wire racks. Bon appétit!

541.   Nut Bars

INGREDIENTS for Servings: 10

½ cup coconut oil, softened	½ cup coconut flour
	1 teaspoon vanilla extract
1 teaspoon baking	

powder	2 eggs, beaten
1 teaspoon lemon juice	2 oz hazelnuts, chopped
1 cup almond flour	1 oz macadamia nuts, chopped
3 tablespoons Erythritol	Cooking spray

DIRECTIONS and Cooking Time: 30 Minutes

In the mixing bowl mix up coconut oil and baking powder. Add lemon juice, almond flour, coconut flour, Erythritol, vanilla extract, and eggs. Stir the mixture until it is smooth or use the immersion blender for this step. Then add hazelnuts and macadamia nuts. Stir the mixture until homogenous. After this, preheat the air fryer to 325F. Line the air fryer basket with baking paper. Then pour the nut mixture in the air fryer basket and flatten it well with the help of the spatula. Cook the mixture for 30 minutes. Then cool the mixture well and cut it into the serving bars.

542.   Hearty Apricot Crumbles

INGREDIENTS for Servings: 4

1 cup fresh blackberries	1 cup flour
½ cup sugar	Salt as needed
2 tbsp lemon Juice	5 tbsp butter

DIRECTIONS and Cooking Time: 30 Minutes

Add the apricot cubes to a bowl and mix with lemon juice, 2 tbsp sugar, and blackberries. Scoop the mixture into a greased dish and spread it evenly. In another bowl, mix flour and remaining sugar.   Add 1 tbsp of cold water and butter and keep mixing until you have a crumbly mixture. Preheat the air fryer to 390 F and place the fruit mixture in the cooking basket. Top with crumb mixture and cook for 20 minutes.

543.   Delicate Pear Pouch

INGREDIENTS for Servings: 4

2 small pears, peeled, cored and halved	1 egg, beaten lightly
2 cups prepared vanilla custard	2 tablespoons sugar
	Pinch of ground cinnamon
4 puff pastry sheets	2 tablespoons whipped cream

DIRECTIONS and Cooking Time: 15 Minutes

Preheat the Air fryer to 330F and grease an Air fryer basket.   Place a spoonful of vanilla custard and a pear half in the center of each pastry sheet.   Mix sugar and cinnamon in a bowl and sprinkle on the pear halves. Pinch the corners of sheets together to shape into a pouch and transfer into the Air fryer basket.   Cook for about 15 minutes and top with whipped cream. Dish out and serve with remaining custard.

544.   Lusciously Easy Brownies

INGREDIENTS for Servings: 8

1 egg	Frosting Ingredients
2 tablespoons and 2 teaspoons unsweetened cocoa powder	1 tablespoon and 1-1/2 teaspoons butter, softened
1/2 cup white sugar	1 tablespoon and 1-1/2 teaspoons unsweetened cocoa powder
1/2 teaspoon vanilla extract	
1/4 cup butter	1-1/2 teaspoons honey
1/4 cup all-purpose flour	1/2 teaspoon vanilla extract
1/8 teaspoon salt	
1/8 teaspoon baking powder	1/2 cup confectioners' sugar

DIRECTIONS and Cooking Time: 20 Minutes

Lightly grease baking pan of air fryer with cooking spray. Melt ¼ cup butter for 3 minutes. Stir in vanilla, eggs, and sugar. Mix well.   Stir in baking powder, salt, flour, and cocoa mix well. Evenly spread.   For 20 minutes, cook on 300F.   In a small bowl, make the frosting by mixing well all Ingredients. Frost brownies while still warm.   Serve and enjoy.

545.   Vanilla Cookies

INGREDIENTS for Servings: 12

2 eggs, whisked	½ cup butter, melted
1 tablespoon heavy cream	2 and ¾ cup almond flour
2 teaspoons vanilla extract	Cooking spray
	¼ cup swerve

DIRECTIONS and Cooking Time: 20 Minutes

In a bowl, mix all the ingredients except the cooking spray and stir well. Shape 12 balls out of this mix, put them on a baking sheet that fits the air fryer greased with cooking spray and flatten them. Put the baking sheet in the air fryer and cook at 350 degrees F for 20 minutes. Serve the cookies cold.

546.   Banana Oatmeal Cookies

INGREDIENTS for Servings: 6

2 cups quick oats	¼ cup milk
4 ripe bananas, mashed	¼ cup coconut, shredded

DIRECTIONS and Cooking Time: 20 Minutes

Pre-heat the Air Fryer to 350°F.   Combine all of the ingredients in a bowl.   Scoop equal amounts of the cookie dough onto a baking sheet and put it in the Air Fryer basket.   Bake the cookies for 15 minutes.

547. Summer Peach Crisp

INGREDIENTS for Servings: 4

2 cups fresh peaches, pitted and sliced	1/2 teaspoon ground cinnamon
1/4 cup cornmeal	A pinch of fine sea salt
1/4 cup brown sugar	1 stick cold butter
1 teaspoon pure vanilla extract	1/2 cup rolled oats

DIRECTIONS and Cooking Time: 40 Minutes

Toss the sliced peaches with the cornmeal, brown sugar, vanilla extract, cinnamon, and sea salt. Place in a baking pan coated with cooking spray. In a mixing dish, thoroughly combine the cold butter and rolled oats. Sprinkle the mixture over each peach. Bake in the preheated Air Fryer at 330 degrees F for 35 minutes. Bon appétit!

548. Crispy Good Peaches

INGREDIENTS for Servings: 4

1 teaspoon cinnamon	3 tablespoon butter, unsalted
1 teaspoon sugar, white	3 tablespoon sugar
1/3 cup oats, dry rolled	3 tablespoon pecans, chopped
1/4 cup Flour, white	4 cup sliced peaches, frozen

2 tablespoon Flour, white	

DIRECTIONS and Cooking Time: 30 Minutes

Lightly grease baking pan of air fryer with cooking spray. Mix in a tsp cinnamon, 2 tbsp flour, 3 tbsp sugar, and peaches. For 20 minutes, cook on 300F. Mix the rest of the Ingredients in a bowl. Pour over peaches. Cook for 10 minutes at 330F. Serve and enjoy.

549. Apple Chips With Dip

INGREDIENTS for Servings: 4

1 apple, thinly slice using a mandolin slicer	1/4 cup plain yogurt
	2 tsp olive oil
1 tbsp almond butter	1 tsp ground cinnamon
	4 drops liquid stevia

DIRECTIONS and Cooking Time: 12 Minutes

Add apple slices, oil, and cinnamon in a large bowl and toss well. Spray air fryer basket with cooking spray. Place apple slices in air fryer basket and cook at 375 F for 12 minutes. Turn after every 4 minutes. Meanwhile, in a small bowl, mix together almond butter, yogurt, and sweetener. Serve apple chips with dip and enjoy.

OTHER AIR FRYER RECIPES

550. Turkey Wontons With Garlic-parmesan Sauce

INGREDIENTS for Servings: 8

8 ounces cooked turkey breasts, shredded	16 wonton wrappers
1 ½ tablespoons butter, melted	3 tablespoons Parmesan cheese, grated
1/3 cup cream cheese, room temperature	1 teaspoon garlic powder
8 ounces Asiago cheese, shredded	Fine sea salt and freshly ground black pepper, to taste

DIRECTIONS and Cooking Time: 15 Minutes
In a small-sized bowl, mix the butter, Parmesan, garlic powder, salt, and black pepper; give it a good stir. Lightly grease a mini muffin pan; lay 1 wonton wrapper in each mini muffin cup. Fill each cup with the cream cheese and turkey mixture. Air-fry for 8 minutes at 335 degrees F. Immediately top with Asiago cheese and serve warm. Bon appétit!

551. Creamy Lemon Turkey

INGREDIENTS for Servings: 4

1/3 cup sour cream	1 teaspoon fresh marjoram, chopped
2 cloves garlic, finely minced	Salt and freshly cracked mixed peppercorns, to taste
1/3 teaspoon lemon zest	1/2 cup scallion, chopped
2 small-sized turkey breasts, skinless and cubed	1/2 can tomatoes, diced
1/3 cup thickened cream	1 ½ tablespoons canola oil
2 tablespoons lemon juice	

DIRECTIONS and Cooking Time: 2 Hours 25 Minutes
Firstly, pat dry the turkey breast. Mix the remaining items; marinate the turkey for 2 hours. Set the air fryer to cook at 355 degrees F. Brush the turkey with a nonstick spray; cook for 23 minutes, turning once. Serve with naan and enjoy!

552. Dijon And Curry Turkey Cutlets

INGREDIENTS for Servings: 4

1/2 tablespoon Dijon mustard	1/3 pound turkey cutlets
1/2 teaspoon curry powder	1/2 cup fresh lemon juice
Sea salt flakes and freshly cracked black peppercorns, to savor	1/2 tablespoons tamari sauce

DIRECTIONS and Cooking Time: 30 Minutes + Marinating Time
Set the air fryer to cook at 375 degrees. Then, put the turkey cutlets into a mixing dish; add fresh lemon juice, tamari, and mustard; let it marinate at least 2 hours. Coat each turkey cutlet with the curry powder, salt, and freshly cracked black peppercorns; roast for 28 minutes; work in batches. Bon appétit!

553. Colby Potato Patties

INGREDIENTS for Servings: 8

2 pounds white potatoes, peeled and grated	1/2 teaspoon freshly ground black pepper, or more to taste
1/2 cup scallions, finely chopped	2 cups Colby cheese, shredded
1 tablespoon fine sea salt	1/4 cup canola oil
1/2 teaspoon hot paprika	1 cup crushed crackers

DIRECTIONS and Cooking Time: 15 Minutes
Firstly, boil the potatoes until fork tender. Drain, peel and mash your potatoes. Thoroughly mix the mashed potatoes with scallions, pepper, salt, paprika, and cheese. Then, shape the balls using your hands. Now, flatten the balls to make the patties. In a shallow bowl, mix canola oil with crushed crackers. Roll the patties over the crumb mixture. Next, cook your patties at 360 degrees F approximately 10 minutes, working in batches. Serve with tabasco mayo if desired. Bon appétit!

554. Mediterranean Eggs With Spinach And Tomato

INGREDIENTS for Servings: 2

2 tablespoons olive oil, melted	4 eggs, whisked
5 ounces fresh spinach, chopped	1/2 teaspoon coarse salt
1 medium-sized tomato, chopped	1/2 teaspoon ground black pepper
1 teaspoon fresh lemon juice	1/2 cup of fresh basil, roughly chopped

DIRECTIONS and Cooking Time: 15 Minutes
Add the olive oil to an Air Fryer baking pan. Make sure to tilt the pan to spread the oil evenly. Simply combine the remaining ingredients, except for the

basil leaves; whisk well until everything is well incorporated. Cook in the preheated Air Fryer for 8 to 12 minutes at 280 degrees F. Garnish with fresh basil leaves. Serve warm with a dollop of sour cream if desired.

555.   Easiest Pork Chops Ever

INGREDIENTS for Servings: 6

1/3 cup Italian breadcrumbs Roughly chopped fresh cilantro, to taste 2 teaspoons Cajun seasonings Nonstick cooking spray 2 eggs, beaten	3 tablespoons white flour 1 teaspoon seasoned salt Garlic & onion spice blend, to taste 6 pork chops 1/3 teaspoon freshly cracked black pepper

DIRECTIONS and Cooking Time: 22 Minutes
Coat the pork chops with Cajun seasonings, salt, pepper, and the spice blend on all sides. Then, add the flour to a plate. In a shallow dish, whisk the egg until pale and smooth. Place the Italian breadcrumbs in the third bowl. Dredge each pork piece in the flour; then, coat them with the egg; finally, coat them with the breadcrumbs. Spritz them with cooking spray on both sides. Now, air-fry pork chops for about 18 minutes at 345 degrees F; make sure to taste for doneness after first 12 minutes of cooking. Lastly, garnish with fresh cilantro. Bon appétit!

556.   Savory Italian Crespelle

INGREDIENTS for Servings: 3

3/4 cup all-purpose flour 2 eggs, beaten 1/4 teaspoon allspice 1/2 teaspoon salt 3/4 cup milk	1 cup ricotta cheese 1/2 cup Parmigiano-Reggiano cheese, preferably freshly grated 1 cup marinara sauce

DIRECTIONS and Cooking Time: 35 Minutes
Mix the flour, eggs, allspice, and salt in a large bowl. Gradually add the milk, whisking continuously, until well combined. Let it stand for 20 minutes. Spritz the Air Fryer baking pan with cooking spray. Pour the batter into the prepared pan. Cook at 230 degrees F for 3 minutes. Flip and cook until browned in spots, 2 to 3 minutes longer. Repeat with the remaining batter. Serve with the cheese and marinara sauce. Bon appétit!

557.   Frittata With Porcini Mushrooms

INGREDIENTS for Servings: 4

3 cups Porcini mushrooms, thinly sliced 1 tablespoon melted butter 1 shallot, peeled and slice into thin rounds 1 garlic cloves, peeled and finely minced 1 lemon grass, cut into 1-inch pieces	1/3 teaspoon table salt 8 eggs 1/2 teaspoon ground black pepper, preferably freshly ground 1 teaspoon cumin powder 1/3 teaspoon dried or fresh dill weed 1/2 cup goat cheese, crumbled

DIRECTIONS and Cooking Time: 40 Minutes
Melt the butter in a nonstick skillet that is placed over medium heat. Sauté the shallot, garlic, thinly sliced Porcini mushrooms, and lemon grass over a moderate heat until they have softened. Now, reserve the sautéed mixture. Preheat your Air Fryer to 335 degrees F. Then, in a mixing bowl, beat the eggs until frothy. Now, add the seasonings and mix to combine well. Coat the sides and bottom of a baking dish with a thin layer of vegetable spray. Pour the egg/seasoning mixture into the baking dish; throw in the onion/mushroom sauté. Top with the crumbled goat cheese. Place the baking dish in the Air Fryer cooking basket. Cook for about 32 minutes or until your frittata is set. Enjoy!

558.   Broccoli Bites With Cheese Sauce

INGREDIENTS for Servings: 6

For the Broccoli Bites: 1/2 teaspoon lemon zest, freshly grated 1/3 teaspoon fine sea salt 1/2 teaspoon hot paprika 1 teaspoon shallot powder 1 teaspoon porcini powder 1/2 teaspoon granulated garlic	1 medium-sized head broccoli, broken into florets 1/3 teaspoon celery seeds 1 ½ tablespoons olive oil For the Cheese Sauce: 2 tablespoons butter 1 tablespoon golden flaxseed meal 1 cup milk 1/2 cup blue cheese

DIRECTIONS and Cooking Time: 20 Minutes
Toss all the ingredients for the broccoli bites in a mixing bowl, covering the broccoli florets on all sides. Cook them in the preheated Air Fryer at 360 degrees F for 13 to 15 minutes. In the meantime, melt the butter over a medium heat; stir in the golden flaxseed meal and let cook for 1 min or so. Gradually pour in the milk, stirring constantly, until the mixture is smooth. Bring it to a simmer and stir in the cheese. Cook until the sauce has thickened slightly. Pause

your Air Fryer, mix the broccoli with the prepared sauce and cook for further 3 minutes. Bon appétit!

559. Chicken Drumsticks With Ketchup-lemon Sauce

INGREDIENTS for Servings: 6

3 tablespoons lemon juice	1/2 teaspoon ground black pepper
1 cup tomato ketchup	2 teaspoons lemon zest, grated
1 ½ tablespoons fresh rosemary, chopped	1/3 cup honey
6 skin-on chicken drumsticks, boneless	3 cloves garlic, minced

DIRECTIONS and Cooking Time: 20 Minutes + Marinating Time
Dump the chicken drumsticks into a mixing dish. Now, add the other items and give it a good stir; let it marinate overnight in your refrigerator. Discard the marinade; roast the chicken legs in your air fryer at 375 degrees F for 22 minutes, turning once. Now, add the marinade and cook an additional 6 minutes or until everything is warmed through.

560. Snapper With Gruyere Cheese

INGREDIENTS for Servings: 4

2 tablespoons olive oil	Sea salt and ground black pepper, to taste
1 shallot, thinly sliced	1/2 teaspoon dried basil
2 garlic cloves, minced	
1 ½ pounds snapper fillets	1/2 cup tomato puree
1 teaspoon cayenne pepper	1/2 cup white wine
	1 cup Gruyere cheese, shredded

DIRECTIONS and Cooking Time: 25 Minutes
Heat 1 tablespoon of olive oil in a saucepan over medium-high heat. Now, cook the shallot and garlic until tender and aromatic. Preheat your Air Fryer to 370 degrees F. Grease a casserole dish with 1 tablespoon of olive oil. Place the snapper fillet in the casserole dish. Season with salt, black pepper, and cayenne pepper. Add the sautéed shallot mixture. Add the basil, tomato puree and wine to the casserole dish. Cook for 10 minutes in the preheated Air Fryer. Top with the shredded cheese and cook an additional 7 minutes. Serve immediately.

561. Baked Eggs Florentine

INGREDIENTS for Servings: 2

1 tablespoon ghee, melted	1/4 teaspoon red pepper flakes
2 cups baby spinach, torn into small pieces	Salt, to taste
2 tablespoons shallots, chopped	1 tablespoon fresh thyme leaves, roughly chopped
	4 eggs

DIRECTIONS and Cooking Time: 20 Minutes
Start by preheating your Air Fryer to 350 degrees F. Brush the sides and bottom of a gratin dish with the melted ghee. Put the spinach and shallots into the bottom of the gratin dish. Season with red pepper, salt, and fresh thyme. Make four indents for the eggs; crack one egg into each indent. Bake for 12 minutes, rotating the pan once or twice to ensure even cooking. Enjoy!

562. Grilled Lemony Pork Chops

INGREDIENTS for Servings: 5

5 pork chops	Fresh parsley, to serve
1/3 cup vermouth	1 teaspoon freshly cracked black pepper
1/2 teaspoon paprika	
2 sprigs thyme, only leaves, crushed	3 tablespoons lemon juice
1/2 teaspoon dried oregano	3 cloves garlic, minced
1 teaspoon garlic salt½ lemon, cut into wedges	2 tablespoons canola oil

DIRECTIONS and Cooking Time: 34 Minutes
Firstly, heat the canola oil in a sauté pan over a moderate heat. Now, sweat the garlic until just fragrant. Remove the pan from the heat and pour in the lemon juice and vermouth. Now, throw in the seasonings. Dump the sauce into a baking dish, along with the pork chops. Tuck the lemon wedges among the pork chops and air-fry for 27 minutes at 345 degrees F. Bon appétit!

563. Onion Rings Wrapped In Bacon

INGREDIENTS for Servings: 4

12 rashers back bacon	1/2 teaspoon chili powder
1/2 teaspoon ground black pepper	1/2 tablespoon soy sauce
Chopped fresh parsley, to taste	½ teaspoon salt
1/2 teaspoon paprika	

DIRECTIONS and Cooking Time: 25 Minutes
Start by preheating your air fryer to 355 degrees F. Season the onion rings with paprika, salt, black pepper, and chili powder. Simply wrap the bacon around the onion rings; drizzle with soy sauce. Bake for 17 minutes, garnish with fresh parsley and serve. Bon appétit!

564.   Party Mozzarella Stick

INGREDIENTS for Servings: 4

12 ounces mozzarella cheese strings	1/4 cup almond flour
2 eggs	1 teaspoon garlic powder
2 tablespoons flaxseed meal	1 teaspoon dried oregano
1/2 cup parmesan cheese finely grated	1/2 cup salsa, preferably homemade

DIRECTIONS and Cooking Time: 40 Minutes
Set up your breading station. Put the eggs in a shallow bowl; in another bowl, mix the flaxseed meal, almond flour, parmesan cheese, garlic powder, and oregano. Dip the mozzarella sticks in the egg, then in the parmesan mixture, then in the egg and parmesan mixture again.   Place in your freezer for 30 minutes. Place the breaded cheese sticks in the lightly greased Air Fryer basket. Cook at 380 degrees F for 6 minutes. Serve with salsa on the side and enjoy!

565.   Breakfast Muffins With Mushrooms And Goat Cheese

INGREDIENTS for Servings: 6

2 tablespoons butter, melted	1 cup brown mushrooms, sliced
1 yellow onion, chopped	1 teaspoon fresh basil
2 garlic cloves, minced	8 eggs, lightly whisked
Sea salt and ground black pepper, to taste	6 tablespoons goat cheese, crumbled

DIRECTIONS and Cooking Time: 25 Minutes
Start by preheating your Air Fryer to 330 degrees F. Now, spritz a 6-tin muffin tin with cooking spray. Melt the butter in a heavy-bottomed skillet over medium-high heat. Sauté the onions, garlic, and mushrooms until just tender and fragrant.   Add the salt, black pepper, and basil and remove from heat. Divide out the sautéed mixture into the muffin tin. Pour the whisked eggs on top and top with the goat cheese. Bake for 20 minutes rotating the pan halfway through the cooking time. Bon appétit!

566.   Filipino Ground Meat Omelet (tortang Giniling)

INGREDIENTS for Servings: 3

1 teaspoon lard	1 green bell pepper, seeded and chopped
2/3 pound ground beef	1 red bell pepper, seeded and chopped
1/4 teaspoon chili powder	6 eggs
1/2 teaspoon ground bay leaf	1/3 cup double cream
	1/2 cup Colby cheese,

1/2 teaspoon ground pepper	shredded
Sea salt, to taste	1 tomato, sliced

DIRECTIONS and Cooking Time: 20 Minutes
Melt the lard in a cast-iron skillet over medium-high heat. Add the ground beef and cook for 4 minutes until no longer pink, crumbling with a spatula.   Add the ground beef mixture, along with the spices to the baking pan. Now, add the bell peppers.   In a mixing bowl, whisk the eggs with double cream. Spoon the mixture over the meat and peppers in the pan.   Cook in the preheated Air Fryer at 355 degrees F for 10 minutes.   Top with the cheese and tomato slices. Continue to cook for 5 minutes more or until the eggs are golden and the cheese has melted.

567.   Western Eggs With Ham And Cheese

INGREDIENTS for Servings: 4

6 eggs	1/2 cup milk
2 ounces cream cheese, softened	1/4 teaspoon paprika
Sea salt, to your liking	6 ounces cooked ham, diced
1/4 teaspoon ground black pepper	1 onion, chopped
	1/2 cup cheddar cheese, shredded

DIRECTIONS and Cooking Time: 20 Minutes
Begin by preheating the Air Fryer to 360 degrees F. Spritz the sides and bottom of a baking pan with cooking oil.   In a mixing dish, whisk the eggs, milk, and cream cheese until pale. Add the spices, ham, and onion; stir until everything is well incorporated. Pour the mixture into the baking pan; top with the cheddar cheese.   Bake in the preheated Air Fryer for 12 minutes. Serve warm and enjoy!

568.   Super-easy Chicken With Tomato Sauce

INGREDIENTS for Servings: 4

1 tablespoon balsamic vinegar	4 Roma tomatoes, diced
½ teaspoon red pepper flakes, crushed	1 ½ tablespoons butter
1 fresh garlic, roughly chopped	1/3 handful fresh basil, loosely packed, sniped
2 ½ large-sized chicken breasts, cut into halves	1 teaspoon kosher salt
1/3 handful fresh cilantro, roughly chopped	2 cloves garlic, minced
2 tablespoons olive oil	Cooked bucatini, to serve

116

DIRECTIONS and Cooking Time: 20 Minutes + Marinating Time

Place the first seven ingredients in a medium-sized bowl; let it marinate for a couple of hours. Preheat the air fryer to 325 degrees F. Air-fry your chicken for 32 minutes and serve warm. In the meantime, prepare the tomato sauce by preheating a deep saucepan. Simmer the tomatoes until you make a chunky mixture. Throw in the garlic, basil, and butter; give it a good stir. Serve the cooked chicken breasts with the tomato sauce and the cooked bucatini. Bon appétit!

569. Baked Eggs With Kale And Ham

INGREDIENTS for Servings: 2

2 eggs	½ cup steamed kale
1/4 teaspoon dried or fresh marjoram	1/4 teaspoon dried or fresh rosemary
2 teaspoons chili powder	4 pork ham slices
1/3 teaspoon kosher salt	1/3 teaspoon ground black pepper, or more to taste

DIRECTIONS and Cooking Time: 15 Minutes

Divide the kale and ham among 2 ramekins; crack an egg into each ramekin. Sprinkle with seasonings. Cook for 15 minutes at 335 degrees F or until your eggs reach desired texture. Serve warm with spicy tomato ketchup and pickles. Bon appétit!

570. Farmer's Breakfast Deviled Eggs

INGREDIENTS for Servings: 3

6 eggs	1 teaspoon hot sauce
6 slices bacon	1 tablespoon pickle relish
2 tablespoons mayonnaise	Salt and ground black pepper, to taste
1/2 teaspoon Worcestershire sauce	1 teaspoon smoked paprika
2 tablespoons green onions, chopped	

DIRECTIONS and Cooking Time: 25 Minutes

Place the wire rack in the Air Fryer basket; lower the eggs onto the wire rack. Cook at 270 degrees F for 15 minutes. Transfer them to an ice-cold water bath to stop the cooking. Peel the eggs under cold running water; slice them into halves. Cook the bacon at 400 degrees F for 3 minutes; flip the bacon over and cook an additional 3 minutes; chop the bacon and reserve. Mash the egg yolks with the mayo, hot sauce, Worcestershire sauce, green onions, pickle relish, salt, and black pepper; add the reserved bacon and spoon the yolk mixture into the egg whites. Garnish with smoked paprika. Bon appétit!

571. Creamed Asparagus And Egg Salad

INGREDIENTS for Servings: 4

2 eggs	1 teaspoon fresh lemon juice
1 pound asparagus, chopped	Sea salt and ground black pepper, to taste
2 cup baby spinach	
1/2 cup mayonnaise	
1 teaspoon mustard	

DIRECTIONS and Cooking Time: 25 Minutes + Chilling Time

Place the wire rack in the Air Fryer basket; lower the eggs onto the wire rack. Cook at 270 degrees F for 15 minutes. Transfer them to an ice-cold water bath to stop the cooking. Peel the eggs under cold running water; coarsely chop the hard-boiled eggs and set aside. Increase the temperature to 400 degrees F. Place your asparagus in the lightly greased Air Fryer basket. Cook for 5 minutes or until tender. Place in a nice salad bowl. Add the baby spinach. In a mixing dish, thoroughly combine the remaining ingredients. Drizzle this dressing over the asparagus in the salad bowl and top with the chopped eggs. Bon appétit!

572. Gorgonzola Stuffed Mushrooms With Horseradish Mayo

INGREDIENTS for Servings: 5

1/2 cup of breadcrumbs	1 ½ tablespoons olive oil
2 cloves garlic, pressed	1/2 cup Gorgonzola cheese, grated
2 tablespoons fresh coriander, chopped	1/4 cup low-fat mayonnaise
1/3 teaspoon kosher salt	1 teaspoon prepared horseradish, well-drained
1/2 teaspoon crushed red pepper flakes	1 tablespoon fresh parsley, finely chopped
20 medium-sized mushrooms, cut off the stems	

DIRECTIONS and Cooking Time: 15 Minutes

Mix the breadcrumbs together with the garlic, coriander, salt, red pepper, and the olive oil; mix to combine well. Stuff the mushroom caps with the breadcrumb filling. Top with grated Gorgonzola. Place the mushrooms in the Air Fryer grill pan and slide them into the machine. Grill them at 380 degrees F for 8 to 12 minutes or until the stuffing is warmed through. Meanwhile, prepare the horseradish mayo by mixing the mayonnaise, horseradish and parsley. Serve with the warm fried mushrooms. Enjoy!

573.   French Toast With Blueberries And Honey

INGREDIENTS for Servings: 6

1/4 cup milk	2 eggs
2 tablespoons butter, melted	1 teaspoon vanilla extract
1/2 teaspoon ground cinnamon	6 slices day-old French baguette
1/4 teaspoon ground cloves	2 tablespoons honey
	1/2 cup blueberries

DIRECTIONS and Cooking Time: 20 Minutes
In a mixing bowl, whisk the milk eggs, butter, cinnamon, cloves, and vanilla extract.   Dip each piece of the baguette into the egg mixture and place in the parchment-lined Air Fryer basket.   Cook in the preheated Air Fryer at 360 degrees F for 6 to 7 minutes, turning them over halfway through the cooking time to ensure even cooking.   Serve garnished with honey and blueberries. Enjoy!

574.   Italian Sausage And Veggie Bake

INGREDIENTS for Servings: 4

1 pound Italian sausage	4 cloves garlic
2 red peppers, seeded and sliced	1 teaspoon dried oregano
2 green peppers, seeded and sliced	1/4 teaspoon black pepper
1 cup mushrooms, sliced	1/4 teaspoon cayenne pepper
1 shallot, sliced	Sea salt, to taste
1 teaspoon dried basil	2 tablespoons Dijon mustard
	1 cup chicken broth

DIRECTIONS and Cooking Time: 20 Minutes
Toss all ingredients in a lightly greased baking pan. Make sure the sausages and vegetables are coated with the oil and seasonings.   Bake in the preheated Air Fryer at 380 degrees F for 15 minutes.   Divide between individual bowls and serve warm. Bon appétit!

575.   Eggs Florentine With Spinach

INGREDIENTS for Servings: 2

2 tablespoons ghee, melted	1/4 teaspoon red pepper flakes
2 cups baby spinach, torn into small pieces	Salt, to taste
2 tablespoons shallots, chopped	1 tablespoon fresh thyme leaves, roughly chopped
	4 eggs

DIRECTIONS and Cooking Time: 20 Minutes
Start by preheating your Air Fryer to 350 degrees F. Brush the sides and bottom of a gratin dish with the melted ghee.   Put the spinach and shallots into the bottom of the gratin dish. Season with red pepper, salt, and fresh thyme.   Make four indents for the eggs; crack one egg into each indent. Bake for 12 minutes, rotating the pan once or twice to ensure even cooking. Enjoy!

576.   Dinner Turkey Sandwiches

INGREDIENTS for Servings: 4

1/2 pound turkey breast	7 ounces condensed cream of onion soup
1 teaspoon garlic powder	1/3 teaspoon ground allspice
BBQ sauce, to savor	

DIRECTIONS and Cooking Time: 4 Hours 30 Minutes
Simply dump the cream of onion soup and turkey breast into your crock-pot. Cook on HIGH heat setting for 3 hours.   Then, shred the meat and transfer to a lightly greased baking dish.   Pour in your favorite BBQ sauce. Sprinkle with ground allspice and garlic powder. Air-fry an additional 28 minutes.   To finish, assemble the sandwiches; add toppings such as pickled or fresh salad, mustard, etc.

577.   Breakfast Pizza Cups

INGREDIENTS for Servings: 4

12 slices pepperoni, 2-inch	Salt, to taste
2 tablespoons butter, melted	4 slices smoked ham, chopped
4 eggs, beaten	1 cup mozzarella cheese, shredded
1/4 teaspoon ground black pepper	4 tablespoons ketchup

DIRECTIONS and Cooking Time: 30 Minutes
Start by preheating your Air Fryer to 350 degrees F. Now, lightly grease a muffin tin with nonstick spray. Place pepperoni into a mini muffin pan. In a mixing bowl, thoroughly combine the remaining ingredients. Bake in the preheated Air Fryer for 20 minutes until a toothpick inserted comes out clean. Let it cool for 5 minutes before removing to a serving platter.   Bon appétit!

578. Country-style Apple Fries

INGREDIENTS for Servings: 4

1/2 cup milk	A pinch of grated
1 egg	nutmeg
1/2 all-purpose flour	1 tablespoon coconut
1 teaspoon baking	oil, melted
powder	2 Pink Lady apples,
4 tablespoons brown	cored, peeled, slice
sugar	into pieces (shape and
1 teaspoon vanilla	size of French fries
extract	1/3 cup granulated
1/2 teaspoon ground	sugar
cloves	1 teaspoon ground
A pinch of kosher salt	cinnamon

DIRECTIONS and Cooking Time: 20 Minutes
In a mixing bowl, whisk the milk and eggs; gradually stir in the flour; add the baking powder, brown sugar, vanilla, cloves, salt, nutmeg, and melted coconut oil. Mix to combine well. Dip each apple slice into the batter, coating on all sides. Spritz the bottom of the cooking basket with cooking oil. Cook the apple fries in the preheated Air Fryer at 395 degrees F approximately 8 minutes, turning them over halfway through the cooking time. Cook in small batches to ensure even cooking. In the meantime, mix the granulated sugar with the ground cinnamon; sprinkle the cinnamon sugar over the apple fries. Serve warm.

579. Crunch-crunch Party Mix

INGREDIENTS for Servings: 8

1 cup whole-grain	1/2 cup almonds
Rice Chex	1/4 cup poppy seeds
2 cups cheese squares	1/2 cup sunflower
1 cup pistachios	seeds
1 cup cheddar-	1 tablespoon coarse
flavored mini pretzel	sea salt
twists	1 tablespoon garlic
2 tablespoons butter,	powder
melted	1 tablespoon paprika

DIRECTIONS and Cooking Time: 25 Minutes
Mix all ingredients in a large bowl. Toss to combine well. Place in a single layer in the parchment-lined cooking basket. Bake in the preheated Air Fryer at 310 degrees F for 13 to 16 minutes. Allow it to cool completely before serving. Store in an airtight container for up to 3 months. Bon appétit!

580. Creamed Cajun Chicken

INGREDIENTS for Servings: 6

3 green onions, thinly	1 ½ cup buttermilk
sliced	1 teaspoon salt
½ tablespoon Cajun	1 cup cornmeal mix
seasoning	1 teaspoon shallot
2 large-sized chicken	powder
breasts, cut into strips	1 ½ cup flour
1/2 teaspoon garlic	1 teaspoon ground
powder	black pepper, or to
	taste

DIRECTIONS and Cooking Time: 10 Minutes
Prepare three mixing bowls. Combine 1/2 cup of the plain flour together with the cornmeal and Cajun seasoning in your bowl. In another bowl, place the buttermilk. Pour the remaining 1 cup of flour into the third bowl. Sprinkle the chicken strips with all the seasonings. Then, dip each chicken strip in the 1 cup of flour, then in the buttermilk; finally, dredge them in the cornmeal mixture. Cook the chicken strips in the air fryer baking pan for 16 minutes at 365 degrees F. Serve garnished with green onions. Bon appétit!

581. Beef And Kale Omelet

INGREDIENTS for Servings: 4

Non-stick cooking	1 tomato, chopped
spray	4 eggs, beaten
1/2 pound leftover	4 tablespoons heavy
beef, coarsely	cream
chopped	1/2 teaspoon
2 garlic cloves,	turmeric powder
pressed	Salt and ground black
1 cup kale, torn into	pepper, to your liking
pieces and wilted	1/8 teaspoon ground
1/4 teaspoon brown	allspice
sugar	

DIRECTIONS and Cooking Time: 20 Minutes
Spritz the inside of four ramekins with a cooking spray. Divide all of the above ingredients among the prepared ramekins. Stir until everything is well combined. Air-fry at 360 degrees F for 16 minutes; check with a wooden stick and return the eggs to the Air Fryer for a few more minutes as needed. Serve immediately.

582. Spicy Potato Wedges

INGREDIENTS for Servings: 4

1 ½ tablespoons	3 large-sized red
melted butter	potatoes, cut into
1 teaspoon dried	wedges
parsley flakes	1/2 teaspoon chili
1 teaspoon ground	powder
coriander	1/3 teaspoon garlic
1 teaspoon seasoned	pepper
salt	

DIRECTIONS and Cooking Time: 23 Minutes
Dump the potato wedges into the air fryer cooking basket. Drizzle with melted butter and cook for 20 minutes at 380 degrees F. Make sure to shake them a couple of times during the cooking process. Add the

remaining ingredients; toss to coat potato wedges on all sides. Bon appétit!

583. Cauliflower And Manchego Croquettes

INGREDIENTS for Servings: 4

1 cup Manchego cheese, shredded	1 teaspoon paprika
1 teaspoon freshly ground black pepper	1 pound cauliflower florets
1/2 tablespoon fine sea salt	2 tablespoons canola oil
1/2 cup scallions, finely chopped	2 teaspoons dried basil

DIRECTIONS and Cooking Time: 15 Minutes
Blitz the cauliflower florets in a food processor until finely crumbed. Then, combine the broccoli with the rest of the above ingredients. Then, shape the balls using your hands. Now, flatten the balls to make the patties. Next, cook your patties at 360 degrees F approximately 10 minutes. Bon appétit!

584. Peanut Butter And Chicken Bites

INGREDIENTS for Servings: 8

1 ½ tablespoons soy sauce	1 teaspoon sea salt
1/2 teaspoon smoked cayenne pepper	32 wonton wrappers
8 ounces soft cheese	1/3 teaspoon freshly cracked mixed peppercorns
1 1/2 tablespoons peanut butter	1/2 tablespoon pear cider vinegar
1/3 leftover chicken	

DIRECTIONS and Cooking Time: 10 Minutes
Combine all of the above ingredients, minus the wonton wrappers, in a mixing dish. Lay out the wrappers on a clean surface. Now, spread the wonton wrappers with the prepared chicken filling. Fold the outside corners to the center over the filling; after that, roll up the wrappers tightly; you can moisten the edges with a little water. Set the air fryer to cook at 360 degrees F. Air fry the rolls for 6 minutes, working in batches. Serve with marinara sauce. Bon appétit!

585. Salted Pretzel Crescents

INGREDIENTS for Servings: 4

1 can crescent rolls	1/2 cup baking soda
10 cups water	2 tablespoons sesame seed
1 egg, whisked with 1 tablespoon water	1 teaspoon coarse sea salt
1 tablespoon poppy seeds	

DIRECTIONS and Cooking Time: 20 Minutes
Unroll the dough onto your work surface; separate into 8 triangles. In a large saucepan, bring the water and baking soda to a boil over high heat. Cook each roll for 30 seconds. Remove from the water using a slotted spoon; place on a kitchen towel to drain. Repeat with the remaining rolls. Now, brush the tops with the egg wash; sprinkle each roll with the poppy seeds, sesame seed and coarse sea salt. Cover and let rest for 10 minutes. Arrange the pretzels in the lightly greased Air Fryer basket. Bake in the preheated Air Fryer at 340 degrees for 7 minutes or until golden brown. Bon appétit!

586. Zesty Broccoli Bites With Hot Sauce

INGREDIENTS for Servings: 6

For the Broccoli Bites:	1/2 teaspoon granulated garlic
1 medium-sized head broccoli, broken into florets	1/3 teaspoon celery seeds
1/2 teaspoon lemon zest, freshly grated	1 ½ tablespoons olive oil
1/3 teaspoon fine sea salt	For the Hot Sauce:
1/2 teaspoon hot paprika	1/2 cup tomato sauce
1 teaspoon shallot powder	3 tablespoons brown sugar
1 teaspoon porcini powder	1 tablespoon balsamic vinegar
	1/2 teaspoon ground allspice

DIRECTIONS and Cooking Time: 20 Minutes
Toss all the ingredients for the broccoli bites in a mixing bowl, covering the broccoli florets on all sides. Cook them in the preheated Air Fryer at 360 degrees for 13 to 15 minutes. In the meantime, mix all ingredients for the hot sauce. Pause your Air Fryer, mix the broccoli with the prepared sauce and cook for further 3 minutes. Bon appétit!

587. Italian Creamy Frittata With Kale

INGREDIENTS for Servings: 3

1 yellow onion, finely chopped	1/4 cup double cream
6 ounces wild mushrooms, sliced	1 tablespoon butter, melted
6 eggs	2 tablespoons fresh Italian parsley, chopped
1/2 teaspoon cayenne pepper	2 cups kale, chopped
Sea salt and ground black pepper, to taste	1/2 cup mozzarella, shredded

DIRECTIONS and Cooking Time: 20 Minutes
Begin by preheating the Air Fryer to 360 degrees F. Spritz the sides and bottom of a baking pan with cooking oil. Add the onions and wild mushrooms, and cook in the preheated Air Fryer at 360 degrees F for 4 to 5 minutes. In a mixing dish, whisk the eggs and double cream until pale. Add the spices, butter, parsley, and kale; stir until everything is well incorporated. Pour the mixture into the baking pan with the mushrooms. Top with the cheese. Cook in the preheated Air Fryer for 10 minutes. Serve immediately and enjoy!

588. Potato And Kale Croquettes

INGREDIENTS for Servings: 6

4 eggs, slightly beaten	1 cup kale, steamed
1/3 cup flour	1/3 cup breadcrumbs
1/3 cup goat cheese, crumbled	1/3teaspoon red pepper flakes
1 ½ teaspoons fine sea salt	3 potatoes, peeled and quartered
4 garlic cloves, minced	1/3 teaspoon dried dill weed

DIRECTIONS and Cooking Time: 9 Minutes
Firstly, boil the potatoes in salted water. Once the potatoes are cooked, mash them; add the kale, goat cheese, minced garlic, sea salt, red pepper flakes, dill and one egg; stir to combine well. Now, roll the mixture to form small croquettes. Grab three shallow bowls. Place the flour in the first shallow bowl. Beat the remaining 3 eggs in the second bowl. After that, throw the breadcrumbs into the third shallow bowl. Dip each croquette in the flour; then, dip them in the eggs bowl; lastly, roll each croquette in the breadcrumbs. Air fry at 335 degrees F for 7 minutes or until golden. Tate, adjust for seasonings and serve warm.

589. Veggie Casserole With Ham And Baked Eggs

INGREDIENTS for Servings: 4

2 tablespoons butter, melted	1 zucchini, diced
1 bell pepper, seeded and sliced	5 eggs
	1 teaspoon cayenne pepper
1 red chili pepper, seeded and minced	Sea salt, to taste
1 medium-sized leek, sliced	1/2 teaspoon ground black pepper
3/4 pound ham, cooked and diced	1 tablespoon fresh cilantro, chopped

DIRECTIONS and Cooking Time: 30 Minutes
Start by preheating the Air Fryer to 380 degrees F. Grease the sides and bottom of a baking pan with the melted butter. Place the zucchini, peppers, leeks and ham in the baking pan. Bake in the preheated Air Fryer for 6 minutes. Crack the eggs on top of ham and vegetables; season with the cayenne pepper, salt, and black pepper. Bake for a further 20 minutes or until the whites are completely set. Garnish with fresh cilantro and serve. Bon appétit!

590. Cod And Shallot Frittata

INGREDIENTS for Servings: 3

2 cod fillets	Sea salt and ground black pepper, to taste
6 eggs	
1/2 cup milk	1/2 teaspoon red pepper flakes, crushed
1 shallot, chopped	
2 garlic cloves, minced	

DIRECTIONS and Cooking Time: 20 Minutes
Bring a pot of salted water to a boil. Boil the cod fillets for 5 minutes or until it is opaque. Flake the fish into bite-sized pieces. In a mixing bowl, whisk the eggs and milk. Stir in the shallots, garlic, salt, black pepper, and red pepper flakes. Stir in the reserved fish. Pour the mixture into the lightly greased baking pan. Cook in the preheated Air Fryer at 360 degrees F for 9 minutes, flipping over halfway through. Bon appétit!

591. Easy Zucchini Chips

INGREDIENTS for Servings: 4

3/4 pound zucchini, peeled and sliced	1 egg, lightly beaten
	1/2 cup parmesan cheese, preferably freshly grated
1/2 cup seasoned breadcrumbs	

DIRECTIONS and Cooking Time: 20 Minutes
Pat the zucchini dry with a kitchen towel. In a mixing dish, thoroughly combine the egg, breadcrumbs, and cheese. Then, coat the zucchini slices with the breadcrumb mixture. Cook in the preheated Air Fryer at 400 degrees F for 9 minutes, shaking the basket halfway through the cooking time. Work in batches until the chips is golden brown. Bon appétit!

592. Easy Cheesy Broccoli

INGREDIENTS for Servings: 4

1/3 cup grated yellow cheese	2 teaspoons dried rosemary
1 large-sized head broccoli, stemmed and cut small florets	2 teaspoons dried basil
	Salt and ground black pepper, to taste
2 1/2 tablespoons canola oil	

DIRECTIONS and Cooking Time: 25 Minutes
Bring a medium pan filled with a lightly salted water to a boil. Then, boil the broccoli florets for about 3

minutes. Then, drain the broccoli florets well; toss them with the canola oil, rosemary, basil, salt and black pepper. Set your air fryer to 390 degrees F; arrange the seasoned broccoli in the cooking basket; set the timer for 17 minutes. Toss the broccoli halfway through the cooking process. Serve warm topped with grated cheese and enjoy!

593. Italian-style Broccoli Balls With Cheese

INGREDIENTS for Servings: 4

1/2 pound broccoli	4 eggs, beaten
1/2 pound Romano cheese, grated	1/2 teaspoon paprika
2 garlic cloves, minced	1/4 teaspoon dried basil
1 shallot, chopped	Sea salt and ground black pepper, to taste
2 tablespoons butter, at room temperature	

DIRECTIONS and Cooking Time: 25 Minutes
Add the broccoli to your food processor and pulse until the consistency resembles rice. Stir in the remaining ingredients; mix until everything is well combined. Shape the mixture into bite-sized balls and transfer them to the lightly greased cooking basket. Cook in the preheated Air Fryer at 375 degrees F for 16 minutes, shaking halfway through the cooking time. Serve with cocktail sticks and tomato ketchup on the side.

594. Hearty Southwestern Cheeseburger Frittata

INGREDIENTS for Servings: 2

3 tablespoons goat cheese, crumbled	2 eggs
2 cups lean ground beef	½ onion, peeled and chopped
1 ½ tablespoons olive oil	½ teaspoon paprika
½ teaspoon dried marjoram	½ teaspoon kosher salt
	1 teaspoon ground black pepper

DIRECTIONS and Cooking Time: 30 Minutes
Set your air fryer to cook at 345 degrees F. Melt the oil in a skillet over a moderate flame; then, sweat the onion until it has softened. Add ground beef and cook until browned; crumble with a fork and set aside, keeping it warm. Whisk the eggs with all the seasonings. Spritz the inside of a baking dish with a pan spray. Pour the beaten egg mixture into the baking dish, followed by the reserved beef/onion mixture. Top with the crumbled goat cheese. Bake for about 27 minutes or until a tester comes out clean and dry when stuck in the center of the frittata. Bon appétit!

595. Philadelphia Mushroom Omelet

INGREDIENTS for Servings: 2

1 tablespoon olive oil	1 bell pepper, seeded and thinly sliced
1/2 cup scallions, chopped	2 tablespoons milk
6 ounces button mushrooms, thinly sliced	Sea salt and freshly ground black pepper, to taste
4 eggs	1 tablespoon fresh chives, for serving

DIRECTIONS and Cooking Time: 20 Minutes
Heat the olive oil in a skillet over medium-high heat. Now, sauté the scallions and peppers until aromatic. Add the mushrooms and continue to cook an additional 3 minutes or until tender. Reserve. Generously grease a baking pan with nonstick cooking spray. Then, whisk the eggs, milk, salt, and black pepper. Spoon into the prepared baking pan. Cook in the preheated Air Fryer at 360 F for 4 minutes. Flip and cook for a further 3 minutes. Place the reserved mushroom filling on one side of the omelet. Fold your omelet in half and slide onto a serving plate. Serve immediately garnished with fresh chives. Bon appétit!

596. All-in-one Spicy Spaghetti With Beef

INGREDIENTS for Servings: 4

3/4 pound ground chuck	1 bell pepper, chopped
1 onion, peeled and finely chopped	1/2 teaspoon dried rosemary
1 teaspoon garlic paste	1/2 teaspoon dried marjoram
1 small-sized habanero pepper, deveined and finely minced	1/2 teaspoon sea salt flakes
	1/4 teaspoon ground black pepper, or more to taste
1 ¼ cups crushed tomatoes, fresh or canned	1 package cooked spaghetti, to serve

DIRECTIONS and Cooking Time: 30 Minutes
In the Air Fryer baking dish, place the ground meat, onion, garlic paste, bell pepper, habanero pepper, rosemary, and the marjoram. Air-fry, uncovered, for 10 to 11 minutes. Next step, stir in the tomatoes along with salt and pepper; cook 17 to 20 minutes. Serve over cooked spaghetti. Bon appétit!

597. Sausage, Pepper And Fontina Frittata

INGREDIENTS for Servings: 5

3 pork sausages, chopped	2 tablespoons Fontina cheese
5 well-beaten eggs	1/2 teaspoon tarragon
1 ½ bell peppers, seeded and chopped	1/2 teaspoon ground black pepper
1 teaspoon smoked cayenne pepper	1 teaspoon salt

DIRECTIONS and Cooking Time: 14 Minutes

In a cast-iron skillet, sweat the bell peppers together with the chopped pork sausages until the peppers are fragrant and the sausage begins to release liquid. Lightly grease the inside of a baking dish with pan spray.   Throw all of the above ingredients into the prepared baking dish, including the sautéed mixture; stir to combine.   Bake at 345 degrees F approximately 9 minutes. Serve right away with the salad of choice.

598. Celery Fries With Harissa Mayo

INGREDIENTS for Servings: 3

1/2 pound celery root	2 tablespoons sour cream
2 tablespoons olive oil	1/2 tablespoon harissa paste
Sea salt and ground black pepper, to taste	1/4 teaspoon ground cumin
Harissa Mayo	
1/4 cup mayonnaise	Salt, to taste

DIRECTIONS and Cooking Time: 30 Minutes

Cut the celery root into desired size and shape.   Then, preheat your Air Fryer to 400 degrees F. Now, spritz the Air Fryer basket with cooking spray.   Toss the celery fries with the olive oil, salt, and black pepper. Bake in the preheated Air Fryer for 25 to 30 minutes, turning them over every 10 minutes to promote even cooking.   Meanwhile, mix all ingredients for the harissa mayo. Place in your refrigerator until ready to serve. Bon appétit!

599. Traditional Onion Bhaji

INGREDIENTS for Servings: 3

1 egg, beaten	1 ounce all-purpose flour
2 tablespoons olive oil	
2 onions, sliced	Salt and black pepper, to taste
1 green chili, deseeded and finely chopped	1 teaspoon cumin seeds
2 ounces chickpea flour	1/2 teaspoon ground turmeric

DIRECTIONS and Cooking Time: 40 Minutes

Place all ingredients, except for the onions, in a mixing dish; mix to combine well, adding a little water to the mixture.   Once you've got a thick batter, add the onions; stir to coat well.   Cook in the preheated Air Fryer at 370 degrees F for 20 minutes flipping them halfway through the cooking time.   Work in batches and transfer to a serving platter. Enjoy!

600. Easy Greek Revithokeftedes

INGREDIENTS for Servings: 3

12 ounces canned chickpeas, drained	1 chili pepper
1 red onion, sliced	1/2 teaspoon cayenne pepper
2 cloves garlic	Sea salt and freshly ground pepper, to taste
1 tablespoon fresh coriander	
2 tablespoons all-purpose flour	3 large (6 ½ -inch pita bread

DIRECTIONS and Cooking Time: 30 Minutes

Pulse the chickpeas, onion, garlic, chili pepper and coriander in your food processor until the chickpeas are ground.   Add the all-purpose flour, cayenne pepper, salt, and black pepper; stir to combine well. Form the chickpea mixture into balls and place them in the lightly greased Air Fryer basket.   Cook at 380 degrees F for about 15 minutes, shaking the basket occasionally to ensure even cooking.   Warm the pita bread in your Air Fryer at 390 degrees F for around 6 minutes.   Serve the revithokeftedes in pita bread with tzatziki or your favorite Greek topping. Enjoy!

CPSIA information can be obtained
at www.ICGtesting.com
Printed in the USA
BVHW082214050421
604209BV00006B/428